# eCFO

# eCFO

## SUSTAINING VALUE IN
## THE NEW CORPORATION

CEDRIC READ, JACKY ROSS, JOHN DUNLEAVY,
DONNIEL SCHULMAN AND JAMES BRAMANTE

**JOHN WILEY & SONS, LTD**
Chichester · New York · Weinheim · Brisbane · Singapore · Toronto

Published in 2001 by     John Wiley & Sons Ltd,
Baffins Lane, Chichester,
West Sussex PO19 1UD, England

National     01243 779777
International (+44) 1243 779777
e-mail (for orders and customer service enquiries):
cs-books@wiley.co.uk
Visit our Home Page on http://www.wiley.co.uk

*Other Wiley Editorial Offices*

John Wiley & Sons, Inc., 605 Third Avenue,
New York, NY 10158-0012, USA

Wiley-VCH Verlag GmbH, Pappelallee 3,
D-69469 Weinheim, Germany

John Wiley & Sons Australia, Ltd, 33 Park Road, Milton,
Queensland 4064, Australia

John Wiley & Sons (Asia) Pte Ltd, 2 Clementi Loop #02-01,
Jin Xing Distripark, Singapore 129809

John Wiley & Sons (Canada) Ltd, 22 Worcester Road,
Rexdale, Ontario M9W 1L1, Canada

*British Library Cataloguing in Publication Data*

A catalogue record for this book is available from the British Library

ISBN 0-471-49642-1

Typeset in 11/13pt Rotis by Footnote Graphics, Warminster, Wiltshire
Printed and bound in Great Britain by Butler & Tanner Ltd, Frome, Somerset
This book is printed on acid-free paper responsibly manufactured from sustainable forestation, for which at least two trees are planted for each one used for paper production.

# Preface

What is the future role of the chief financial officer and how is it being reshaped by e-business? These two questions are at the heart of this book. Make no mistake, dotcoms will continue to come and go but the Internet is here to stay. The initial euphoria over e-business has died and the world's leading companies are now committed to e-business strategies which make commercial sense. The huge and lasting impact of Internet technology on the CFO and finance function will only intensify. Internet capabilities will be hardwired into operations, and what finance does and how it works will never be the same.

Will finance even exist? Yes, but not as we know it today. What will change? Everything. Finance's mission, its methods, and its reach will all be redefined. Here's a glimpse of the path that lies ahead.

Transaction processing will be fully integrated into Internet traffic. All finance's current work around purchasing and payables, sales and receivables, will be seamlessly conducted via the Internet. Finance's once critical role in this arena will be minimal, focusing on oversight and maintenance.

Managing physical and even working capital will become less and less important. As CFO you'll be custodian of new and different resources—

intangible assets. How you value and nurture these assets will have little in common with today's accounting objectives and practices.

Finance's traditional responsibility for providing and managing accounting information will diminish. Finance departments will no longer control the bureaucracies and infrastructures that gather and guard this data.

What about decision support, or i-analytics—integrated information and intelligence—as we call it at PricewaterhouseCoopers? While decision support will be key to the CFO's evolving role, we believe that eventually a whole new industry will spring up around analytical support services, driven once again by the Internet.

In short, many of finance's well-established and familiar functions will be outsourced or automated. What then will tomorrow's CFO be doing? Presiding over a shrinking empire or staking a claim to uncharted new corporate terrain? As we envision it, the CFO's role will not be diminished but transformed into what we call the *eCFO*. Becoming a true strategic partner to the CEO in making forward-thinking decisions about the future of their company, the eCFO assumes an exciting new role of internal venture capitalist.

Succeeding in this new discipline will require a host of new skills: anticipating industry restructuring, proactively identifying opportunities, justifying investments based on the value they will offer as options in the future, and then creatively managing these options as a portfolio. Meeting these new demands will be rewarding and challenging.

This is the route forward, and we hope that *eCFO: Sustaining Value in the New Corporation* will be an invaluable road map. Our goal is to help guide your way into the future, practically and clearly. Chapter by chapter, you'll find the tools, best practices, research data, and insights you'll need to manage your new role successfully. You'll find frontline advice and real-world examples of the new business models, new valuation techniques, new systems, and new asset-building strategies that are reshaping the finance discipline.

We want to thank all those who contributed to these pages, especially the visionary CFOs who so generously shared their ideas and experiences in their personal introductions to the chapters and in the many case studies. They include Clayton Daley of Procter & Gamble, Tom Meredith of Dell, Renato Fassbind of ABB, Warren Jenson of Amazon, John Coombe of GlaxoSmithKline, Nick Rose of Diageo, Olli-Pekka Kallasvuo of Nokia, Jeff Henley of Oracle, Howard Smith of AIG, Thomas Horton of American Airlines and Stephen Hodge of Shell.

Across PricewaterhouseCoopers, many members of our global practices also offered their expertise and support. Chief among them are Caroline Spicer, Mike Schroeck and John King (Chapter 1); Chris Huckle, Stephen Justice and Robin Lissak (Chapter 2); Likhit Wagle, Michael Duff and Yann Bonduelle (Chapter 3); Michael Mehta, Ben Kettell and Les Barnett (Chapter 4); Wouter Van Der Meer, Malcolm Anthony and Adam Borison (Chapter 5); Brian Lever and Martin Morrell (Chapter 6); David Lindop, John Message and Peter Maxted (Chapter 7); Chris Timbrell, John Granger, Mike Seitz and John Devereaux (Chapter 8); Richard Simpson, Steve Wood and Bernie Segal (Chapter 9); David Pettifer and Louisa Gibson (Chapter 10); Jon Z. Bentley, David Knight, Richard Sandwell, David Narrow and Peter Sedgwick (Chapter 11).

Also very many thanks to the Financial Management Solutions global leadership team, especially John Blackburn, Doug Simpson and Bob Leach, for their support and encouragement throughout the writing of the book. We would also like to express gratitude to those individuals inside and outside PricewaterhouseCoopers who provided valuable writing and editing input; they include Karin Abarbanel, Linda Gatley, Barkley Murray, Sara Valente, Bill Wartman, Simon Caulkin and Janayea Howe. Special acknowledgment goes to our external advisors, including Doug Dorrat from VisionCube, Andrew Campbell from Ashridge, Amory Hall from Akasha Media, and to the team at John Wiley for their patience and professional support.

Cedric Read, Jacky Ross, John Dunleavy,
Donniel Schulman and James Bramante
March 2001

# Contents

Contents

*Contents*

# CHAPTER 1

# Finance in the e-Business World

## MOVING A GLOBAL BRANDED GOODS COMPANY INTO THE e-WORLD

*Clayton Daley, CFO*
Procter & Gamble

*As a branded products company, our challenge is always to add value for our consumers. The core of that challenge at P&G lies in technology—developing and marketing products that are demonstrably better to the consumer than competitive offerings.*

*With P&G's market capitalization listed at about eight or nine times book value, it's pretty obvious that the greater part of our assets are not those that are on the balance sheet. That intangible value is a combination of the value of our brand names and of our franchises, supplemented by the R&D and the people in our organization.*

*Over the last decade we have used shareholder value as a unifying concept. We are trying to get everyone—people in finance, marketing, R&D, product supply, and those who deal with our customers—to understand that their activities should be directed toward improving value for the shareholder. When we introduce any forward-looking business plan, we ask ourselves, If the business successfully implements this strategy, is it a value-building strategy or not?*

*P&G has managed to sustain reasonably good financial performance over time because we focus on the long term. That means having the discipline to invest in R&D and components of the marketing mix that keep our franchises strong. Last year we announced what I think is the most significant reorganization in our history, converting our company from a geographic product and profit model to a global product and profit model. We've moved to global product management because we view ourselves as a technology company, not just a marketing company. As such, our R&D dollars must create technologies that have broad applications across the world, in both developed and developing markets.*

**e-Commerce will have a significant impact on the finance function. We're going to be right in the middle of B2B, managing orders, receivables and payables.**

*This reorganization, which we call Organization 2005, has had a significant impact on the finance organization. Most of the accounting and transaction processing activities are now in the shared services organization, while our local infrastructure management is now handled in what we call the market development organization.*

*In addition, e-commerce is influencing our future. In finance, business-to-business (B2B) is the most ubiquitous. It will be in the interest of corporations to agree on standards for B2B commerce as quickly as possible. Much of the cost reduction and working capital improvements available through Web-based B2B commerce will depend on there being standard interfaces; managing different protocols for different suppliers would defeat the purpose.*

*We're implementing a business-to-employee (B2E) strategy that is part of our shared services vision, in which our employees will use our intranet essentially to manage their own human resources records.*

*But probably the area that gets the most media attention is business-to-consumer (B2C). We are going to participate in that space, but we're going to enter it carefully. Existing distribution channels are often the best means of getting our products to our consumers. It's more efficient for our consumers to buy Charmin toilet paper at a Wal-Mart store than to order it on a Web site. But there are certainly some product lines that are more suited to e-commerce. In fact, we have introduced a line of prestige, personalized skin and beauty care products distributed directly to consumers over a Web-based site.*

*Undoubtedly, e-commerce will have a significant impact on the finance function in general. Finance is going to be right in the middle of B2B, managing orders, receivables and payables.*

*I think that most e-commerce investments will lend themselves to the kind of analysis that you would conduct with any investment where your goal is to create shareholder value. While the predictability of B2C profits and cash flows is likely to be much more volatile than traditional investments in the business, you still must bring financial discipline to that part of your portfolio.*

*Increasing shareholder value in this market also means growing the value of intangibles; at P&G, this includes R&D, marketing and people. It's always been a challenge for finance to add value in the R&D process—developing portfolio analysis techniques, using real options to get a better handle on the real value of R&D. Once we've developed those technologies and those options, what do we do with them? Can we license that technology? Can we sell it? Can we partner with somebody? How do we derive maximum value out of the R&D portfolio?*

*We also become involved as e-commerce impacts marketing. How do we evaluate the effectiveness and the efficiency of our various marketing programs? Are we getting good value for those dollars? e-Commerce advertising has not been very cost-effective or efficient, but that will change over time. A forward-thinking finance organization is going to figure out how to get in front of this evolving industry, rather than being pulled along by it.*

*The final component is* people. *I think their value is sometimes understated; in this company we really believe that people drive results. As we move into the next century, we certainly believe that good people management skills are essential to maintaining value for the shareholder.*

*Technology is definitely changing the playing field in finance competencies. The challenge lies in determining what techniques to use and keeping valuation techniques relevant. I believe that ERP systems are enablers, but not solutions in and of themselves. Investments in materials management systems and business planning systems pay off, but they're not sufficient. You can have the best systems in the world, but if you have an inherently inefficient forecasting and planning process, they aren't going to do much for you.*

*Over time the role of finance people will evolve. Historically, financial managers have spent more time on traditional transactional processing and accounting. In the future, analysis techniques will be readily available to everyone in the organization; financial managers will be challenged to rise above their traditional roles to become more like generalists, in terms of their ability to add value to the business.*

*The world out there says that the tenure of the CFO shortens every year. My view of the CFO's role is relatively simple: how do you add value from your office? That's what I think the challenge has been and will continue to be. Do I think there will continue to be a finance function? I believe there will be. I can certainly envision, though, that it will be very different from its role in the past. I think the traditional functions may tend to blur over time. And I think it will be important for finance people to embrace that change rather than resist it.*

---

Like the shot heard round the world, the e-business revolution is challenging even the best-run and most successful companies. We've seen the rise and fall of dotcom start-ups on Nasdaq and we've seen Fortune 500 companies like P&G make their business-to-business debuts. All the companies interviewed for this book believe unequivocally that the Internet will have a fundamental and positive impact on their businesses. Undoubtedly global economic growth is, and will continue to be, fueled by the Net. The issue for the world's leading companies is not *whether* to invest in e-business, it's *how*.

To keep pace, CFOs are waging competitive battles on many fronts: streamlining their finance functions, investing in new technologies, pushing for globalization, implementing shareholder-value-based measurements, improving decision support, becoming true business partners.

In *CFO: Architect of the Corporation's Future* we positioned the CFO as an *architect* using shareholder value to redesign and reshape the business, framing visions for finance which stretched across areas of the CEO and strategy.[1] But the CFO landscape is changing. Globalization, industry convergence, and shareholder value are as relevant today as they were then. What we underestimated was the *velocity*–the speed of change, the speed of globalization, the speed of industry convergence, and most importantly, the speed of technology—as evidenced in the explosive growth of the World Wide Web and e-business.

"For the last 11 consecutive quarters, we have had a return on invested capital that is the envy of most industries—in excess of 150%, creating great shareholder value. While we are pleased, we are not satisfied. We have a lot more headroom to increase this return. The Internet will help us." These comments were made by Tom Meredith, managing director of Dell Ventures; at the time he made them, he was Dells's CFO. Currently, Dell generates more than 40% of its business via the Internet, has negative working capital, a four-hour manufacturing lead time, and adjusts its advertising and pricing strategy in real time. That's velocity!

But how do you get there? As CFO you need answers to some of the tough questions raised in this chapter:

- How is e-business transforming finance?

- How do the new Internet business models change existing business economics?

- What is their impact on investment appraisal, resource allocation, capital requirements?

- How do you communicate your new Internet investment expectations and strategies to investors?

- How is the role of the finance function changing?

- How do *you* add value?

## NEW OPPORTUNITIES FOR VALUE CREATION

The single most important driver of change for most CFOs today is the business-to-business (B2B) e-revolution. B2B is changing the rules of competition: companies are being forced to innovate continuously simply to keep up. Internet ventures are joining forces with well-established companies to launch B2B initiatives. Most traditional business principles still hold true in the new economy, but imagination, insight and courage are needed to succeed in the world of virtual business.

Brands, customers, intellectual property and human resources, intangible assets like these are now driving value and partnering decisions. External alliances and outsourcing vehicles, such as value-added communities

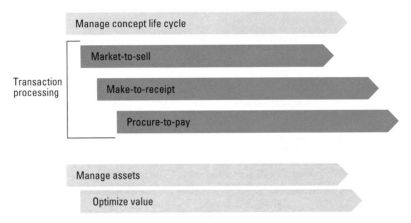

**Figure 1.1** *Breaking up the company's traditional value chain*

(VACs), are being formed to exploit new opportunities for trading over the Internet. Industry-specific (vertical) communities are being organized to promote supply chain efficiencies, as seen in automotive manufacturing, the chemical industry, and grocery (FMCG) trade exchanges. Function-specific (horizontal) communities are sprouting up that cut across industries to address common business issues, such as HR services, information technology, and procurement.[2]

What does all this mean for your company? Business processes such as market-to-sell, make-to-receipt, and procure-to-pay can be separated from your core business concept, the source of your inherent competitive advantage, be it a brand, intellectual capital, a product or a customer interface (Figure 1.1). In the future these unbundled processes may be positioned in VACs. The CFO is still concerned with the glue that holds the value proposition together–the processes for managing assets and optimizing value.

For the CFO this fundamental shift–from optimizing the value of *individual* businesses to optimizing a *network* of businesses–presents major new challenges. There is little precedent on which to build business scenarios. The investor market, while generally receptive to Internet-related investment, is volatile. As the old-economy business model is transformed into the new-economy model, where should you focus your assets to ensure value creation?

As new strategies are brought to market, the CFO's vision will need to

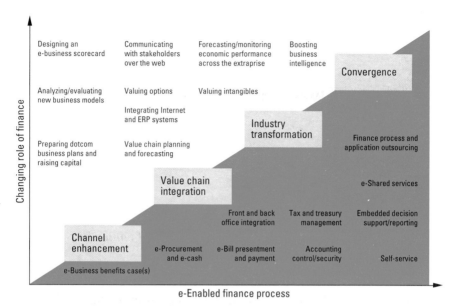

**Figure 1.2** *e-Business strategy development: the impact on finance roles and processes*

change, too. Figure 1.2 shows the changes that are likely to impinge upon traditional finance roles and processes at each stage in the execution of a company's e-business strategy from its simplest form, channel enhancement, to ever-increasing levels of complexity.

## UNDERSTANDING WEBONOMICS

Old-economy companies invested in such physical assets as manufacturing sites, distribution sites, office buildings and telecommunications infrastructure. Understandably, the CFO focused on improving return on capital and investment, EBITDA and asset turns, and making investments that exceeded the cost of capital. Companies focused on spurring improvements in time to market, customer responsiveness, inventory management, and supply chain logistics. More recently the focus shifted to increasing cash flow.

In the emerging new economy, however, corporate value is increasingly tied up not in physical assets but in intangible assets. This is affecting even

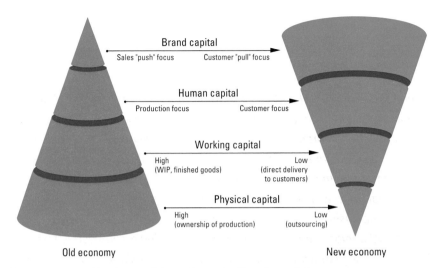

**Figure 1.3**  *e-Business drives decapitalization of the company*

traditional companies. In fact, research has shown that more than 78% of the S&P500's market value now flows from intangibles. New-economy companies have accelerated this trend dramatically. Figure 1.3 shows how a B2B e-business has far more capital tied up in brands and people than in working and physical capital.

How does this affect shareholder value and financial management practices? Cash flow remains vital. As a new e-business model takes off, cash is invested rapidly in acquiring customers, advertising and brand development, hiring new talent, and building Web sites. Short-term profits are less important than growth and sustainability. At some point, cash burn becomes a crucial performance measure.

## Creating Options for Growth

e-Business companies may experience ever-increasing losses, even as they build increasingly valuable intangible assets. Furthermore, as they grow by expanding their customer base and their presence on the Web, they are creating *options* to pursue new business opportunities. To keep pace, old-economy companies investing in major new e-business ventures must develop and fine-tune new valuation models. As the following case study shows, the stakes can be huge.

Case Study
Transformation through e-Investment

*The chairman of a global high-tech solutions provider was asked to sign off on a proposed $1 billion investment in e-business. His team's "simple" objective: to transform the corporation from a traditional, vertically organized company into a radically new, customer-centric organization through a huge cash infusion.*

*Most of the company's senior managers viewed the proposal as a "no-brainer," particularly as their major competitors were following similar paths. However, the business in its current form was driven by hard economic value added (EVA) numbers, and the CFO had made specific growth commitments to Wall Street. The justification to the board for the e-business investment was a fluffy concept of "enhanced customer value." It simply didn't stack up in EVA terms.*

*Instead of rubber-stamping the e-business venture, the chairman and CFO asked some probing questions. Four seemingly intractable problems emerged:*

1. *The discounted cash flow (DCF) numbers simply didn't work; e-business could not be justified in traditional cash flow terms.*

2. *The "enhanced customer value" proposition could not be quantified in financial terms.*

3. *The CFO did not know how to communicate effectively the proposed e-business investment package to Wall Street.*

4. *In the heart of the business's operations, people were concerned about how e-business would affect performance.*

*The solution? A whole new set of financial management principles, built around the customer-centric e-business perspective. The new approach had four components:*

1. *New financial analytics, involving the use of real options, which accommodated the inherent uncertainties of the e-business world.*

2. *An approach to determining customer lifetime value involving the attribution of future revenues, costs and investments.*

3. *An investor relations program in synch with the company's underlying e-business strategy, and a strong emphasis on communicating both goals and results.*

4. *A new e-business scorecard with differential shareholder-value-based incentives for those involved in the e-business investment portfolio.*

*The CFO's plan of action led to a sea change in financial management for the entire company. Investment allocation processes were overhauled. Major changes in planning and budgeting processes were initiated. Performance metrics were turned on their head. And a forceful communication program drove the strategy and its benefits home to investors.*

---

With its goal of connecting with customers, e-business demands a new set of analytics to value and manage proposed initiatives. And so the CFO faces a new challenge: creating a financial model for the new business that takes into account options, identifies the drivers behind emerging customer value propositions, and then links them both to shareholder value.

Investment appraisals for new-economy companies have to embrace risk, uncertainty and optionality. Such appraisals must also factor in three components of shareholder value: known cash flows from the existing business and related known projects; options for growth, future opportunities to exploit current investments; and speculation, the froth from the volatile investor (day-trading) market.

Most valuation methods can accommodate only one execution route to shareholder value creation. The discounted cash flow (DCF) approach, for example, reflects a single path that cannot cope with the uncertainty and rapidly changing market conditions of e-business. Techniques such as real options valuation (ROV) provide a more complete picture of future value by building upon proven DCF techniques, decision analysis, and option pricing models.

## Developing a New-Economy Mindset

Reconciling *what customers value* with *what creates value for shareholders* is a major challenge for the CFO. What's more, linking together shareholder value, customer value and real options value– and building them into the financial management processes of your company–requires a major reorientation. The old-world mindset is steeped in a traditional accounting concept–historically assessing physical assets. The new-world mindset is based on sustainable value creation.

To make the shift, follow these principles:

- *Focus on the future, not the past.* Value your business for what it can generate in the future, rather than on results delivered in the past.

- *Think intangible, not tangible.* Focus on managing the value of intangible assets, such as customers, brands and R&D, rather than on the value of physical assets, such as premises, plant, and stock.

- *Pursue growth, not reduction.* Concentrate on initiatives that open up new opportunities. Treat cost reduction as an opportunity for releasing resources that can be invested in growth, rather than as an end in itself.

- *Create loops, not lines.* Implement new resource management processes which flex with the changing business models; make your planning and reporting disciplines dynamic and iterative, rather than tying them to linear time frames.

- *Build windows, not walls.* Develop customer-based metrics that monitor business performance from a number of different analytical windows. Avoid information in functional silos by using tools that provide line of sight and transparency.

Select the best tools, especially best-of-breed solutions, to integrate systems as required, rather than necessarily picking one solution that tries to do everything. Structure financial management services to mirror the global aspirations of your organization as a whole, and aim for global consistency rather than focusing on new process and system implementations that are primarily geared to the needs of local territories.

Above all, the CFO and the finance function have two different and often conflicting roles to play in the new corporation: acting on the one hand as *flexible business partners* teaming up through joint ventures and alliances to create new e-businesses, and on the other hand as *disciplined professionals* sustaining the corporation's reputation and brand value, stakeholder relations, and long-term performance.

## APPLYING OLD-WORLD DISCIPLINES IN THE NEW CORPORATION

e-Business provides substantial opportunities for creating value. This in turn requires an understanding of the new value drivers that are fueling the new economy. At the same time, all the CFOs who contributed to this book made it clear that the financial management disciplines that had served them well in the old economy should be applied more than ever in the new. It's the context that's changed, and the speed required. Most important, what's needed is a dose of reality.

It's one thing to talk about new financial management principles and practices, but it's another to implement them. And how do you cope with the reality of developing a new e-business alongside an existing traditional business model—with all the attendant resourcing, reporting, and structural conflicts?

Figure 1.4 shows the evolution of the finance function through the 1980s and 1990s, then the move in 2000 toward *virtuality.* Finance has been getting smaller, with more emphasis on decision support, and is now

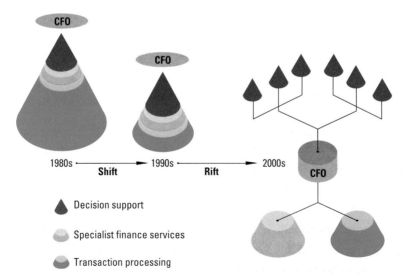

Figure 1.4 *Toward a dispersed finance function*

becoming physically more fragmented. Increasingly transaction processing occurs in remote shared services and is sometimes outsourced. Decision support is embedded in business units. And specialist support services operate at a commercial arm's length. As a result, the CFO is now at the center of a web of relationships.

The Internet provides an exciting vehicle for step changes in performance—further, deeper cost reductions in transaction processing and new ways to share decision-support data across functional lines. What new demands on finance are created by new e-businesses? What are their structural implications? Above all, how must you overhaul your finance vision—continuing to implement best-practice improvements while accommodating emerging e-business needs?

CASE STUDY
Redefining the Finance Vision

*A fast-moving company in the entertainment and media industry is developing a new digital business, sharing the customer, content and production assets of existing business units. The company has grown rapidly from a traditional newspaper business into a large magazine publisher. It has done this organically, through its expertise in launching new titles to targeted audiences, major acquisitions in the UK and Germany, and diversification into related media activities, such as television.*

*Each publication was formerly a profit center in its own right and had its own finance support. Once the company had reached a size and maturity where it could benefit from joint marketing, advertising and back-office services, publications were combined with other media into customer-oriented networks. The entertainment network, for example, combined radio, TV and magazines aimed at the music interests of younger consumers.*

*This evolving customer network concept created challenges for the company's traditional financial planning and reporting structures. The CFO began shaping a new vision for finance. At the same time, the CEO and top team focused on e-business. They created Virtual, a new division bringing together current and planned Web-based investments. This new division would exploit*

*B2B online opportunities, creating new revenue streams and leveraging consumer networks.*

*Investors reacted positively to the digital strategy and so did the share price. The objective: to transform the company's size and value by taking content and audiences into an e-commerce environment. By separating out the digital business, the company created a new enterprise with its own ownership culture, attracting new talent, providing fresh motivation and incentives, and creating a dynamic goal—rapid investment in new digital opportunities.*

*The CFO and global finance team revisited the finance vision. Shareholder value creation was still at the top of the agenda, and so was implementing value-based management through key performance indicators, balanced scorecards, and streamlined planning and reporting processes. The vision for transaction processing was still relevant, based on shared services and a common systems platform.*

*But the digital business had some specific needs that finance had to meet:*

- *Online statistics updated in real time for performance monitoring.*

- *Accelerated financial reporting, and an instant, or virtual, closing process.*

- *Support in evaluating new business opportunities requiring more of a venture capital approach and less emphasis on fixed annual budgets for resource allocation.*

- *Corporate finance skills for joint venture partnering, externally funded acquisitions, and potential spin-offs.*

*The CFO recognized that the changes needed would affect the whole business. By taking responsibility for online operations away from existing offline business, Virtual could undermine the company's established performance management framework. Ways of working together toward common corporate goals had to be found in an environment where incentive structures differed, intangible assets were to be shared, and the new digital business was to function virtually, with a small staff and few physical assets.*

*The solution? Each business, including Virtual, has its own shareholder value improvement targets, tailored scorecards, and tailored decision support. Although there is potential for double counting, decision-support systems are being put in place that are flexible enough to report revenues, costs, and assets from a number of perspectives.*

*The new digital business is accelerating company-wide adoption of finance best practices. Speed, flexibility and responsiveness are the criteria for the new shared services operation—now needed more than ever—supported by new systems platforms and streamlined resource management. Finance skills are changing even more radically than they would have without Virtual. Today there is less emphasis on routine and more emphasis on being true business partners in achieving shareholder value growth.*

---

The company in the case study is not unusual in pursuing financial best practices. Certainly all major companies should have a vision for finance and strive for continuous improvement. And everyone must meet the challenges of e-business by creating standalone business entities under one corporate umbrella, by integrating e-business approaches into existing operations, or by pursuing e-business alliances with a range of partners.

## HOW IS e-BUSINESS RESHAPING THE FINANCE FUNCTION?

Our research shows that finance lags behind customer management, procurement, and supply chain management in the adoption of e-business practices. This isn't surprising, since the value of doing business over the Internet lies primarily in the *sell-side* and *buy-side* portions of the value chain. However, momentum is building for the adoption of Internet technologies *inside* the boundaries of the corporation.

The role of finance in the e-business world now expands beyond transaction processing and decision support, into actually making a difference in performance improvement. e-Business initiatives can be ordered around the three roles for finance, as shown in Figure 1.5.

In a recent survey we asked CFOs to project the impact of e-business on their companies' finance function. It yielded these aggregate results:

- *In two years' time, what percentage of your revenues will be derived from e-business?*

  Some 70% of respondents thought at least a quarter of their revenue would be sourced through e-business; 15% thought that e-business would account for more than half of revenues; and 15% of respondents thought that e-business would have no impact at all.

- *What percentage of your costs will be sourced through e-business?*

Some 65% of respondents thought at least a quarter of their costs would be sourced via the Internet; 25% thought e-business would account for more than half of their costs; and only 10% of respondents thought that e-business would have no impact.

- *Which aspect of your finance function will be most affected by e-business?*

Not surprisingly, billing and payment processes were selected as the functions most likely to be substantially affected by e-business, followed by treasury and cash processes. Decision-support processes, such as reporting, metrics, and investment appraisal, were seen as less likely to be affected, although they were still viewed as investment priorities by the CFO. In all, 50% of respondents intended to invest in Web-enabled management information and data warehousing. Data protection and security inevitably ranked high on the CFO agenda.

The bottom line? Most CFOs predicted that e-business would have a major impact on their businesses and their finance processes. But few professed to know what that impact was likely to be in terms of changes to finance strategy, decision support, transaction processes, finance organization,

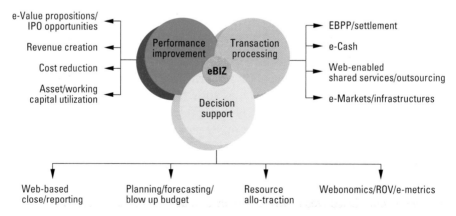

**Figure 1.5** *e-Business financial initiatives*

and systems. Also, the future role of the CFO was unclear. While some believed it would be unaffected by e-business, fully half those surveyed foresaw major changes.

Undoubtedly, the growth of new e-markets will stretch existing finance skills. Customer analytics, online performance reporting, and the use of emerging integration technologies present new challenges in decision support. The trends toward Web-enabled shared services and outsourcing mean a whole new set of skills. These new skills are needed, not just to meet demanding new service levels and cost benchmarks, often according to a contract, but also to master the specialized technical knowledge required by the following shifts:

- From traditional month-end routines, to the virtual close.
- From traditional budgeting, to targets based on real-time lead indicators.
- From an emphasis on historical accounts, to rolling forecasts.
- From traditional invoicing, to electronic bill presentment and payment (EBPP).
- From traditional payroll and procurement, to self-service.

There are a bewildering number of new process improvement opportunities and new technologies from which CFOs can choose. Our survey showed that the biggest barrier to successful implementation of an e-business strategy was the *lack of a clear vision*. Resistance to change and outdated skills were both close behind.

The story of the virtual close at Cisco is well known. Although radical improvement in the closing process does not generate a huge amount of shareholder value in its own right, the indirect benefits are substantial. This case study takes finance best practices in transaction processing and decision support, and combines them with the latest Internet technology.

CASE STUDY
The Virtual Close at Cisco

*Five years ago, Cisco was growing rapidly and acquisition activity was intense, but business systems were unlinked and overwhelmed by the huge volume of data. Against this backdrop there was a firmwide mandate to keep costs and headcount under control. It was clear that financial reporting processes had to be improved.*

*In FY95 it took 14 days for Cisco to close its books globally. Today a global flash report is produced by noon on day one following the close; a worldwide trial balance in full line-item detail is produced by the end of day one; and complete reporting packages are available by the end of day two, then worldwide sign-off with analysis on day three.*

*Among the key items of information flowing to management daily, online and in real time, are bookings, revenue, order status, margins, and expenses. According to CFO Larry Carter, "The virtual close has enabled us to dramatically improve the accuracy of financial information and significantly speed up the time it takes to produce critical data." How has Cisco achieved this success? Through six key building blocks:*

- Management commitment: *targets are set each year for the top executives. The annual finance goals include specific targets for improvements in the closing process. This is reinforced by the CEO, John Chambers.*

- Process reengineering: *low-hanging fruit was addressed first; a workgroup approach was taken to resolve specific problems and issues. There were no sacred cows, everything was reviewed for automation. Better forecasting was needed to set accruals and reserves rapidly. Standardized processes were developed to expedite month-end closing for each main location worldwide. Flash reporting was introduced, materiality limits for cutoffs set, and cross-charging minimized. Ultimately, Cisco implemented a worldwide chart of accounts, integrated various source systems, standardized using one consolidation tool, and automated intracompany transactions.*

- The linking of finance with IT: *finance and IT are no longer viewed as a cost center, but as a value-adding strategic partnership, delivering the latest technology solutions to business problems. Finance, just as other functions, has to find the trade-off between IT investment in applications and headcount spending. This motivates the creation of projects that can achieve a payback cycle of less than 12 months.*

- Web-based applications: *Cisco Web-enabled both reporting applications (such as executive information, revenue reporting, expense tracking, and gross margin movements) and employee tools (such as online travel reimbursement, online catalog purchasing, and worldwide sales commissions).*

- Standard network systems architecture: *Cisco's network systems architecture is standardized on Oracle. This standardization applies not only to database management, development tools and physical infrastructure, but also to application packages, whatever their focus: ERP, decision support, or e-commerce.*

- Continuous review: *metrics were created to measure the quality and cycle time of key activities; these became known as "close metrics." Monthly-close postmortems were instituted to communicate implementation issues and successes. Crucially, ownership for the close metrics was assigned to managers at various levels across the organization. The monitoring of results is decentralized at the business unit level, and even at account level.*

*Cisco claims that its Internet and internal business applications save it millions of dollars every month. Yearly improvements in productivity of 20% or more are being achieved in transaction processing areas such as accounts payable, accounts receivable and payroll. But perhaps the greatest benefit of the virtual close lies in the new ability of Cisco to monitor and analyze continuously the critical information necessary to run its business effectively.*

---

As this case study shows, implementing a vision for finance, be it in the old economy or the new, still means adopting a radical but robust approach to process reengineering, combined with technology and relentless improvement. But the e-business world does offer finance a completely fresh opportunity to add value as a business partner.

## Finance Value Propositions

The contribution finance can make by using the Internet can best be framed through *finance value propositions*. These identify the business case for change (expressed in terms of shareholder value improvement), the options at each major decision point, and the resulting risks and uncertainties. Finance value propositions fall into three main categories:

- *Capital utilization:* decapitalizing the old-economy business by shedding physical assets and improving operating efficiencies in order to build intangible assets in the new-economy business. This finance value proposition focuses on value chain analysis, asset disposals and working capital improvements, as well as on increasing intangible asset values, reducing operating costs, and most importantly, releasing funds for reinvestment in growth.

- *Building the extraprise:* participating in e-markets, leveraging value-added communities, working with new partners, developing and supporting new economic models. This finance value proposition is built around competitive financing, business planning, managing resources, broadening shared services, and outsourcing applications and business processes.

- *Integrating new technologies:* taking advantage of Internet technology to convert data into information then into knowledge, Web-enabling business processes, and integrating financial transactions and decision support. This finance value proposition is built around developing business intelligence and streamlining financial management processes.

The CFO interviews conducted for this book revealed numerous examples of how finance can use the Internet to add value to every aspect of the business.

e-Settlement   A large multinational telecom provider had complex billing arrangements for many small customers as well as for a few very large ones. Receivable balances were spiraling out of control. The solution was to install a Web-based facility for resolving customer disputes, to reengineer the collections process, and improve credit screening through the modeling of customer behavior. Electronic bill presentment and payment (EBPP) was added to the functional capability of the systems. The benefits? A 60% reduction in cycle time for customer dispute resolution, additional revenues, and a major reduction in bad debts.

EBPP is a relatively new technology. For the biller, it means lower clerical costs, new customer marketing opportunities, and advance cash flow. For customers, the value proposition is less clear but it does give them control over payments and the ability to view and manipulate data online. To implement EBPP, billers have two options: presenting billing information on their own Web site (biller direct) or using a third-party service provider (consolidator).

e-Procurement   A consumer products company sought to reduce the cost of externally purchased non-production-related goods and services. Purchasing cards had been introduced but poorly implemented, resulting in a mushrooming of the supplier base. The spend across suppliers was analyzed, and e-procurement software was selected. Standard multi-supplier catalogs were created, and the entire procure-to-pay cycle was Web-enabled. Additionally, automated time and expense reporting was implemented for some 2,000 users. The benefits? Elimination of maverick buying, prenegotiated contracts and discounts, and clerical efficiencies. A 10% cost reduction target was easily exceeded.

> *Shareholders in e-markets may create additional value through transaction fees, service charges, and subscriptions from participating companies, on both the buy side and supply side.*

Many companies in the same industry are now collaborating to form e-markets—trade exchanges that benefit from combined purchasing power, efficiencies in maintaining standard supply catalogs, and shared business services. Shareholders in these e-markets may create additional value through transaction fees, service charges, and subscriptions from participating companies, on both the buy side and the supply side.

Web-enabled shared services   An energy company had implemented a shared services operation for finance in each of its continental theaters: the Americas, Europe, and Asia-Pacific. It wanted to achieve a 30% savings increase through outsourcing. Reengineering improvements were identified, process scope established, service and operating level agreements defined, and contracts with an outsourcer agreed upon. Processes flowing between the company and the outsourcer were Web-enabled, including transaction data, workflow, and management reporting.

Outsourced shared services can be expanded beyond the finance back office into human resources, procurement, and IT infrastructure. The scope can be widened still further to cover the front office and decision support. Using the Internet, previously dedicated shared service centers can be opened up commercially to other companies. These can be linked to trade exchanges, leading to further front- and back-office integration, Web-enabled forecasting, and data exchanges among partners. The shared services operation can thus be converted from a cost center to a profit center and into an initial public offering.

Integrated decision support  Experience shows that transaction processing propositions can create shareholder value by reducing either cost or working capital. Value propositions for decision support are more difficult to justify. How do you assess the additional economic benefits of external business intelligence, customer lifetime value information, cost-to-serve data, and Web-based reporting? Only in terms of closing the shareholder value gap—the difference between what shareholders expect and what the company can deliver.

> *How does the CFO assess the economic benefits*
> *of external business intelligence, customer lifetime*
> *value information, cost-to-serve data, and*
> *Web-based reporting?*

The case for decision-support information for new e-business operations is driven by the need for speed and flexibility. Proven benefits include real-time drilldown, accessibility to online information and e-metrics, and greater insight into how to create customer and shareholder value. But perhaps the most important benefits of decision-support information lie not in the data itself, but in the more responsive management processes it allows, including resource allocation, budgeting, and rolling forecasts. The end result? Tighter linkage between strategic aspirations and front-line operational activities.

## THE eCFO's AGENDA

This book is intended to help shape the eCFO's agenda. Its key theme is the sustained creation of shareholder value in an e-business world. But how can you translate this lofty goal into reality?

The chapters that follow draw upon our independent research, intensive discussions with CFOs, and best practices. Each chapter is introduced by a leading CFO, describing the key challenges they face. Chapter by chapter, those challenges have three main themes:

- *Planning future performance:* it's not enough for today's CFO to analyze shareholder value and implement value-based management. You must stand on the front line with your CEO, searching out opportunities, crafting deals, and designing new business models (Chapter 2). Then your priorities will be to communicate value creation potential to investors, probe assumptions behind the new value drivers—often with little track record to build on—and keep score dynamically on how the new business is doing (Chapter 3). Your next goal: educating management on how to value intangible assets by overturning accounting conventions and providing a new focus on value creation (Chapter 4).

- *Allocating resources and evaluating the results:* your agenda must challenge traditional resource management processes; achieving success will depend on your appetite for taking risk, being creative, and seeing potential investments as options for growth (Chapter 5). Then go one step further: abandon the budget (Chapter 6). To do all this, you'll be investing more in systems: getting the most from your existing ERP suite while integrating new e-business solutions (Chapter 7).

- *Defining new structures:* your contribution going forward increasingly will be focused on preparing the corporation for the inevitable and constant structural change. The corporation's cost base will be slow to react, so radical overhaul may become an ongoing feature rather than a one-off event (Chapter 8). You must decide between acquisitions and alliances, and how to integrate them, taking advantage of the Internet (Chapter 9). Not that the role of the corporate center should escape scrutiny. You are a primary player in updating this value proposition (Chapter 10). What about the structure for finance? What form shall it take? Web-enabled, shared? Yes. But outsourced as well? Maybe. Virtual? Almost certainly (Chapter 11).

Like all chapters, this concludes with an eCFO checklist to guide your way.

# eCFO CHECKLIST

## DESIGN NEW BUSINESS MODELS
Do you search out new e-business opportunities? Can you convert these into robust value propositions? Does your finance function play a leading role in implementing new models? Have you realigned your finance processes?

## OPTIMIZE SHAREHOLDER VALUE
Do you understand how the market values your e-business investments? Have you analyzed the new value drivers? Have you created an e-business scorecard?

## GROW INTANGIBLES
Do you know how to value your corporation's intangible assets? How regularly do you update your valuation results and communicate them to investors? Are your managers' investment priorities directed toward growing intangibles?

## RETHINK RESOURCE ALLOCATION
Do you focus on attracting rather than allocating resources to new initiatives? Do you look at your investments as options for growth? Do you know when to spin on, spin in or spin out?

## BLOW UP THE BUDGET
How effective is your annual budget at responding to the new economy? Do you use key performance indicators for targeting and rolling forecasts for monitoring? Could you abandon budgeting altogether?

## DELIVER A NEW SYSTEMS VISION
Have you realized the full benefits of ERP? Do you know how to integrate your e-business solutions? Do you have a dynamic set of tools for gathering and reporting business intelligence in the new economy? Have you developed the business case for a CFO portal?

OVERHAUL YOUR COST BASE
Do you understand how your new business models impact existing cost structures? Have you benchmarked costs externally and set stretch targets? Do you reinvest savings in innovation and growth?

UNLOCK VALUE FROM ACQUISITIONS AND ALLIANCES
Do you plan postacquisition integration ahead of the deal? Do you take account of cultural fit? Do you stay focused on closing the value gap? Have you considered the advantages of alliances over acquisitions?

REINVENT THE CORPORATE CENTER
Does your corporate center create or destroy value? Are you refocusing investment on those discretionary activities that add value to business units? Have you developed a performance contract for the center?

MOVE TOWARD A VIRTUAL FINANCE FUNCTION
Are your finance processes fully Web-enabled? Have you extended your decision-support service throughout the extraprise? Could you go further with outsourcing? Will your finance function exist at all in 2010?

# CHAPTER 2

# Designing New Business Models for Value Creation

## DIRECT FROM DELL'S CFO

*Tom Meredith, Managing Director Dell Ventures, and former CFO*
**Dell Computer Corporation**

*I think the challenges facing Dell can probably be broken down into people and models. The Dell business model is predicated on being direct. It is centered on the customer experience, bringing value through a series of propositions tied to moving goods in a more compressed time period, shrinking distance, and lowering cost.*

*The Internet is an almost perfect extension of the direct model as a perfect one-on-one segmentation. It leads to almost perfect information, in almost perfect time and almost perfect pricing. In consequence, the Internet is transformational across industries.*

*For some time we have used "fast-cycle segmentation" at the customer level. After all, it is the customers who buy the product that create the value. We looked for trends or common characteristics across customer sets, and as a business grew large we split it into smaller units. The growth of the split segments would invariably exceed the growth of the combined segments. At first our own colleagues bridled at having their job responsibility narrowed; now most of senior management understand the model: to have your business split up is actually a sign of success.*

*The Internet transforms business; the Web changes everything. We know the Internet has had a tremendous effect on Dell and on our stakeholders—our customers, our employees and our suppliers. We use the Internet externally and internally, and we also use an extranet capability. In each case we seek to bring more value to our stakeholders by compressing time and distance, and shrinking cost. Effective use of the Internet is about value creation.*

*Dell's growth rate has continued to surpass all but perhaps one or two companies. In the context of our space, we are the fastest growing, lowest cost, most profitable, open systems vendor on the face of the planet. The Internet has driven greater efficiencies and scaling opportunities and, I suspect, generated significantly more volume.*

*Since the Internet provides unprecedented access to information, entities can now trade bits of information, forming alliances to produce a product, a service or an experience. This enhances shareholder value while providing great customer solutions.*

**The Internet has allowed us instantly to provide data, information analyses, analytic and decision support that historically would have taken us days or weeks or months to obtain.**

*Six or seven years ago, Dell had at least 300 suppliers providing 80% of its building materials; today 30 suppliers account for those materials. This creates a more vulnerable set of relationships among Dell and our suppliers. We can share information on design, quality, product, and pricing, and we are in a more continuous feedback loop. Most of our top suppliers also now embrace an extranet relationship with Dell, and that's delivered tremendous leverage to our company.*

*I think the industry is only beginning to understand the true drivers of value creation in the Internet economy. Capital markets are responding very favorably to experimental models, pouring money into the anticipation of promise.*

*Shortly after I joined Dell as CFO, we clarified a number of key focus areas. They included liquidity, profitability and growth, and more specifically, a metric called return on invested capital. The Internet has enabled us to leverage the cycle times to help our overall liquidity and, frankly, our returns. Often we trade off margin dollars in exchange for faster growth, while trying to deliver a consistent, balanced and sustainable set of results for our shareholders.*

*At Dell we have tried to quantify the value added by the Internet. Three years ago we began to measure Web-enabled revenues per day, and in a short period of time we determined that nearly 40% of our revenues were Web-enabled. Which means we earned roughly $30 million of revenue per day across the Net.*

*That's a great metric—it really focuses one's attention on exactly how far we've come as an organization. But I think the real news is the activity that underpins those numbers. It's the advent of e-commerce. All companies are now feeling the e-commerce imperative—a need for scaling at a greater and faster rate. Also, as information becomes more ubiquitous, how do we offer it to our customers in a valuable way? How do we create and maintain a relationship with our customers that is deeper than the buy and sell transaction?*

*One means is to leverage our sales and support capabilities via the Internet to give our customers better product information and a better price. At Dell we have over 27,000 premiere Web pages enhancing the customer experience, providing service, support, and order status, as well as over 35,000 pages of technical support.*

*Inside our company, the Internet has allowed us instantly to provide data, information analyses, analytic and decision support that historically would have taken us days or weeks or months to obtain. Finance has always examined the questions, What did we learn and what do we do next? But now our business decision-makers, line managers, and operations folks expect these answers immediately.*

*At Dell we are very, very focused on maintaining our low-cost model and our low-cost position in the marketplace. The Internet helps us here as well. For example, commodities that go into systems have historically depreciated roughly half to one point a week. Because the Internet allows us to share data directly with the supplier, our marketing and finance people can now provide current, accurate pricing information to the decision-makers in the field. We can then pass on those lower component costs in lower total system pricing, which helps maintain our very competitive position in the marketplace.*

*I think it was Peter Drucker who said in the early sixties that the worker would be responsible for the information age. That still holds true. And ironically, the thinking that helped achieve our market position is probably not going to bring us to the next level. Now leadership, including myself, must get managers to embrace a new level of thought. In hiring, we're interested in people who understand the anticipation and promise of the Web. The biggest risk for any business today is the race for talent.*

*Dell's new competitors will largely be Web-related and legacy-free. We're in a good competitive position, but going forward we will have to do some things differently. While we are careful to maintain our position in terms of incumbent competitors, we're also building the new Internet direct Dell model to deliver our value proposition for both shareholders and customers.*

*Among CFOs there's a universal belief that either you can embrace the Internet, or be victimized by it as a function. This is prompting finance functions to examine how they will transform themselves over time. CFOs have to address the short, intermediate and longer-term impact of the Internet on their companies. At Dell we have lots of discussions around the "beyond the box" experience. That experience can include financing, access to the Internet, a branded portal strategy; it can include peripheral equipment, or accessories.*

*The Internet also demands agility. When companies like Dell become bigger, they add more products, extend geographies, and increase their staff—they become more complex organizations. But building a backbone, a stronger foundation, also builds in certain rigidities. It's a challenge for finance professionals to bridge the gap between rigidity—the strong organization—and the agility of the Internet.*

*Part of the solution is moving from an independent control environment to one that is interdependent, both externally and internally. You can't hire 8,000 people, as we did two years ago, and be personally involved in every executive decision. You have to trust your new colleagues and allow them the agility and the freedom to move more rapidly.*

*Another example of the rigidity/agility discussion really centers on Dell's approach to segmentation, fast-cycle segmentation in particular. Segmentation allows us to focus on specific customer segments and their commonality, whether the segment is an individual, a business, or an educational institution. As we segment, the finance world recreates historical data to determine whether past trends are carrying through. If the trends are favorable, we leverage them; if they're not, we determine how to adjust that business and thus improve our overall profitability.*

*So segmentation prompts a whole set of questions around the backbone, challenging you to ask why not as opposed to why.*

---

Dell has made a success of taking its existing direct sales business model and putting it on the Internet. As a result, it is regarded as a market leader in its sector and has superior economic performance. Companies in other sectors are also making major investments in software, hardware, communications and content—often framing new products and services—to transform the way they do business. Why do we have this phenomenon? For two main reasons:

- New technology is making it possible to connect businesses and people globally. The arrival of the Web, digital technology, WAP, and other emerging connectivity technologies have made it not only easier but *cheaper* for people to communicate, not by a small margin but by a quantum factor.

- New levels of connectivity have changed marketplace economics by reducing the barriers to entry for new players. These new players seize value creation opportunities, becoming a competitive threat to established companies.

Because the new market opportunities are open to more players, there is a sense of urgency: the view still prevails that the first player to reach the market captures the most market share *and value.* But there is also a growing sense of realism, as we begin to learn about what works well and what doesn't in Internet investments. Many of today's leading companies are rethinking or even reshaping their business models. The new economic assumptions will have to withstand hard scrutiny and testing, and CFOs will have to be clear on the business case. Corporate involvement in business-to-business exchanges, for example, continues to grow fast despite concerns that many exchanges, even successful ones, won't make much money. The benefits of participation in e-markets may be greater than the returns on e-market investments. Once built, however, it's unlikely that exchanges will be dismantled even though they may struggle to achieve critical mass and profitability.

This chapter identifies the drivers which are changing business models and provides guidance for CFOs on the learning experienced so far in setting up e-business—practical cases which draw out some of the economic realities and dispel some of the hype.

## THE DRIVERS OF CHANGE

Why and how are business models changing? Here are some of the drivers behind change:

- *Increased specialization*: there is a renewed focus on what's core to the business; this is leading to an increase in outsourcing and disintegration of the traditional value chain through partnering. The challenge: meeting customer needs when the company specializes in only one segment of the value chain.

- *One-to-one customer relationships:* there is better understanding of customers' individual needs and increasing personalization of customer treatment, providing the opportunity for more targeted marketing and customer leverage.

- *More pull and less push*: business is increasingly customer-led rather than production-driven. Supply chains have to be more flexible and responsive. Conversely, companies are using the Web to find new channels, markets, and customers to fill unutilized capacity—more push, less pull!

- *Redefined trading relationships:* new markets are being created, new value-added communities are emerging, and business partnerships are becoming more substantive.

- *Self-service:* employees and customers have increased access to tools and services, giving more control to individuals.

Figure 2.1 shows how the enterprise business model can be viewed in three segments: the buy side (suppliers), the sell side (customers) and the inside (infrastructure). For many companies, the Internet breaks down the traditional barriers between these segments by making it possible to create networks of enterprises, including outsourced partners.

Take this example, in which barriers with suppliers have come down. A major engineering conglomerate has developed a trading network, a Web-based link to its suppliers that enables them easily and quickly to make bids for its components contracts. It features an electronic catalog, the ability to make electronic purchases, and the option of paying online with an electronic credit card. The system has cut procurement cycles in half, processing costs by a third, and the cost of goods purchased by up to 50%. The company now does well over $1 billion worth of Web-based

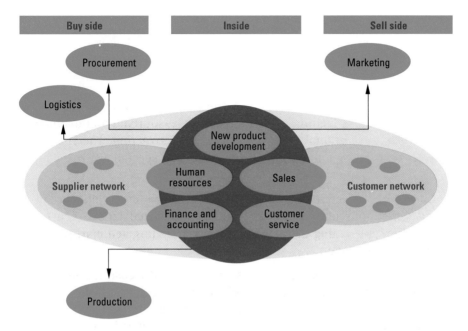

Figure 2.1   *The networked enterprise*

business annually. The number of suppliers has come down, and the remaining ones have become more efficient.

Take another example, in which barriers both with customers and internally between functions have come down. A high-tech company does 80% of its sales over the Web. Customers select from an electronic catalog, are helped to get their order exactly right, and can track its progress online. The whole process of ordering, contract manufacturing, fulfillment, and payment is automated. The CFO claims that 55% of orders pass through the company's system without being touched by anyone. "We just collect the money," he says. He reckons that the company is saving over $500 million a year by using the Web. Indeed it could not have maintained its growth rate without it.

Despite these success stories, many of the finance executives of the established companies interviewed for this book have a healthy cynicism; they've seen the Internet bubble grow and burst. They may themselves use the Internet freely for personal and domestic purposes, but they are considerably more cautious when it comes to experimenting with their businesses. Why? Apparently, it's the other functions in the business which have most to gain from the Internet: marketing and sales, through more direct connectivity with the customer; procurement, manufacturing and logistics, through more direct connectivity with suppliers and customers; and human resources, through more direct connectivity with the employee community. But for the finance community there are many risks to face: disruption to established financial management disciplines, loss of control over spending and accounting transactions, systems failure and, most importantly, potential loss in profitability.

The CFO has to be ahead of the game, with answers to these questions:

- Where and how do we create shareholder value in our business model, today and in the future?

- Which of our customers provide us with the most value? How do we evaluate our customer investment and measure the returns?

- What new pricing structures are appropriate in the e-business world?

- What is the optimal configuration for our infrastructure?

- How much investment should be tied up in both physical assets (including working capital) and in intangibles (including brands, R&D, and technology)?

In *Leading the Revolution*, Gary Hamel encourages us to think beyond new products and services to entirely new business concepts that meet deep customer needs in unconventional ways.[1] CFOs are in one of strongest positions to think through the economics of new business concepts, holistically and concretely. Hamel has created a useful framework for "unpacking the business model." This framework describes business models as having four main components: the customer interface, the core business strategy, the strategic resources required, and the value network that surrounds the company (suppliers, partners, coalitions). Core competencies, strategic assets, and core processes have to be combined, or configured, through a unique set of linkages to support the core strategy.

Underpinning the business model are four interrelated factors that determine its profit potential:

- *Efficiency*: the business model must deliver customer benefits at optimal cost.

- *Uniqueness*: the business model must be unique (in concept and execution) in ways that are valued by customers.

- *Fit*: the business model must be internally consistent; all its components must reinforce each other and work together toward the same end goal.

- *Profit boosters*: to achieve superior returns, the business model should benefit from competitor lockout, strategic economics such as scale or focus, or as in Dell's case, its inherent operating agility.

How is this theory borne out in practice? Next we review the range of new business models that different companies are adopting and analyze the underlying economic lessons they offer. The examples should assist CFOs in designing economically attractive new business models. They include an auction-based Internet start-up, an electronics company investing in new distribution channels, an e-market in the utilities industry, and a business-to-employee portal in a high-tech company.

## WHAT CAN ESTABLISHED BUSINESSES LEARN FROM INTERNET START-UPS?

Successful Internet businesses seem to have common strengths: sustainable competitive advantage and a clear rationale as to why the business should be online. Management should share an understanding of how the core business is intended to deliver profits. The technology used should be strong in both functionality and scalability. Above all, there is no substitute for an excellent and committed management team, capable of winning investor confidence and delivering growth.

CASE STUDY
The Formative Years of an
Internet Company

*The founding directors came together to prepare a business plan some three years ago. Among them, they had previous experience in Internet service provision, online publishing, and corporate finance. The business model was founded on the auction house concept of commission-based services for putting buyers and sellers together. As with all business-to-consumer start-ups, the first rounds of funding were required for the Web site, staffing and advertising, both online and offline. Revenues were to arise from commissions, agency sales, and listing fees.*

*The directors' plan did not require them to make a profit for the first two years; it was presented to financiers as a capital investment. After two years the company was still in a loss position, with costs exceeding revenues. But the business was seen to be successful, both in taking market share away from competitors and in acquiring similar businesses in its sector. Investment in fixed assets, with the exception of computer systems, was minimal and most of the funding went into the technology and building of the brand.*

*The original strategy has remained intact, but some aspects of the operating economics have been intentionally changed. The company abandoned holding inventory for resale and relied purely on agency commissions with no dis-tribution responsibility.*

*What lessons has the company learned so far? It is essential to have a strong management team that is totally dedicated to making the new business model work. Investors will back superior management teams because they know their markets, track their competitors closely, and understand the strengths and limitations of the model they've created. The company has avoided some of the more common, often fatal errors made by others, such as growing too quickly, overdoing the publicity or making promises to customers they can't fulfill, usually through poor Web site design or weak logistics.*

---

Successful Internet company management teams like the one in this case study have a sound appreciation of the business model fundamentals, and a passion for customer service tempered by a clear sense of financial control.

## USING THE WEB TO PROTECT AND ENHANCE REVENUES

In business-to-business (B2B) e-business, channel enhancement is often more about redesigning internal processes, creating an environment of standardization, and reducing costs than about absolute revenue in-crease and integrating a company with other entities. In contrast, *pure play* business-to-consumer (B2C) Internet retailers focus almost entirely on revenue growth, or more accurately, customer capture. But as many dotcoms are discovering, integration of back-end processes and systems are necessary components of a long-term strategy for sustainable growth.

Deciding what business model to adopt in dealing with your B2B customers can be difficult. How far should your Internet links extend into the customer's value chain? How much value-added service should you provide, not only to your customers but also to your customers' customers? What are the effects on existing distribution channels? What's the payback? Consider the case of an electronic consumer goods supplier that has these issues to tackle as it implements an extranet with a dealer network fragmented across a continent.

CASE STUDY
B2b: Big Business Dealing with Small
Businesses over the Web

*A consumer electronics manufacturer and distributor is implementing a global e-business project, initially focusing on 14 countries in Europe. The market for the goods (televisions, hi-fi, etc.) is mature, the products have little competitive differentiation, and customers are becoming more sophisticated buyers. The company's response is focused on improving service levels as well as competing on price.*

*The dealer network varies from country to country. In the UK it is concentrated on a few multiple retailers with a high market share. In most of the countries, however, a large number of small independent dealers have the majority of the market and therefore, from the manufacturer's viewpoint, these dealers are expensive to service and a lot less profitable. But the company cannot ignore this sizable market and initiated the e-business program with the twin objectives of improving service levels to independent dealers and reducing cost to serve.*

*The new B2b extranet is designed in three functional tiers (Figure 2.2).*

- With the dealer: *this tier covers traditional transaction processing, from order to payment and dealer servicing. Dealers can order from the manufacturer and pay on the Web, and they can view the manufacturer's catalog online. But the end consumer transactions are handled entirely by the dealer.*

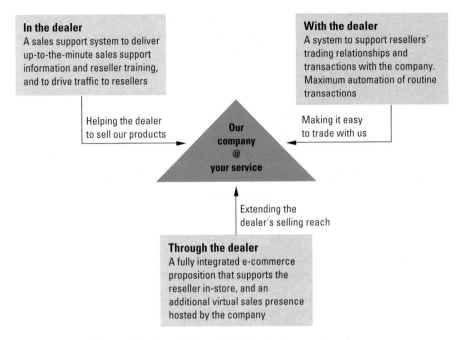

**Figure 2.2** *Strengthening links with the dealer network*

- In the dealer: *this tier is being extended so that the manufacturer can more directly support sales and service activity via the Web through to the end consumer on the dealer's premises. For example, a small dealer will be able to access and order from the full manufacturer's catalog online, even when carrying only minimal stock on the premises. Furthermore, consumers will be able to view products and make buying decisions online. New Web-based processes are being introduced by the manufacturer to train dealer sales-people, to register consumer guarantees, and to monitor stock status in the supply chain.*

- Through the dealer: *this tier goes one stage further. The manufacturer will have direct access over the Web to the dealer's customer base for joint direct marketing with the dealer. Here the manufacturer becomes more of a host to the dealer, providing the dealer with Web site design, delivery and content services.*

*The business case for the initiative was based primarily on cost savings. Depending on the functional tier implemented—the extent to which the extranet is extended through the dealer to service the customer directly—savings of 5–15% are expected in the cost to serve. These savings arise from reductions in the frequency of sales rep visits, stock obsolescence, and processing costs.*

*Incremental revenue benefits accruing from the higher service levels are more difficult to ascertain, although measurable improvements in dealer satisfaction levels are being achieved with a positive sales knock-on. Other revenue-based measures have also started to improve, such as sales volume, average purchase value, and revenue per store. Not only does the new system create more selling opportunities for the manufacturer, but it reduces the amount of cash tied up in inventory and working capital in the supply chain, for the benefit of consumers, dealers, and the manufacturer.*

*Customers and dealers have so far reacted positively to pilot implementations in selected countries. Preparations are now being made for a full global rollout to build on the success in Europe.*

---

Technology-driven initiatives such as this case study can pay back the original investment in under two years. What worked well in this particular case were the clarity of vision for service improvement and the robustness of the business case for cost reduction. Implementing an e-business project tends to be a journey of exploration, there are few precedents from which to learn. Staying focused on the business case requires traditional program management discipline.

When new e-based sales channels are introduced in consumer goods industries, the existing dealer network can be threatened by what is seen as a potential new competitor. Good communication is required if the manufacturer is to maintain the motivation of dealers throughout implementation. The dealers need to share in the benefits and be convinced of the manufacturer's ability to deliver the new solution.

In certain industries, such as high-tech, manufacturers are not so dependent on retail dealer networks and customers are more willing to buy online. In these industries the economics of the sell-side business model can be improved if customers wish to configure their own purchases, as in the case of Dell. Allowing the customer to configure the product online helps the seller reduce inventories and achieve just-in-time-for-customer production. Dell is also able to react online to aggressive competitor pricing strategies. Since Dell and its customers have a one-to-one relationship over the Web, customers' buying patterns, product preferences, and price sensitivities can be monitored and acted upon, sometimes within hours.

Perhaps the greatest potential for new revenue results when the Web-enabled sales channel allows entry into new markets in which the company does not already have a physical presence, for example, moving from a saturated US market to an underdeveloped European or Asian market. A company can add a sales channel without changing its basic business model. However, if the company truly expects to increase customer loyalty, customer service or sales by this new channel, then radically different processes must be put in place to manage the channel. As the success of the sales channel takes off, scalability becomes key. Companies serious about e-business can move forward in one of two ways: by using Web technology to strengthen their distribution network, or by trying to migrate their current sales model into a direct Web-enabled channel.

CASE STUDY
Migrating to a New Direct Sales Model

*A US retail chain, with an extensive national presence in shopping malls but without an Internet operation, found its growth being limited by the rapid expansion of B2C Web sites that sold similar products at lower prices. Because of the Internet, newcomers were able to establish their businesses quickly and cheaply, without the need for extensive physical inventory, costly retail location or experienced sales personnel, although they would need to spend up to around $50 million on marketing to obtain visibility.*

*Initially, the retail chain responded by increasing the number of special promotions it ran in its stores, offering deeper discounts on more products than it had in the past. While this kept inventory turns high, the CFO realized that this would eventually become self-defeating. Even though the chain purchased in far greater quantities than its Internet competitors, it would never be able* consistently to underprice them because it had a much higher fixed overhead. Short of massive store closings, that wasn't going to change.

The CFO was charged with reconfiguring the organization's business model to counteract its new competition and regain market share. After conducting a study, the CFO recommended that the company quickly move to establish a substantial Internet operation at an estimated cost of $75 million spread over two years.

Although the start-up costs were high, the CFO argued that the investment would add economic value. Once the initial staff, hardware, and software were in place, the Internet would reduce the organization's ongoing costs of doing business on multiple fronts: the cost of online sales would be much lower than in-store transactions and additional savings could be found by handling procurement, back-office transactions, and HR functions on the Web.

> **The company wasn't cannibalizing its bricks-and-mortar business. The Internet retail operation capitalized on its brand and large customer base, complementing its stores rather than competing with them.**

Getting into e-commerce would allow the company quickly to expand its retail presence by capitalizing on its brand and its reputation for quality and attentive service. It could add, remove or take on new lines of merchandise instantly and inexpensively online. Plus the company would obtain far more extensive customer data on Internet shoppers than it obtained on traditional shoppers, making it possible to have pinpoint marketing and information sharing between the two operations.

The CFO also pointed out that the company would essentially be establishing a new franchise. The future of the Internet is undefined but positive, and the prevailing outlook is that the sooner an entrant gets in, the better. It would also improve the company's image, since retailers without a robust Internet presence are thought by consumers to be out of touch. And despite the volatility of this market segment, those who are doing innovative work on the Internet have generally benefited on the stock market, creating new value for their shareholders.

The CFO established the Internet business as an independent entity, with separate funding and reporting. That enabled the parent company to obtain *partial backing from venture capitalists and some of its business partners, while keeping the start-up losses the Web site would suffer from damaging the balance sheet of the parent. The independent status also allowed the Internet operation to move as rapidly as e-commerce requires, and to offer key employees the stock options that are necessary to attract top candidates.*

*After a year the company conducted a study of its online operation. It discovered that the majority of its Internet shoppers were:*

- *People who live outside major metropolitan areas*
- *People who dislike or don't have the time for shopping*
- *People who have specialized needs and require hard-to-find products*
- *People who want to do extensive comparison shopping before buying*

*Customers who continued to shop in the chain's stores tended to be:*

- *People concerned about the security and privacy of purchasing online*
- *People who lack the equipment or knowledge for gaining access to the Internet*
- *People who enjoy the social experience of traditional shopping*
- *People who live near existing stores*

*The data indicated that the company wasn't cannibalizing its bricks-and-mortar business by establishing a retail operation on the Internet, and after some initial adjustments to product mix and special promotions, its e-business enterprise produced satisfactory revenues. The chain fortified its mall sales by refocusing those stores on their areas of strength and value, such as purchasing advice and personal service.*

*Even though the first Internet businesses established the Web as a place where goods were sold at steeply discounted prices, the company refrained from this practice. Instead, the e-commerce operation capitalized on its brand and large customer base, complementing its stores rather than competing with them. The CFO then leveraged the learning of the B2C start-up by exploring the B2B options available to the chain.*

As this case study illustrates, for established enterprises to maximize the economic value they receive from B2C investments, they must alter their business model enough to compete with dotcom rivals, without losing those attributes of the model on which they have built their brand. The customers are in charge, and if you don't understand and satisfy their demands, someone else will. Fortunately, every time they visit your Web site, consumers leave a trail of information about their wants and needs.

## EXPLOITING e-MARKETS

e-Markets are online marketplaces that serve specific industries and participants belonging to the same supply chain. e-Markets link buyers and sellers globally by enabling them to manage, buy, sell, and trade products and services with greater efficiency, which ultimately reduces operational expenses. Although most e-markets remain in their developmental stages, evolutionary changes mean that the B2B marketplace is likely to grow exponentially, potentially reaching $200 trillion in worldwide capital market value over the next 10 years.

For example, Transora.com was launched in June 2000. This e-market initially comprised at least 20 of the world's leading food, beverage and consumer products companies, including Coca-Cola, Kraft Foods, Kellogg and Nabisco. They came together to explore ways of boosting efficiency in the FMCG industry supply chain. Realizing that B2B transactions increasingly take place over the Internet, the companies faced a choice of developing their own online market structures with suppliers, or *all coming together* at one time and building one marketplace.

The participants of this open, standards-based e-market exchange now represent nearly 40% of the players in the global consumer products industry. Today 50 businesses have invested $240 million; the e-market provides participants with procurement, vendor and product catalogs, online order management, supply chain collaboration, and financial services. Transora.com expects the efficiencies of these and other online offerings eventually to save participating companies up to 10% of the cost of offline procurement methods.

By consolidating such daily business processes in a standard online environment, the once complex transactions between participating suppliers, manufacturers, and distributors are now greatly simplified. They're not just dealing with prices. It's about collaboration and communication among the many participants that are required to make a product show up on the shelf at the right time. Consumers, in turn, should reap the benefits of these efficiencies through reduced prices and an increased variety of goods in stores.

A key benefit of the e-market will be increased speed and liquidity of transactions for participating companies. "Transora.com will offer a single connection to a broad array of services and exchanges on the Internet, providing ease of connectivity and associated cost efficiencies," comments one participant.

Not all e-markets are on the scale of Transora.com, nor organized globally around a vertical industry. Some companies just invest initially in their own enterprise-wide buy site; others in procurement portals which may be horizontally organized, i.e., buyers join together across a number of industries to purchase relatively low-value-added non-production-related materials such as office supplies. Some, like utilities, may cover a limited geographic region.

Each of these business models will have its individual economic characteristics, all based fundamentally on reducing the cost of procurement. But the larger, more sophisticated e-markets have additional revenue-creating opportunities such as subscriptions, rentals, and transaction and auction fees. These revenues can come not only from buyers but also from suppliers, who may also have to pay market-site access, hosting and integration fees.

But all these e-market models are in their infancy; it may take many years for their true economic viability to emerge. The CFO should develop a sound business case for the investment at the outset. Consider this case study on a consortium of utility companies that are preparing for a potential industry-wide procurement portal.

CASE STUDY
Demonstrating the Economic Viability of an e-Market Company

*A consortium of utilities businesses wanted to build a procurement portal to link many hundreds of suppliers with their own businesses and ultimately several dozen others. The investments were significant; they would have to buy the software to run the portal, customize it, research participant requirements,* set up a company, recruit staff, and so on. Then people had to be convinced to participate and to pay for doing so. Sizable one-off and recurring fees were needed to cover the investment, before any incremental return could be generated; the buyer and supplier take-up projections were key.

Assessments of how many buyers and suppliers might participate and the rate at which they were likely to join would determine the size and timing of investment in setting up the portal; they would also support the revenue projections. So what questions had to be answered to prove the opportunity viable?

- Who would want to be party to a joint venture rather than simply a user of the portal?

  Although there's huge interest in e-business, in business-to-business, caution reigns. Participants must ensure their representatives are closely involved in the analysis process. The potential rewards are huge, but the risk is significant. Buy-in is critical, so the consortium had to be sure there would be enough participants to make it work.

- How many buyers and suppliers would participate and how quickly could they be acquired?

  Volume is key. Many suppliers to one buyer may be feasible. Many to many is much better. While suppliers may feel compelled to conform, the motivation may be different for customers. Early on, the portal founders will need to sell the concept to potential customers. The key is the percentage of total pro-curement that could be channeled through the portal. From the viewpoint of suppliers, it makes most sense to segment high-value purchases, such as raw materials and capital goods. The important thing is to get a critical mass of customers and suppliers.

- How would people be charged for use of the portal?

  Would a joining fee and annual access fee be acceptable, or should par-ticipants be charged per transaction? With few existing portals to refer to, it's difficult to decide the right price structure. e-Business pundits claim that transaction costs will tend to zero, which suggests that an annual fee would be most appropriate. But this is unlikely to cover short-term costs while the critical mass of participants builds. The total annual cost to both buyer and supplier must be lower than the benefits of participating. Existing portals and industry benchmarks for procurement transactions provide a starting point for examining alternative pricing strategies; discussions with poten-tial participants will confirm the best mix of annual and transaction-based fees.

- *What volume of transactions would be expected?*

For a transaction fee structure to be supportable, volume data is critical. This also affects the system's size. Potential participants would be obliged to provide data on the volume of all transactions processed through the portal—purchase orders, goods receipt notes, sales orders, invoices, shipping notes, and payments. Such information is not always readily available. The critical issue is how sensitive variations in these transaction volumes might be, both to profits and operational performance. Transaction volume can have a significant impact on the size of transaction fees and their relation-ship with an annual access fee. In this case the portal company would have to quadruple the transaction fee to generate the same revenue as a mix of transaction and annual access fees.

- *What would be the content of the portal?*

Would there be a charge to suppliers for adding and maintaining catalogs of items in the portal? While there aren't many precedents, today's portals do charge for this service.

- *Do other revenue streams exist?*

For example, would there be revenue from holding auctions, selling man-agement information, advertising sponsorship, exchange transactions? The answer is yes (Figure 2.3). But the issue is timing. The most common additional revenue source, buyer-and-seller auctions, can generally be introduced quickly. In contrast, selling information, perhaps for inventory and distribution management, would be a feasible service only when sufficient data is available via the portal.

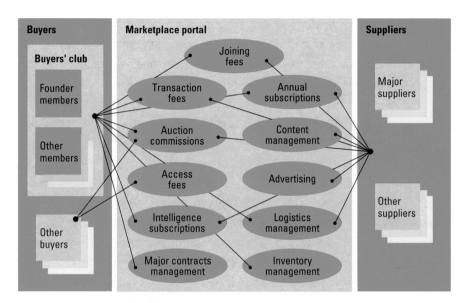

**Figure 2.3** *Typical revenue potential for a marketplace portal*

- *What would be the hardware and software costs of building the portal?*

  *There are several suppliers of off-the-shelf portal software. Each offers a different mix of up-front and ongoing licenses, maintenance, and consultancy. Additional hardware may be required, depending on whether the portal is a separate entity or a wholly-owned company. The decision-making process around software and hardware is identical to that in any system design—specification of requirements, proposals from potential suppliers, and a cost-benefit assessment. Typical costs are $15–20 million.*

- *Would any other software or system changes be required?*

  *Other systems may need to be built around the portal itself, a billing system for example. Buyers and suppliers may also need to enhance their systems to secure access. These requirements should all be addressed by portal software suppliers and form part of the cost-benefit analysis.*

- *What other start-up costs are likely?*

  *A new idea requires marketing. A new business needs legal advice and financial management. New systems and procedures demand training. With*

*little in-house expertise to draw on, companies may also need external con-
sulting support. Typically, half a new portal's total investment is represented
by these secondary start-up costs.*

- *What organization would be needed to support the portal?*

*Whether it operates within an existing business or as a joint venture, infra-
structure is required. Typically, a joint venture in a sizable business requires a
full management team. As participants increase, so will the customer
support staff. Dotcom expertise can be costly. Attracting the right people
requires six-figure salaries for the CEO, operations director, and other key
staff. Senior technical and financial salaries follow market norms. Overall,
people costs can consume 10% of an operating budget. Choice of location
influences these costs and is driven by proximity to the right people, and
possibly taxation issues. One option is to outsource processes such as billing
and call center services.*

- *How will the portal business be set up and valued?*

*The main consideration here is whether or not a flotation is anticipated.
Potentially large returns could encourage initial participants to take shares
in a separate company and simply write off the up-front investment. Altern-
atively, it may be necessary to borrow funds and treat the portal as any other
operating investment. It is important to evaluate the cash flow implications
using an appropriate weighted average cost of capital. The valuation should
be based on discounted cash flows with a perpetuity; this offers the most
reliable picture of the worth of the business. The rest depends on dotcom
market sentiment!*

*Tried and tested techniques of discounted cash flow and sensitivity analysis
showed a payback period for the proposed portal in excess of four years and a
return of 26%, hardly the pot of gold at the end of the Internet rainbow. In the
analysis, the portal company was valued at a conservative one-tenth of the
revenue multiple that had been driving dotcom prices sky high.*

*But members of the consortium recognized that business-to-business e-
opportunities are about taking something you do already and doing it better, in*

*this case procurement. The benefits case for the portal embraced cost savings within participating businesses, both buyers and sellers, as well as cash generation. For example, it would streamline the procurement process and help match supply and demand more effectively.*

*Clearly, the savings plus even the most modest realization of cash benefits made the portal a worthwhile proposition. And real options analysis of future growth revealed potential for greater shareholder value creation in anticipation of an IPO.*

---

## OPTIMIZING THE SUPPLY CHAIN THROUGH e-COLLABORATION

Collaborative planning via the Internet provides an environment for integrating demand and supply-side processes to achieve reduced inventory levels, shorter supply chain cycle times, and reduced supply chain costs. It encourages partnering between retailers and manufacturers, and between manufacturers and their suppliers, through comanaged processes and shared information.

In the US an industry group of retailers and manufacturers has set up a collaborative planning, forecasting and replenishment (CPFR) business model. This initiative aims to improve the partnership between retailers and their suppliers. Today more than 30 companies participate, including retailers such as Wal-Mart and Kmart, manufacturers such as Procter & Gamble and Sara Lee, and IT partners such as Hewlett-Packard and SAP. The concept has been extended to Europe and is running pilots in four countries. Figure 2.4 sets out the collaborative processes for both retailers and suppliers. Here are some of the benefits:

- *Synchronization*: by generating feasible, optimized plans and schedules, and replanning when conditions change.

- *Inventory reduction*: by providing better visibility of information relating to forecasts, orders and plans for anticipating consumer demand and providing for collaboration with channel partners.

- *Responsiveness*: by reducing time to detect demand, commit, produce and fulfill, leading to improved replenishment cycles and increased sales.

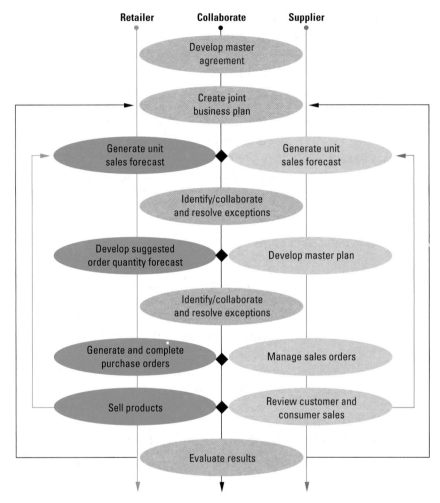

**Figure 2.4** *Collaborative planning, forecasting and replenishment processes*

Experience of this type of CPFR e-business initiative has so far shown reduced inventory levels of 18–40%, increased inventory turns of 20–70%, reduced production cycle times of up to 70% and reduced goods returns of 5–20%. An effective demand planning tool is a critical foundation for collaboration. Don't underestimate the importance of technology infrastructure—Internet connectivity affects systems performance.

But success during implementation requires more than just technology. Standard supply chain processes should be developed by partners;

pilot implementations are useful to prove new process viability and value. Roll out the new CPFR strategy to key suppliers in waves, with initial emphasis on important, high-volume or high-velocity suppliers. The development and implementation process for CPFR itself should be collaborative. Supplier insights add value. A collaboration agreement prior to going live puts the focus on achieving results.

Supply chain collaboration is a good example of *external* connectivity over the Internet and the value to be obtained by combining different companies' business models. Connectivity *internally* over intranets, and on into the external world, can also create value by linking employees together and changing the internal business model.

## THE BUSINESS CASE FOR B2E

What is B2E connectivity? B2E, or business-to-employee, means using the Internet to develop the relationship between the business and the employee in a new way. It's direct, it's personal, and it can be very cost-effective. A B2E enterprise information portal (Chapter 7) is the *corporate home page* for employees. It provides an entry point for finding and connecting other sites on the corporate intranet. The B2E portal is a personalized, ever-changing mix of news, resources, applications and e-commerce options; it becomes the desktop destination for everyone in an organization and the primary vehicle by which people do their work.

From the CFO's viewpoint, the B2E portal has tremendous potential for cutting across functions and business units, allowing employees to manage their own data and transactions, and providing a ready-made vehicle for sharing information and knowledge. It also offers a useful boost to corporate communications and the gathering of business intelligence. It's content can be divided into four application categories:

- *Employee connectivity*: comprising corporate financial information, competitive intelligence and corporate communications, connected to online learning, employee self-service applications and pay-related information.

- *Operational systems*: including cross-functional management reporting, workforce planning, performance measurement and other operational applications (customer, finance, supply chain).

- *Workgroup collaboration*: ranging from discussion forums and newsgroups to document management, Web conferencing and instant messaging.

- *External connectivity*: linking customer extranets, partner portals and external intelligence feeds to the intranet.

To the business, the financial benefits of a B2E portal include reductions in clerical work, operational cycle times and cost. To the employee, it's a tool that can simplify work by providing personalized information access anywhere, anytime. The value proposition encompasses *qualitative* benefits such as enhanced productivity, improved management information, improved connectivity and employee satisfaction, and *quantitative* benefits focused on reduced transaction processing costs, elimination of redundant infrastructure and associated maintenance costs.

But B2E is more than this. It can help to reshape the overall business model. Automotive companies are using B2E to shorten product development life cycles; oil companies are restructuring their internal operating models to improve productivity; pharmaceutical companies are using B2E to integrate corporate cultures following megamergers; telecommunications and entertainment companies are using B2E to attract and retain talent by securing employee mind share.

Consider the development of the B2E portal in the following case study; it shows how one leading high-tech company has gone about global implementation.

CASE STUDY
Implementing a Global Employee Portal

*A leading high-tech company has a vision for a "smarter Internet," one that enables organizations to invent new ways of doing business. The company believes any business asset or process can be delivered as a service across the Net.*

*The CEO set the target of reducing infrastructure costs by $1.5 billion to fund the company's entry into e-services. For the HR organization, which had already undergone a transformation, this meant doing something radically different. The company decided to look at moving HR work onto the Web; this* *progressed to a feasibility study for an employee portal. Since much of the basic processing for HR was already Web-enabled, the next step was channeling all employees' personal information through a portal.*

*HR-related costs are targeted to fall by 30%, a substantial cut, and new processes and procedures should allow HR staff to focus on services that add value to the business. Although initially the business case focused on reducing infrastructure costs in HR, finance and IT, subsequently the portal was seen as a tool for managing Internet use generally. For example, it has led to initiatives for consolidating the number of servers, for better coordinating content management, and for making more efficient use of the network.*

*These improvements, taken together, represented a total $200 million in cost savings. Much of the benefit derived from giving employees responsibility for managing their own data and extracting information. As the original HR project developed into an initiative for moving all infrastructure work onto the Web, a true enterprise-wide B2E portal has emerged. The scope ranges from financial processes (such as pay and expenses) to simple e-procurement applications (such as travel supplies) and workplace applications (such as office space scheduling). The portal is also used for a range of new processes, such as inducting a new employee and doing it consistently worldwide.*

> **Initially the business case focused on reducing the company's infrastructure costs in HR, finance and IT. Subsequently the portal was seen as a tool for managing Internet use generally.**

*The B2E portal was first released in the fall of 2000. This release is global, it is accessible by all employees and it has become a framework for business process transformation, even in functions such as sales and marketing. The content includes features such as myFrontpage, myData and myJob.*

*The next release will address myGroup and myWorkspace, ensuring that employees can collaborate over the Internet, making the portal the one place they go to do everything. As planned, the portal will address personal as well as work needs, such as managing personal finances.*

*The journey hasn't been easy. Implementing a B2E portal involves complexity and commitment. Integrating business processes on the Web challenges functional boundaries: integrating different languages, metrics, systems and tools. The company has moved from being primarily US-based (with a dominant manufacturing model) to being truly global (with a model based more on sales, services and consulting). Here are some of the learning points for portal implementation:*

- *When forming implementation teams, combine functional and technical expertise.*

- *When making savings in headcount, cut back on offline services; ensure that self-service takes over.*

- *Don't be too ambitious too early; break the project into manageable phases.*

*In essence, the company's B2E portal not only provides customers with a real-life example of how to apply e-technology in changing an existing business model, it also provides a vehicle for driving change across the enterprise.*

---

Experience in implementing new B2E models has shown the importance of starting with accurate and reliable operational processes and information. The implementation of a B2E program should be preceded by a cleanup initiative for existing and new Web content.

## MANAGING YOUR PORTFOLIO OF BUSINESS MODELS

Most bricks-and-mortar companies have allowed their e-business investments to develop opportunistically. Today most major companies have an e-business strategy with a clear vision, a robust process for evaluating and prioritizing investment opportunities, and guidelines for execution. Many CFOs are in the difficult position of internal venture capitalist; as such, they can become the gatekeeper on behalf of the board of directors, advising on the size and balance of risk in the e-business portfolio.

CASE STUDY
Endesa Builds a Net Factory

*Endesa, the leading electricity utility in Spain, has diversified into telecommunications and new technologies. CFO Jose Luis Palomo says, "Our vision is much more than a utility. We're building a new business portfolio in the most attractive segments: mobile telephony, cable, digital TV and, most importantly, Internet services and industry portals." Endesa's market capitalization has grown steadily to $25 billion, of which 65% is in the core electricity business in Spain, 20% in electricity interests internationally (mainly South America), and 15% in telecommunications. "We are fortunate in having a positive cash flow of $4 billion per annum," comments Palomo.*

*"Our overall objective is to double the company's intrinsic value in less than five years. Sustaining growth, improving profitability, optimizing the cost of capital and mobilizing our intangibles are critical to achieving this. We manage our business as a strategic portfolio, concentrating on core competencies and competitive skills, and proactively checking each business unit for strategic fit and value creation. In my role as CFO, I regularly advise the board on buying, selling, sharing, or keeping business units."*

*What are the intangibles that Endesa aims to mobilize? The company has a strong customer base (over 27 million customers), a strong supplier base (annual purchases in excess of $3 billion), and proven skills in developing companies in new markets, combined with its core management skill in energy and telecommunications. Palomo continues, "We're going to leverage this intangible base via new business initiatives such as trading, e-business, and value-added services." The company has three main e-business investments that are likely to extend and change its business model, creating a Net factory, as Endesa calls it.*

- *Business-to-business: Endesa is creating an electronic business trade exchange by combining its purchasing power with that of other external partners in an Internet-based exchange connected to common suppliers.*

- *Business-to-customer: Endesa is enhancing and extending its services to its extensive customer base (both domestic and business) by using the Internet as a main distribution channel.*

- Technology-related Internet investments: *Endesa will invest $400 million during the next five years in mobile/Internet WAP services; in remote electronic metering and related services; and in Powerline, data and voice traveling over the electricity distribution network.*

*Endesa's Net factory will manage the transfer of knowledge and skills between its core business and the new initiatives. But the B2B trade exchange, known as Endesa Marketplace, will be set up as an independent investment. Palomo comments, "We've formed Endesa Marketplace to cope with the enormous growth in B2B e-business over the next few years. In our vertical market, we intend to be the first utility company to offer our suppliers and partners a sophisticated e-business solution. We're currently linked through the Net with 1,000 of our top suppliers, doing $2 billion worth of trade per year in Spain and Latin America. We expect Endesa Marketplace to give us $60–120 million in savings alone in our procurement chain.*

*"Linking up with other partners in our own and other industries should generate $200 million in revenues for Marketplace as a business model in its own right. In addition to generating procurement savings, transaction and license fees, we have the potential to generate revenues from logistics, financial services, advertising and content management. And there are, of course, potentially big capital gains. We hope to take this new business to IPO and create further shareholder value as a result."*

As CFO you will by now have evaluated, and possibly taken to implementation, a number of e-business initiatives: B2C, B2B or B2E. Now bring it all together and take a detailed look at your portfolio as a whole. How many *ideas* does your company have in its innovation bank? How many e-business *experiments* are being conducted across the company? How many new *ventures* are being nurtured? And, most importantly, how many big new *businesses* are being built? You can expect to have thousands of ideas, hundreds of experiments, tens of ventures, but perhaps only one or two big new businesses.[1]

Leading-edge companies are rationalizing their e-business portfolios,

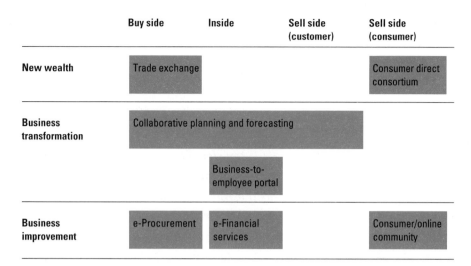

|  | **Buy side** | **Inside** | **Sell side (customer)** | **Sell side (consumer)** |
|---|---|---|---|---|
| **New wealth** | Trade exchange | | | Consumer direct consortium |
| **Business transformation** | Collaborative planning and forecasting | | | |
| | | Business-to-employee portal | | |
| **Business improvement** | e-Procurement | e-Financial services | | Consumer/online community |

Figure 2.5  *A framework for evaluating e-business initiatives*

incorporating many promising initiatives into their core businesses and singling out a few as big business opportunities in their own right. Figure 2.5 sets out a framework for mapping initiatives from across the enterprise, identifying whether they're from the sell side, the buy side or the inside. It also helps you differentiate those initiatives which merely represent an incremental business improvement from those which potentially can transform the business or be spun off as independent wealth-creating businesses:

- *New wealth*: these opportunities often require a separate entity; the key capabilities of established large corporations are different to those required for new e-business ventures that expand the boundaries of the company's traditional business model and markets. What's required in this circumstance is a *vision to reality* evaluation process. Implementation needs to be supported through an incubator with shared support services. External specialist skills often have to be imported.

- *Business transformation*: these opportunities are treated as specific initiatives with their own stretch targets. The strategic imperatives are set top-down by the corporate center, but each business unit has its own implementation program. Evaluation takes into account existing capacity and skills within the organization.

- *Business improvement*: these opportunities are often functionally led and are treated as extensions of existing processes. The scale of investment and its impact on the business may still be significant, but the level of change is less disruptive compared to new wealth and business transformation initiatives.

The CFOs of some of the world's leading companies are quite often faced with various joint ventures, e-commerce portals and a plethora of other e-business initiatives. In addition, they're often responsible for a venture capital fund to launch new ideas globally and across vertical markets. The biggest barrier to changing the business model using e-business is lack of resources committed to implementation. What's needed is a targeted investment budget of the right scale for the expected value impact. You need clear criteria for funding at group, business unit, and initiative levels, with a facility for subsequent tracking.

# eCFO CHECKLIST

## REEVALUATE YOUR CURRENT BUSINESS MODEL
Determine where in the value chain you create the highest returns for shareholders. Benchmark externally against the best. Assess the new opportunities created by the Internet.

## FOCUS YOUR e-BUSINESS INVESTMENTS WHERE YOU HAVE CLEAR COMPETITIVE ADVANTAGE
Prepare a thorough business case for going online. Avoid the mistakes of many Internet start-ups. Keep tight control over costs and cash; go to market with proven technology; plan how you will sustain customer service levels. Regularly reexamine the original economics for going online.

## PROTECT AND ENHANCE REVENUES WITH A ONE-TO-ONE CUSTOMER STRATEGY
Understand what the customer values and personalize all touch points. Determine predicted revenues and costs over the lifetime of customers; invest in the most profitable. React fast with competitive pricing. As you build new online distribution channels, maintain a clear strategy for the old.

## CONSIDER JOINING WITH YOUR COMPETITORS IN AN e-MARKET
Secure early cost savings with e-procurement. Benefit further by combining your purchasing power with others. If you can, get into an e-market early; secure a founding equity stake. Build a business model which could create longer-term opportunities for incremental revenue and shareholder value.

## DECAPITALIZE YOUR SUPPLY CHAIN
Partner collaboratively with suppliers who you trust to take on the physical asset and inventory investment. Only invest in those parts of the supply chain where your specialist expertise is essential to assure customer service.

**DEVELOP A VALUE PROPOSITION FOR B2E**
Take advantage of employee portals to make cost savings and
efficiency improvements, and to create additional value through
extraprise-wide knowledge sharing.

**TAKE A PORTFOLIO VIEW OF YOUR e-BUSINESS
INITIATIVES**
Scan business units and functions for missing opportunities for
value creation, business transformation, and process improvement.
Prioritize initiatives according to enterprise capabilities and the
people resources needed for execution.

# CHAPTER 3

# Optimizing Shareholder Value: From EVA to e-Metrics

## VALUATION AND STRATEGIC BUSINESS DECISIONS

*Renato Fassbind, CFO*
ABB

At ABB we serve a wide range of customers in power transmission and distribution; automation; oil, gas, and petrochemicals; building technologies; and in financial services. We currently employ about 160,000 people in more than 100 countries.

While no other company in our core markets can match our resources today, we are not complacent. We recognize that just as globalization and technological change are sources of competitive advantage, they can also be threats to our future. Hence we need to be agile as well as large. Through a commitment to entrepreneurial values—speed, flexibility, and frontline management responsibility—we intend to move early, anticipating change rather than just reacting to it. These are the keys to our long-term growth and profitability.

Our corporate strategy going forward is clear. We will continue to expand into knowledge- and service-based sectors while reducing our dependence on heavy-asset businesses. This strategic shift will reduce our capital requirements, helping us maximize the return on our invested capital.

*Why are we driving through a value-based management (VBM) program? The answer goes to the heart of what we in finance are about.*

*First, our challenge in finance is to provide forward-looking forecasting and value-planning assistance to businesses. By providing value-based information, we can support our businesses through better operational and strategic decision making.*

*In addition, investor relations are important to ABB. With our strong focus on VBM and our strategic response to current competitive issues, I expect the market to reward ABB's planned growth in value. Hopefully, too, shareholders will recognize us as a dynamic global company—a company that moves into new growth areas decisively, creating ever more value.*

*There are barriers to internalizing value-based principles. Some of our people are still looking back, basing decisions on historical data. In some areas, book values are still the standards against which managers are measured. We have to turn this mindset around and encourage future-oriented, market-value thinking. We want our people to understand that they are benchmarked against the market and not against internal, historical budget data. VBM provides the framework for this cultural change.*

**Ultimately, we see all our systems linked in some way to the Web, including our core financial systems. We will need the right metrics to understand the e-business value proposition.**

*VBM also gives us a transparent backdrop against which to assess our business portfolio. With it, our management will be able to make tough choices, some of which may require divesting businesses that do not promise to create value for ABB. We are only in the first of a four-year program, but already I am confident that VBM will support better strategic decision making across our organization.*

*e-Commerce is an extremely challenging issue for ABB, as it is for our entire industry. It will certainly change many of our business processes; we are already adjusting our service by giving customers the ability to buy products from us via the Internet. Ultimately, we see all our systems linked in some way to the Web, including our core financial systems that support e-commerce. We will need the right metrics to understand the e-business value proposition, just as we need the right metrics to manage the rest of our business portfolio.*

*Competing in the e-world demands completely new concepts and new ways of doing business. Developing those innovations is possible only in an encouraging environment. Our job is to foster that environment and motivate our people, while forecasting the future value we expect to create. My personal goal is to see that we reach as many of our employees as possible with our message about value creation—a significant challenge given the decentralized nature of our global operation.*

---

ABB has been cited by *Industry Week* as one of the 100 best-managed companies, a first for its field. ABB is also a traditional "bricks and mortar" company seeking to move away from capital-intensive industries into service-based, knowledge-driven markets. Its value-based management program is intended to introduce principles of value creation throughout its diverse businesses. At the same time, like so many companies, ABB recognizes that a new set of value metrics is required to thrive in today's e-driven economy.

In particular, as companies consider investing in e-business initiatives, they find standard cash-based valuation techniques difficult to apply for a simple reason: in many instances the strategic objectives that drive e-business growth cannot be easily or meaningfully quantified in cash flow terms. This problem is compounded by the seemingly irrational behavior of the stock market toward Internet stock values.

In *CFO: Architect of the Corporation's Future* we focused on applying fundamental principles of shareholder value and stressed the importance of cash. Cash is king! That's what the message was. Investors use cash to value both a company's existing business and its future growth potential. Today most of the world's leading companies have adopted economic value added (EVA) or some form of cash-flow-based valuation as the basis for analyzing their shareholder value. Ironically, however, just as more CFOs are using cash-driven valuation techniques, they are becoming acutely aware of the limitations that such approaches impose.

In the old "bricks and mortar" economy, where tangible assets reigned supreme, it made perfect sense that known cash flows dominated the perception of shareholder value. But in today's new economy there's been a major change: intangible assets have outstripped tangible assets in importance.

The result? Actual cash generation capacity isn't the major factor in market capitalization—it's the potential for creating cash in the future as reflected in the options for growth that a company exhibits. This is what really counts in today's marketplace. In the eyes of investors, cash alone is no longer king; options for growth have emerged as an increasing proportion of a successful company's total market capitalization. Analysts are struggling to find a way to assess these options. One approach that many have embraced is real options valuation (ROV); it offers promise but it's complex and time-consuming. As we'll see, a new valuation lexicon is emerging.

In the e-business world, capital itself is becoming digitized in the form of intangible assets such as intellectual content, customer empowerment, trustworthiness, know-how, brand reach, and innovation. How should these be measured? How are competitive advantage and market share gauged when new technologies emerge at Internet speed?

Whatever else has changed, one thing is clear: the world's leading corporations stay that way by delivering sustainable returns over time. Winning companies have a single-minded focus on value creation in the broadest sense. From this vantage point, our goal in this chapter is threefold: to explain the limitations inherent in widely used valuation techniques; to explore the impact of e-business on shareholder value; and to present *seven dynamics of value creation*, a new set of metrics that can be applied to e-business initiatives. As more and more traditional companies investigate e-business ventures, we find increased confusion. Our aim is to clear away the fog and set you on a path to sensible, realistic performance measurement.

## THE SEVEN VALUE DRIVERS REVISITED

*CFO: Architect of the Corporation's Future* made the case for the transition from earnings to cash, moving from an accounting-based earnings approach to EVA and other cash-based valuation methods. The evolution and characteristics of these methods are shown in Figure 3.1. EVA has an advantage over earnings in taking into account the cost of capital consumed. But it has a major disadvantage when compared to free cash flow: it is still based on historical asset values and only measures a single point

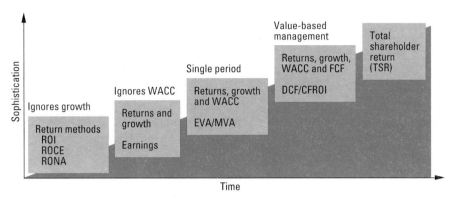

**Figure 3.1** *The evolution of valuation techniques*

in time. The free cash flow approach correlates most closely with actual share price performance and is a multiyear measure, since it is based on future projections of cash flows.

Why is free cash flow so important? The simple answer: because of its impact on the valuation process. Corporate value is assessed on the future free cash flow that investors expect a company to generate over a defined time frame less the cost of capital. Put another way, companies create shareholder value only if they generate returns that exceed their cost of capital.

There are seven key drivers that contribute to shareholder value creation (Figure 3.2). Turnover growth and cash profit margins determine how much cash a business generates. The cash tax rate, the amount of tax paid, determines how much cash flows out, along with major investments in the business in the form of fixed assets and working capital expenditures. The sixth driver is the weighted average cost of capital (WACC); this is the rate of return expected by investors based on the risk they associate with the business and its capital structure (the ratio of debt to equity). The final driver is the competitive advantage period (CAP); this is the time frame in which the market expects your business to create value by generating returns that are higher than its cost of capital.

These seven key drivers of shareholder value are critical to success, yet in today's disruptive economic climate, they tell only part of the valuation story. Underpinning these seven value drivers are seven dynamics that exert huge influence in the e-business world: customer focus, brand equity, management capabilities, business design, content, timing and

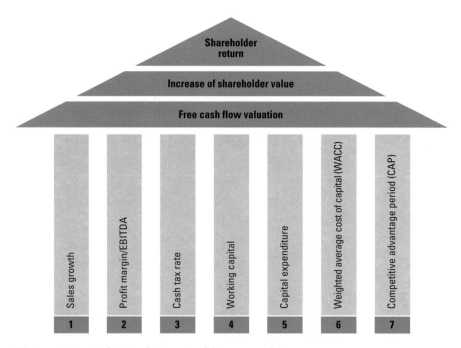

**Figure 3.2** *Value is determined by seven drivers*

agility. These seven dynamics reflect a new language, and an emerging set of metrics, that investors are using to describe and assess options for growth, the primary source of value in today's e-business economy. As we'll see later on, measuring performance using these seven dynamics can help you plan and implement a value-based e-business strategy.

## CRITICAL VALUATION CHALLENGES

Why are shareholder value principles so difficult to implement in today's business climate? The quick answer is that cash flow economics measures only a limited number of the characteristics that make a company valuable. In today's marketplace, factors difficult to quantify, such as perceived competitive advantage, the capacity for innovation, first-mover advantage, and recruiting track records, are all seen as contributing to success. With this in mind, let's take a closer look at major valuation issues facing today's CFOs.

CASE STUDY
Embracing Value-Based Management
and e-Business at TPG

*TNT Post Group, or TPG, is comprised of the original Dutch Postal Company and TNT, a courier service company. The combined group has three businesses: Mail, Express and Logistics. TPG was recently voted number three in its industry by the* Financial Times, *but its share price performance has been affected by the hype for Internet stocks.*

*TPG is implementing value-based management for a number of reasons. By focusing on key performance indicators (KPIs), TPG plans to link external value driver assumptions used by investors to its internal strategy. Through value-based management, TPG intends to strengthen the relationships among profit margin drivers, working capital, and capital expenditures to enhance its projected share price performance.*

*TPG's goals are to be the recognized world leader in its three business areas and to achieve above industry average growth and profitability by pursuing focused acquisitions and developing value-added services for its customers. Value measures are being implemented at all levels at TPG: corporate, divisional, business unit, and reporting units. At each level, they will be tailored to economic value, economic profit targets, and KPIs.*

*TPG is building a strategy for e-commerce delivery and logistics that will drive its future growth in shareholder value. e-Business is already totally reshaping its customer relationships: customers are making shipments via the Internet; they want parcels tracked and delivered using the Internet. Keeping service levels high requires new software tools and protocols; supply chains are also much more transparent. Beyond this, e-business is transforming TPG's HR and finance processes, systems and valuation mechanisms for investment appraisal.*

---

As TPG moves forward to redefine its approach to valuation in the new economy, its situation highlights many of the challenges facing other companies as well:

- *Treating capital as a major constraint.* Despite recent market swings, capital continues to be available for commercially viable projects. As a result, capital is often not the major factor constraining growth; a scarcity of new ideas, know-how and talent, and/or management capability is far more likely to inhibit expansion. In fact, some companies find that the more they grow, the less capital they require; customers fund their working capital and suppliers fund their manufacturing capacity. The message? In today's marketplace, you're missing the point if you base your business decisions on a free cash flow formula that has cost of capital as its divisors. It can skew your valuation analysis considerably.

- *Using DCF in a volatile marketplace.* Free cash flow and shareholder value are based on a discounted cash flow (DCF) calculation. Different scenarios are averaged and then built into value driver assumptions. This approach has serious problems, particularly in a volatile economy. In uncertain environments, such as created by the e-business advances, cash flows cannot be predicted far into the future. DCF therefore has limited application as a basis for investment appraisal. In the real world, you make decisions over the life of a project, exercising different options at different stages as new information emerges and circumstances unfold.

- *Making valuation unnecessarily complex.* Time and again, we find that top management unnecessarily complicates its shareholder value measures. Fully implementing EVA, for example, requires up to 180 accounting adjustments in areas such as depreciation, advertising, and R&D. Such extensive fine-tuning often leads to unnecessary complexity. While constant adjustments may benefit top management, they slow everyone else down. When shareholder value programs are implemented at the business unit level, less is best. The simpler the metrics, the easier they are to translate into concrete performance improvement goals.

- *Undervaluing implementation.* Shareholder value policies are usually decided at corporate headquarters. Often this results in "ivory towerism." Presentations on the importance of shareholder value are zealously delivered to business unit CFOs, but little attempt is made to translate financial assumptions made at the corporate level into meaningful targets for business units; even less attention is paid to framing useful measures at the operational level. With poor follow-through, even the best shareholder value program quickly fades away.

- *Using measurement as a substitute for action.* Companies facing fundamental difficulties with their inherited cost base or massive industry upheaval should be wary of launching major shareholder value campaigns. A shareholder value drive is *not* the solution to deeply rooted structural problems. Companies should be equally careful not to mislead themselves into believing that their current share price, supported by shareholder value calculations, frees them from the need to make fundamental cost reductions in order to remain competitive. Investors frequently build their cost reduction expectations into share price and then demand that management deliver on them. Chapter 8 addresses the issue of how companies can streamline costs while refocusing resources on growth and innovation.

Real options valuation (ROV) techniques can be applied to e-business initiatives and other investment decisions with uncertain outcomes (Chapter 5). Briefly described here, the options approach treats risk as an asset or opportunity. In a turbulent environment, risk is unavoidable and flexibility is essential; if treated as options, investments in these circumstances can grow in value the more volatile or risky the environment becomes.

CASE STUDY
A High-Tech Company Uses ROV to Build
an e-Business Strategy

*A top-tier technology company was slow to recognize the impact of the new economy and found itself under enormous competitive pressure. e-Business posed a challenge to every aspect of its existing business model: how it developed and manufactured products; how it managed customer relationships; how it marketed and distributed globally; and how it conveyed its value proposition to customers, shareholders, and employees.*

*The immediate challenge: assessing a range of e-business initiatives to determine which offered most value. As a first step, the company identified its customers' core needs and which of those needs were the most important drivers of customer value. Next it probed the underlying assumptions of shareholder value creation for each proposed initiative.*

*Management flexibility or "optionality" was critical to understanding how different initiatives could add value—highlighting the benefits of real options valuation. Selling a new product exclusively over the Web in current markets, for example, could trigger several future options, from offering additional products over the Internet to expanding single or multiproduct sales into untapped markets.*

*During the next phase of e-business investigation, the shareholder impact of each initiative was quantified, including the "option value" inherent in each potential decision and the risks associated with each initiative. It was determined that carefully selected e-business initiatives could add over $1.2 billion in value.*

---

## WEBONOMICS: e-BUSINESS MEETS SHAREHOLDER VALUE

The recent dramatic depression of dotcom company share prices has sharpened our appreciation of the basics. Consider what Credit Suisse First Boston said at the height of the boom: "Internet stocks are the paradox of Wall Street. Their valuations have skyrocketed with no seeming connection to fundamentals. Everything seems backwards: The faster many Internet stocks grow sales, the greater their reported losses. And the more money they lose, the greater appetite investors appear to have for these stocks. Is it reasonable that Amazon's equity market value is more than six times the combined value of Barnes & Noble and Borders? Should a new media company like Yahoo! really trade at over 280 times estimated earnings, while a traditional print media company like the New York Times trades at 17 times? These questions have prompted some investors to claim that we are in a new age where old rules do not apply. We disagree."

So do we. The old rules *do* apply; in fact, they're more important than ever. As we noted earlier, the fundamental drivers of value are the same for e-business ventures as they are for traditional companies. Other fundamentals:

- *Cash*: the value of a security (or any other asset) is the value of the cash flows it will generate.

- *Timing*: dollars received early are worth more than dollars received later.

- *Risk*: safer dollars are worth more than riskier dollars.

- *Purchasing power*: dollars that can buy more goods are worth more than dollars with lower purchasing power; that is, inflation matters.

- *Liquidity*: dollars flowing out of liquid assets are worth more than dollars flowing out of assets that can be sold only at great expense or with difficulty; that is, flexibility matters.

If these basics still apply, what has changed? Quite a lot, actually. The Internet has proved to be more than a relentless growth engine. It's also a "disruptive technology," simultaneously redefining consumer lifestyles, how companies operate, and the interaction between the two. By accelerating the pace of investment, e-enabled technologies are also transforming the capital market system.

> ***Despite recent market upheavals, the Internet is
> accelerating the flow of cash and this is likely to fuel
> continued demand for e-business investment.***

All this is having a far-reaching impact on the dynamics of value creation, so much so that we have coined a new term, "Webonomics," to reflect the pervasive nature of what's happening. To understand better how e-business is affecting the valuation environment, let's look at some key influences.

Individual investors gain ascendancy    Is there any doubt that we've entered the age of the individual investor? Not any more. It's probably not too much to say that small investors were the critical factor during the great 1990s bull market. Their pension plans have supplied steady infusions of new capital. With the help of the Internet, they have broken down many barriers that once separated Wall Street from Main Street—barriers to information, low commissions, and initial public offerings (IPOs). Share ownership is also becoming more widespread. In the US alone, the number of households that own stock grew from 28% in 1989 to 48% in 1999. Collectively, individual investors have something they never really had before—power.

Online investment is also surging. The number of Internet brokerage firms grew from 30 in 1997 to more than 140 by the end of 1999. By the year 2003 it is expected that more than $3 trillion will be invested online, up from zero in 1997. Currently online stock trading represents 50% of all retail trades in the US. Along with changing investment patterns in Europe and worldwide, this signals a huge influx of capital. In 1980 the world stock of equities, bonds and cash totaled some $11 trillion. By 2000 these financial assets exceeded some $80 trillion. In the US, venture capital investment in entrepreneurial companies rose from $700 million in 1980 to $20 billion in 2000.

The bottom line? Despite recent market upheavals, the Internet is accelerating the flow of cash and this is likely to fuel continued demand for e-business investment. For CFOs this means two things: (1) access to capital and (2) mounting pressure to identify and invest in the most promising e-business opportunities.

New ways emerge to maximize shareholder value    e-Business technologies are helping to boost performance and profitability by improving customer service, reducing costs, increasing the efficiency of business processes, and creating new revenue streams. All this is creating value in exciting new ways:

- Opening new channels for reaching customers

- Streamlining value chain activities to release hidden assets

- Leveraging new channels and the value chain to deliver more benefits to customers

Every forward-thinking company needs to make decisions about selecting and managing e-business initiatives based on a quantitative understanding of what delivers value to customers, venture partners, and shareholders. This brings us to our next point.

Current valuation approaches come under stress    When levels of turbulence are very high, levels of understanding (as to what the future holds) are relatively low. Traditional cash flow projections are rigid and linear. In the e-business environment, cash flow projections have to be flexible and iterative. They have to accommodate choices (options) early in the investment cycle then throughout Accommodate information changes. Accommodate risk-level changes. Accommodate resource changes. Accommodate timing and priority changes. Accommodate management changes. Accommodate technology changes.

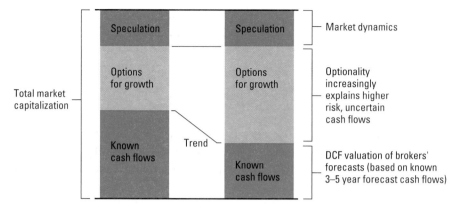

**Figure 3.3**  *Trends in market capitalization*

To assess e-business initiatives properly, it is necessary to take valuation techniques to the next level. Dynamic tools like ROV build on DCF, decision analysis, and option pricing models to offer a more complete picture of the future. The primary tenet of ROV is that asset value is intimately linked to asset management.

Embracing new valuation tools like ROV can help investors do a far better job of figuring out *how* to assess e-business opportunities. But when it comes to knowing *what* to look for, the answer remains simple and unchanging: investors value companies based on future cash flows tempered by market speculation (Figure 3.3). A company's share value is made up of three elements:

- *Known cash flows:* these are cash flows anticipated by investors based not only on current expectations but also on information in the public domain related to short-term cash flows (within 3–5 years) arising from new products already in the pipeline, market development plans, and recent acquisitions.

- *Options for growth:* these expected cash flows are based on investors' views of a company's ability to generate superior returns well into the future. They do not relate to concrete, known projects. Rather, they are subjective and based on investor confidence in corporate management, a company's flexibility and agility in reinventing itself, and its historical track record. The bottom line: anticipating how successfully a company will exploit any and all options for growth. Essentially, this comes down to assessing its ability to generate and sustain competitive advantage.

- *Speculation:* day traders are gaining critical mass. Typically, these speculators invest for the sole purpose of making short-term profits. The degree of speculation in a company's share price in itself creates volatility, something which long-term investors and the company's management cannot predict and should largely ignore.

These three sources of expected cash flow are reflected in a company's share price and their mix can vary tremendously by company. Companies that are viewed as industry leaders consistently outperform their sector peer groups in share price growth by significant margins. GE, Merck, Coca-Cola, and Lloyds TSB, for example, have options for growth that are valued aggressively by investors and tend to have little speculation in their share price.

The mix of cash flow components can also differ by industry sector. Consumer electronics and automotive manufacturing, for example, have more than 50% of their share value tied up in existing business assets. Companies in the high-tech and e-business sector, such as Dell, Amazon, and Cisco, have very aggressive investor expectations concerning future growth built into their share price. They are also less reliant on physical assets as a source of capital.

## THE e-MARKETPLACE

So what is driving value creation in today's e-enabled economy? How can you identify the value drivers of e-business performance, translate them into e-metrics and use them to support your overall corporate strategy? Before answering these questions, we need to explore key forces that are shaping the e-marketplace.

### Diverse and Interconnected Revenue Streams

e-Business enables companies to generate revenue using diverse means. The result: simple revenue drivers in the traditional cash flow model are replaced by a complex, interconnected set of revenue streams.

- *Reach:* capturing new customer segments, expanding geographically, and leveraging Internet-enabled ability to enter new markets that were once closed due to poor economics.

- *Using customers as salespeople*: opening up wider distribution channels. Internet customers make their own choices, effectively selling to themselves and to others.

- *Alliances and partnerships:* exploiting customer information through referrals or cross-selling to provide commission revenue, advertising revenue, and revenue sharing.

- *Mass customization*: target marketing through leveraging knowledge about customers to tailor specific offerings to their needs.

- *Customer information:* selling customer information to other companies is a growing revenue source.

- *The network effect*: buyers and sellers in a network become more valuable to users as the user base expands; the value of the network grows exponentially as the number of users grows arithmetically.

- *Pooling and netting:* instantaneously recording revenues and expenditures creates a new cash flow dynamic; netting them off and investing surplus cash in overnight markets is standard.

- *Flexible capacity:* switching customers to alliance partners when demand exceeds supply, and sharing the profits.

## Changing Patterns of Customer Profitability

The competitive advantage period used in the Internet business model differs from traditional cash flow valuation models. Intangible assets that once conferred competitive advantage, such as brands, may lose value; others, such as customer experience, may increase in value.

- The locus of value is shifting from brands to customers; as customers grow in importance as a source of competitive advantage, brand value is being redefined.

- New intermediaries are appearing on the Internet; their allegiance is to the customer rather than the supplier. Known as navigators, they generate advertising income by attracting customers, offering advisory services, and enhancing customer support.

- Due to navigators, companies that sell their products on the basis of advertising and marketing face fresh economic pressures: differentiation through branding becomes more challenging and price more of a factor.

- New economic models emerge: a customer loyalty model based on customer experience rather than advertising; a brand preference model based on goods sold at commodity prices.

## Changes in Relationships between Sales and Fixed Costs, Sales and Margins

Fundamental differences in the cash economics of business models will become increasingly important.

- Costs are not linked directly to revenue: incremental customer acquisition costs fall dramatically as the business grows; margin potential is exponential.

- The more customers you acquire, the lower your incremental cost to service them, including brand costs, advertising costs, and distribution costs.

- Margin potential is much higher than for a traditional, bricks-and-mortar company since traditional companies have to invest in physical assets to service additional customers. For example, an online supermarket requires substantially lower investment in physical assets to service additional customers than its traditional counterpart.

- The margin driver in the traditional cash flow model has a more linear, predictable relationship with revenue growth. In the Internet model, the fixed to variable cost relationships change; lower fixed-asset investment creates economies of scale.

## Cash Is Coming in Faster

In traditional cash-flow-based valuation models, working capital is treated as a cost. In the Internet world, it is seen as a revenue generator.

- Cash generation has accelerated. Traditionally a product was built and sold then cash came in (Figure 3.4). Companies like Dell operate on a new model; they sell first, get the cash, and then build, leading to accelerated cash inflows and decelerated cash outflows.

| Slow | Medium | Fast |
|------|--------|------|
| Build | Sell | Cash in |
| Sell | Cash in | Customer |
| Cash in | Build | Sell and fulfill |

Figure 3.4 *Models of cash generation have changed*

- The Internet model is moving toward negative working capital. Internet companies like Amazon have gone one step further; they generate cash (externally and internally), acquire the customer then sell and reinvest the cash generated to fuel even greater customer growth.

## Cash Is Burning Faster

Capital markets are beginning to scrutinize burn rates more closely (Figure 3.5). Too low a burn rate and the market perception is that you are not growing your business fast enough. Too high a burn rate and investors begin questioning when they will see returns.

- In an e-business environment, burning cash in order to grow is accepted as one of the costs of doing business.

- The Internet business model is constantly investing cash to build its intangible assets, not tying it up in fixed assets or brand development.

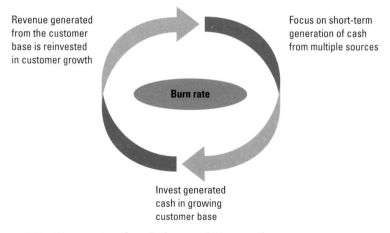

Figure 3.5 *Burn rate of cash for market growth*

- The burn-rate cycle operates differently from that of a traditional business. Companies generate diverse streams of revenue very quickly, invest that revenue immediately in acquiring new customers, and then extract additional revenue from new customers to reinvest in acquiring still more customers.

## Different Approaches to Fixed-Asset Investment

New business models are leading companies to reexamine their approach to fixed assets as well as their tax strategies.

- New e-business models provide the opportunity to leverage fixed capital investments in new ways. When purchasing a car, for example, you could make your selection using one company's showroom and inventory, but buy it over the Internet using another company's purchasing power to lower your cost. Autobytel has built a successful e-business operation on just this premise.

- The Internet also offers the opportunity to leverage other companies' products and services via completely new combined offerings that attract new customer bases. This also has a positive impact on the longer-term investment levels required.

- This approach applies not only to physical asset investments; intangible assets, such as brands, content, and R&D, can also be leveraged more easily in this way. Conversely, airlines with surplus capacity can offload it through online travel auction companies without sacrificing normal pricing policies, improving their asset utilization.

- Low investment in fixed assets gives companies the flexibility to relocate from high-tax to low-tax territories. There is a strong trend to either outsource or create arm's-length commissionaire structures to optimize tax position.

## e-BUSINESS: THE SEVEN DYNAMICS OF VALUE CREATION

How can you measure e-business success? Today's best CFOs understand that the key drivers of shareholder value remain unchanged and link them to a set of relative performance measures, leading their businesses toward,

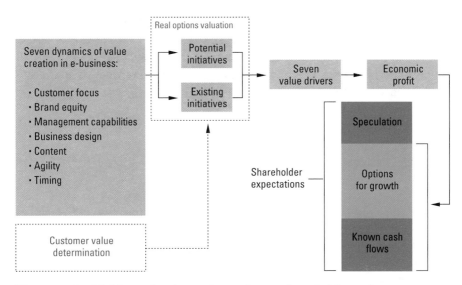

**Figure 3.6** *Linking e-business dynamics to shareholder value*

for example, above industry average revenue growth, margins and capital efficiency (fully leveraging both tangible and intangible assets). But CFOs and investors alike know that e-business and the focus on customer value are having a clear impact on traditional valuation (Figure 3.6). Studies of Internet companies and investor valuations of those companies suggest that emerging e-metrics seek to evaluate seven dynamics: customer focus, brand equity, management capabilities, business design, content, agility, and timing.

## Customer Focus

In the e-world, customers have more choice and faster access. They're better informed and better able to identify and profit from price variations. Viewing the customer not as an external *target* but as an integral part of the business, enlightened companies design their strategies and operations around relentlessly enhancing customer satisfaction.

When evaluating any e-business initiative, CFOs need to look carefully at its unique customer value proposition and ability to build and *sustain* long-term customer value. How intimately does the e-business know its current customer base? How vigorously is it developing new markets? What barriers to entry does it face? Do customers prefer to cherry-pick or deal with one vendor offering a comprehensive solution? Is there a tracking system in place to monitor customers' needs? Is the e-business aggressively developing next-generation products or services? Does it have a coherent system for leveraging customer knowledge? Is it fully exploiting the network effect? How well is it balancing pricing pressures, switching costs, and brand loyalty? Is it using metrics like retention, stickiness, and eyeball time?

## Brand Equity

Though appearing rarely on balance sheets, brand equity—the value derived from public perceptions of a company's brand name—greatly influences the capital market's estimation of the competitive advantage period. Strong brand equity lets the company attract and retain the right customers, strategic partners, employees and investors, and generate a premium for its offerings. Building on a vibrant brand franchise, the company can also transition more easily into new product and service lines, and convince its customers to follow. By focusing the company on being a *brand developer* and outsourcing noncore activities, the CFO can reduce capital expenditure.

## Management Capabilities

Management talent and expertise are always key valuation considerations. Both capital markets and venture capitalists pay close attention to management track records and credibility when appraising investment options. In e-business, a shortage of experienced managers puts a high premium on this requirement.

> *Does management have a clear vision of how it will generate sustainable value and a real-world plan for realizing it? Is your management team agile and insightful enough?*

According to a group of senior analysts, "Quality of management is the single most visible differentiator between Internet companies." And another e-business commentator says, "For large established companies, the single biggest impediment to e-biz blueprint planning is lack of consistent attention from top management. Without deep investments of time and energy from CEOs, CFOs and other senior executives, companies simply cannot achieve the cultural, strategic and technical changes required to navigate their ships in e-biz waters."

Rigorously scrutinize management reputation, creativity, and innovation. Does management have a clear vision of how it will generate sustainable value and a real-world plan for realizing it? Is your management team agile and insightful enough to capture opportunities in strategic alliances, work with shifting relationships, create new offerings, and drive new markets? Can it "sell" its vision effectively enough to attract the best talent and skills? Are there incentives for entrepreneurial thinking and execution (Chapter 4)? Can management effectively court investors' confidence, communicate options for future growth, and demonstrate superior sustainable performance?

## Business Design

More than ever, capital markets pay attention to the way a company generates economic returns—its business design—and how this adapts over time. What do they look for?

- *Is the e-venture's business design capable of delivering on its customer value proposition?* The markets attach high values to innovative business designs aimed primarily at meeting the anticipated needs of customers. Likely to attract an even higher valuation is a business design that is equipped to meet unanticipated customer needs.

- *Is the business design tight?* Transparency of information and market demand for a greater understanding of value creation require a tight business design to attract investors, reduce their risks, and lower their cost of equity.

- *Does the business design reflect the company's differentiated capabilities?* It's difficult to succeed in the new economy simply by being lowest-cost provider. Differentiation by, for instance, product characteristic or value-added service is likely to be a bigger factor in growing sales and options.

- *Is the business design robust?* If not, then competitors can more easily enter the market, drawing attention to its flaws and attacking its weaknesses.

## Content

According to Forrester Research, "Content alone draws 75% of consumers back to their favourite Websites." The challenge for the CFO is to value the content a company offers on its Web pages as an intangible asset. Is it providing the right content from customer *and* shareholder value standpoints? Other crucial questions concern control over information. Does content development happen internally or is it outsourced? Who owns the intellectual property rights? How will content be protected in a strategic alliance?

## Agility

Responsive companies moves fast and first to take advantage of new opportunities. With equal adeptness, they walk away from non-value-creating business areas. Key strengths include an adaptive culture in which people learn readily and manage change effectively. Flexibility is key—streamlining through shared services and outsourcing—or shifting to an optimal tax location. Consider using velocity as a metric. Probe entry and exit strategies.

## Timing

"When the rate of change inside the company is exceeded by the rate of change outside the company, the end is near," comments Jack Welch of GE. In valuing an e-business, speed is a prime concern. But so too is careful assessment of how to apply an appropriate approach at an appropriate pace.

A large global, traditional company will have to think through very carefully how it exploits new e-business options. If the company decides to grow an e-business initiative *internally*, then its investments will be evaluated against traditional quarter-by-quarter profit metrics. If the company decides to grow it through a separate corporate vehicle, i.e. *externally*, the investment will be evaluated against burn-rate metrics. The parent company will need to decide what profit return targets are required and their timing. Get this wrong and you could either starve the start-up of much needed capital or pour money into a losing proposition.

This burn-rate factor will affect the corporate's view of its cost of capital in its traditional cash flow valuation model. The corporate does not have to fund new ventures on its own; partnerships, alliances, and other investment vehicles all provide alternative financing sources. The corporate will need to reconsider its longer-term financing strategy, its hurdle rates for investment appraisal, and its capital structure.

CASE STUDY
Using the Seven Dynamics to Pinpoint Promising
e-Business Opportunities

*A global consumer products company with a strong stable of highly valued brands was viewed by investors as a well-run organization with an excellent cost-cutting track record and substantial incremental cash flows. However, investors perceived few options for growth compared to its competitors. As a result, its share price was lagging and its traditional business model was under enormous pressure. The company needed to signal forcefully to investors the potential strength of its growth options, particularly in the e-business arena, in a language they could understand.*

*Using the seven dynamics of value creation, the company identified promising e-business growth opportunities in Europe. As a first step, finance used the seven dynamics to assess the competitive environment the company faced. This identified the strengths and weaknesses of existing business models in its industry, especially in the area of wholesalers and retailers; the relative brand strength and agility of current and future competitors; the timing of new innovations and technologies; areas where customer focus was strong and where it was weak.*

*The company also viewed the content offerings of the food industry as a whole and its key competitors, especially the potential for bundling new products and services. Also assessed were the current management capabilities of competitors. This comprehensive analysis identified the major strategic questions that any growth initiative would have to address. For instance, how can we avoid channel conflicts with key partners?*

*Using the seven dynamics as an analytical tool enabled the company to identify key opportunity areas that offered attractive options for growth. The seven dynamics also proved useful as a tool for comparing and evaluating the various growth options identified. The most promising options were then fed into a DCF-based forecasting model where the relative weightings applied to the seven dynamics were used to gauge potential cash flow impact. The company subjected the initiatives with the greatest cash flow potential to further financial modeling.*

---

As demonstrated here, the seven dynamics of value creation in e-business provide a powerful tool for assessing the competitive environment, identifying potential growth options, comparing and ranking the options for growth identified, and communicating these back to investors in language that they understand and are looking for from corporate management.

## BUILDING A BALANCED e-BUSINESS SCORECARD

In light of all these factors, how do you begin to assess the market value of e-business initiatives, whether you're pursuing an external alliance or building internal capabilities? In particular, how do you relate e-business performance to the seven key drivers of shareholder value we discussed earlier in this chapter? In working with diverse companies to evaluate e-business opportunities, we've developed a highly flexible approach for creating an "e-business scorecard" that has widespread application. The scorecard is designed around an emerging set of key performance indicators that drive business in today's Internet-enabled economy; Figure 3.7 shows an example for an offline publishing company's new digital operation.

CASE STUDY
An e-Business Operation Builds a
Balanced Scorecard

*The parent company of a new Internet venture is in the media and publishing business. In the late 1990s it found that, almost overnight, more than 90 different Web sites had sprung up across its magazine and radio holdings, all of which were operating independently and without the oversight of top management.*

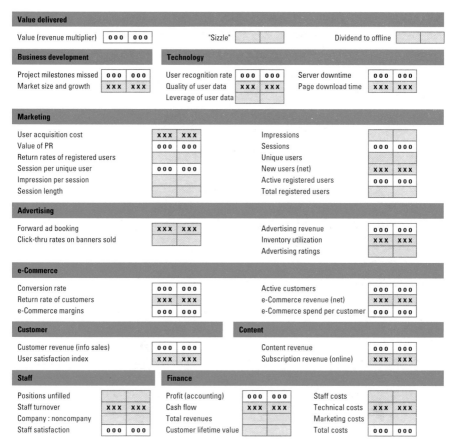

**Figure 3.7** *e-Business scorecard (illustrative example)*

*This burgeoning Internet activity raised some pivotal questions: How much is all this costing us? Are we making any money? How can we channel all our scattered Internet resources into a viable digital business and create new revenue streams?*

*Ultimately, the parent company decided to combine all its Internet activities into a standalone enterprise. Once this decision was made, it faced a fundamental challenge: how to develop and apply e-metrics, new performance measurements that could be applied in an e-business context and correlated with the key drivers of shareholder value. It responded by developing a balanced e-business scorecard, a flexible tool that's linked to business strategy. Here's how:*

- Step 1: *working with a small team including key board members, the CFO and the chief of operations, the company conducted two intensive workshops over 10 days. In the first workshop, participants described their strategy for the new e-business initiative they had created: what they wanted to achieve and what critical success factors would contribute to reaching their strategic goals. Building on the experience of other Internet companies, a total of 150–200 business drivers were identified. They covered a broad range of functional areas, from advertising to technology.*

- Step 2: *to determine which key performance indicators (KPIs) should be built into the balanced scorecard, a dynamic performance measurement model was created; it included all the 150–200 business drivers initially identified. This master model was used in the second workshop.*

- Step 3: *next, key functional categories, such as advertising, marketing, content, e-commerce, technology, and portfolio management were pinpointed. All the business drivers were clustered by category. Key business drivers were selected within each category that management felt was strategically important. In all, 45 KPIs emerged from the master list of business drivers. These were grouped into 15 cluster categories. In advertising, for example, one KPI was forward advertising booking, which drives advertising revenues. Another KPI was click-through rates on banner ads; if these rates are high, advertisers are willing to pay higher fees.*

- Step 4: *the next step was to define each business driver by giving it a name and deciding how it would be measured, how often it would be reported, the time period reflected, who owned the data, and what the strategic goal of the measure would be.*

- Step 5: *a system was designed for delivering the data in a scorecard visual format. This captures information on the 45 KPIs and then aggregates it according to the definitions outlined. The model is complicated but versatile. It allows management to view information on a site-by-site level and a consolidated level, and to adopt business-to-business and business-to-consumer perspectives.*

As this case study suggests, the scorecard is a dynamic tool that can be adapted as new data flows in and is reviewed for strategic impact. It also provides a solid foundation for valuation. The KPIs are linked to business strategy and to the seven drivers of shareholder value. These measures can be used to gauge the overall value of the business on an ongoing basis.

## KEEP YOUR EYE ON THE PRIZE

Creating value is central to your role as CFO, and the pressure to demonstrate continually increased shareholder value will only grow. While some find this daunting, others relish the challenge. Those who feel equipped to meet it know that the road to success is a one-way street. It lies in delivering sustainable returns over time. This is what superior performance is built upon. This is what fuels shareholder value creation.

> *In today's confused and often unpredictable business climate, it takes confidence to focus on what really matters and courage to stick to the fundamentals.*

In today's confused and often unpredictable business climate, it takes confidence to focus on what really matters and courage to stick to the fundamentals. At the same time, it's reassuring to know that valuation principles you've relied on in the past are resilient enough to help you guide your company's future. As you navigate today's stormy e-business waters, don't lose sight of the fact that you have ample tools at your command to make the tough, insightful decisions required to maximize shareholder value.

# eCFO CHECKLIST

## VIEW YOUR e-BUSINESS INITIATIVES AS VALUE-CREATING INVESTMENTS

Resist the impulse to view e-business activities differently from a valuation perspective. Treat your e-business ventures as viable value-creating investments in terms of both performance measurement and expectations.

## FOCUS ON THE NEW ECONOMICS OF e-BUSINESS

To survive in the brave new business world, factor volatility into every decision. Redefine risk. The capacity for innovation, first-mover advantage, and other factors difficult to quantify are now part of the valuation mix.

## UNDERSTAND THE SEVEN DYNAMICS OF e-BUSINESS

Make sure that any e-business initiative you launch is linked to your business strategy and to the seven value drivers. Understand and address the seven dynamics that underpin those drivers.

## MONITOR YOUR CASH BURN RATE EARLY AND OFTEN

Capital is chasing a limited number of solid e-business opportunities; it's not surprising that cash is being consumed at an alarming rate. In this environment, it's easy to view a high cash burn rate as par for the course. Investors are beginning to abandon this "anything goes" attitude and you should too. Decide what's acceptable and what's not, and then monitor cash outflows rigorously.

## BUILD AN e-BUSINESS SCORECARD TO TRACK PERFORMANCE

Before you can accurately assess the value of an e-business opportunity, you need to identify and apply appropriate performance measurements. The balanced e-business scorecard is built around an emerging set of key performance indicators that drive business in today's Internet-enabled economy. It is a highly responsive tool that's linked to your strategic goals.

IMPLEMENT e-BUSINESS METRICS QUICKLY AND FLEXIBLY
Operating at Internet speed is essential in today's economy. In
order to fuel value creation at an acceptable pace, you need to
"dynamize" your performance measures. View metrics as
responsive and evolving business drivers rather than a static set of
tools.

AIM FOR SUSTAINABLE PERFORMANCE
EVA and other valuation approaches are only a means to an end.
Whether it's built on bricks or Internet clicks, the real goal of any
venture is superior sustainable performance.

KEEP YOUR STRATEGIC OPTIONS OPEN
Flexibility is the name of the game in today's marketplace. Focus
on the future; ensure that every available option is pursued to the
fullest and that it drives value creation.

# CHAPTER 4

# Growing Intangibles: From Valuation to Maximization

## VALUING AND MANAGING INTANGIBLE ASSETS

*Warren Jenson, CFO*
Amazon.com

*At a high-growth Internet company like Amazon.com, we are keenly aware that, in order to expand and change at the pace required, we have to have the financial basics in place, with strong controllership. We believe this speeds our progress, enabling us to grow even faster than we would otherwise.*

*What lies behind our success at Amazon.com so far? Our relentless focus on the customer in every decision, every action we take, and every new product we introduce. We assess what we can do for our customers, and then we rapidly build scale—a platform on which we can repeat the process as quickly as possible. Our priority is to create value for our customers; then we look for the returns we think we can generate.*

*Our share price is driven by several factors. First, our customer base; we have 16 million customers globally and we're building valuable relationships. Our challenge is how to leverage that customer base to generate even more customers and provide more and better services for those that we have. Our share value is also driven by the options we have before us, some of which we don't even know about today. Looking at companies like Amazon.com, the question is, What value can be created given the networks we have in place? What is the option value in owning a share of Amazon.com today, given the nature of the opportunities in front of us in the years to come?*

*As far as investment decisions are concerned, we use option theory, determining whether the cost of not entering early is so high that we must invest today, even though traditional wisdom would suggest we wait. This is a land rush; the companies that are capable of building the networks, growing the customer base, attaining a franchise of loyal customers around the world— they'll be the winners.*

*Customer acquisition costs vary for every company, but for a start-up company in today's Internet environment, those costs are extremely high. To drive customer acquisition costs down, we leverage the power of our network, satisfying our customers in every way possible so that viral marketing will lead others to Amazon.com.*

> **The value of the brand is created by first creating value for the customer; it's a self-reinforcing mechanism. The better we serve customers, the greater our brand equity.**

*Since customer relationship management is our most valuable asset, we are intent on keeping our customers well informed, giving them everything they want to know about a product, including whether their neighbors and friends (in their virtual buying community) liked it too. We know an enormous amount about our customers. We mine our data, but never in a way that would jeopardize the bond between those customers and our company.*

*The notions of brand and customer go hand in hand. The value of the brand is created by first creating value for the customer; it's a self-reinforcing mechanism. The better we serve customers, the greater our brand equity.*

*In this new Internet economy, company balance sheets will be very different. We do everything we can to maximize invested capital. We don't see the need for high levels of invested capital; we're looking to drive toward triple-digit returns over time. Yet when we talk about intangible value, ultimately this is measured in cash flow. By intangible value we mean new customers added and how frequently they return to our site. We assess our investment by spending per customer and how well we served customers from quarter to quarter in terms of the percentage of our on-time orders.*

*Our people are another important asset. We have assembled a team pulled from best-practice leaders anywhere and everywhere; from start-ups and major corporations, and we use their skills to the best of our capabilities.*

*The Internet will not wait; it's a cultural, not geographical, phenomenon. It requires substantial investment up front to gain scale fast. The opportunity will not last forever. We have to be represented in as many places, with as many products, as quickly as possible; building the brand, the franchise, and the customer relationships. We think our biggest challenge is one of execution in the face of insurmountable opportunity.*

---

Bill Gates once remarked, "Our primary assets, which are our software and our software-development skills, do not show up on the balance sheet at all." Intangibles, a company's combined nonphysical assets, can't be measured in conventional accounting terms. In many companies they barely register on management's agenda.

Yet though few companies manage or measure intangibles, investors certainly value them. Consider the growing gap between stock market valuations and a firm's book value. The median ratio of market to book values for US companies has more than doubled in the past 25 years. In some cases, such as Microsoft, Amazon and Dell, physical assets now account for a tiny proportion of market value.

Many CFOs can calculate to the dollar what they spend on R&D, advertising or training people. But measuring the returns from brands, know-how, intellectual property, and customer relationships is proving far more challenging. Companies that learn to value and leverage their intangible assets will win out over those that don't. Indeed, survival depends on it. That is what this chapter is about.

What do we mean by intangibles? We use the term to denote the combined "soft" assets: the unique patents, software, brands, trademarks, logos, franchises, R&D, ideas, expertise, and relationships—with which a company leverages its physical assets to create returns for shareholders. First in this chapter we look at why intangibles are becoming so important and how they are influencing valuation and investment decisions. Then we show in practical terms how CFOs can come to grips with some of the categories of intangibles that have most impact on a company's value:

- Customers

- Brands

- R&D

- Intellectual property and copyright

- Reputation

- People

## WHY ARE INTANGIBLES SO IMPORTANT?

A company's market value is driven by its anticipated earnings potential –the net present value of its future economic profits. Assets underpin the capital that is invested to achieve those future cash flows. Even in manufacturing, success is increasingly dependent on intangibles such as R&D, customer relationships, branding, and management agility. Tangible assets like property can be leased and manufacturing outsourced. In fact, some analysts argue that Nike and Benetton, which don't manufacture their own products, actually have more value as virtual companies than if they owned their own production facilities.

As a source of value, intangibles have been growing in importance at the expense of physical assets for many years. The Internet has amplified this trend in three ways. First, it has speeded up the shift from tangibles to intangibles and taken it global. Second, by enabling supply chains and business models to fragment and reassemble in many different forms, the Internet has put intangible assets at the heart of business. For a Yahoo! or an eBay, their new business model *is* what they are. Third, the Internet makes intangibles more mobile and tradable. Content of all kinds is shared, repackaged and repurposed. Music and film are prime examples.

Unfortunately, accounting practices have failed to keep pace with the changing nature of the corporate asset base. For example, some intangibles are assigned value if they are acquired (i.e., money changes hands) but not if they are internally generated. If they are valued then brands may have to be depreciated, ignoring the fact that powerful brands can steadily increase in value over a potentially limitless lifetime. Not surprisingly, lack of transparency and consistency in valuing intangibles has fueled the volatility of Internet stock prices.

Some skeptics, CFOs among them, believe that intellectual assets will never be meaningfully measured. Intangibles, they argue, can vanish overnight: a brand can be damaged by rumor or failure, a patent can expire, a technology can be superseded. In their view, reporting on intangible assets may confuse investors.

As this suggests, techniques for valuing intangibles are in their infancy. Yet CFOs have no choice but to start measuring, monitoring, and managing their companies' intangibles for compelling reasons:

- *Markets value intangibles.* Identifying and communicating the value of intangibles can have a profound effect on market views of company performance and potential. Yet intangible assets are often systematically underreported and therefore undervalued. The results of our recent cross-sector study emphasize this point (Figure 4.1).

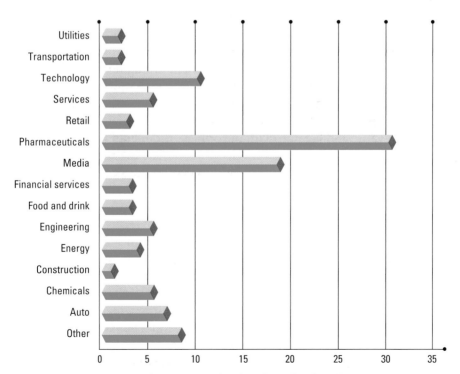

**Figure 4.1** *Market value as a multiple of net book value*

- *Intangibles drive investment.* It goes without saying that capital allocation—investing to achieve maximum increases in economic and shareholder value—is the CFO's most important responsibility. To make sensible decisions about the balance between physical and intangible investments, companies must be able to value their R&D, customer relationships, brands, human capital, and intellectual property.

- *If you can't measure it, you can't manage it.* Because intangible assets are generally unreported, they are invisible. Because they are invisible, they are underexploited. Most companies currently only attempt to value intangibles in response to a crisis, perhaps a takeover bid. Very few manage them systematically or strategically, or even at all. For example, organizations commonly fail to:

  - understand the breadth and depth of their knowledge and capability base, missing opportunities for cross-selling
  - leverage intellectual property like patents, thus failing to exploit possible revenue streams from licensing
  - recognize the potential of their brands, and so can't see where to invest to increase their value

In short, for most companies intangibles are an untapped source of competitive advantage. As CFO you face an urgent task: building a framework that links intangibles with the new economy and allows both physical and nonphysical assets to be managed and nurtured. How? By developing metrics to value and capitalize on the critical intangible assets examined in the following sections.

## ENHANCING CUSTOMER VALUE

Peter Drucker has written that the central purpose of any business is to create a customer. Today the corporate customer base is increasingly recognized as a pivotal asset. For many new-economy players, it may be their largest resource. How effectively they leverage that customer base can spell the difference between success and failure.

Customer lifetime value is a concept that many companies find useful in assessing the value of their customer base.[1] It encompasses total customer profitability—any and all revenues created throughout the life of a company's relationship with a given customer. On the cost side of the equation are all the expenses associated with acquiring, serving, and retaining that customer. At its simplest level, value is created by generating revenues from the delivery of products and services to customers that exceed the cost of the delivery process.

Understanding, managing, and improving the value of the customer base raises important questions for the CFO:

- *Does your company have customer relationships that provide profitable long-term growth?*

  In today's e-business world, customers have greater choice, more awareness of competitive offerings, and are more likely to churn. In many business-to-consumer businesses, nurturing the customer to breakeven has become a critical discipline. Banks offer cash incentives to try new products, phone companies give mobiles away free, and retailers use loss leaders to attract customers into their stores.

- *Do you really understand who your customers are, where they come from, and how much they contribute?*

  Each customer's value to the business should be continuously monitored, managed, and improved. Analysts typically find that 80% of a company's profits are generated by 20% of its customers. A telecommunications company surveyed its subscribers and found that 6% contributed 40% of the revenue, but these high-value customers were costly to serve with a breakeven point of 32% (Figure 4.2). Although for low-value customers the breakeven point was relatively low, the churn of those customers was more than double that of the high-value segment; high-churn customer groups have a shorter life cycle and therefore lower lifetime value.

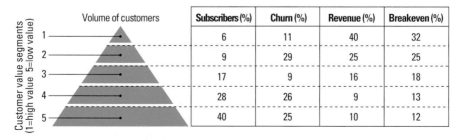

| | Volume of customers | Subscribers (%) | Churn (%) | Revenue (%) | Breakeven (%) |
|---|---|---|---|---|---|
| 1 | | 6 | 11 | 40 | 32 |
| 2 | | 9 | 29 | 25 | 25 |
| 3 | | 17 | 9 | 16 | 18 |
| 4 | | 28 | 26 | 9 | 13 |
| 5 | | 40 | 25 | 10 | 12 |

*Customer value segments (1=high value 5=low value)*

**Figure 4.2**  *Understanding customer value for a telecoms company*

- *How do you deploy resources to acquire and retain the right customers?*

  With markets close to saturation and customer costs spiraling out of sight, simple market share objectives are a recipe for disaster. Most organizations are searching for new strategies focused on customer and shareholder value. The key: defining all customer-value-driven activities (e.g., campaigns and sales targets) at an individual customer level to ensure personalization.

- *Does your investment in CRM systems properly address customer value?*

  Many companies use customer relationship management (CRM) systems, including call centers, sales and marketing, and customer service tools, to integrate customer-oriented processes across departments and lines of business. Such projects improve operational efficiency but they do not necessarily enhance customer retention and value. Some CRM systems provide insufficient intelligence on customer profiles, break-even modeling, and potential lifetime value. Likewise, activity-based management techniques used by some firms to identify customer and product revenues, costs, and profitability often do so only for some customer segments.

 CASE STUDY
Introducing Customer Lifetime
Value Measures

*A medium-sized European mobile phone operator competing fiercely for a greater share of high-value commercial business was alarmed to find that the cost of customer acquisition was skyrocketing without obvious benefit to revenues or profit. With the market nearing saturation, the board decided that growing its existing customer base was essential to consolidating its market position and regaining financial health. That meant improving customer intelligence and service.*

*With the aid of a software specialist, the company built a system to consolidate contracts into meaningful customer entities and track costs and revenues on a lifetime basis. The system also generated many other nonfinancial measures, enabling the operator to assess value and breakeven exposure for each customer. Using customer usage profiles, it drew up an investment plan based on direct marketing. This immediately increased cross-sales success rates by more than 200%.*

*Next it reorganized its customer care department and CRM systems to distinguish between high- and low-value customers. The company now uses this intelligence to develop and tailor the pricing of new products according to current profitability, customer lifestyles, or loyalty-based incentives. As the company moves heavily into the Internet world with 3G networks, portals will be tailored to each customer and products priced uniquely, based on customer lifetime value measures.*

*The effect of these changes on churn has yet to be established. However, management is confident that the long-term improvements in customer satis- faction achieved by small investments in customer value will yield dramatic improvements over time.*

---

Many companies have tried to value customers using standard rates of return or net present value. While these metrics may work for assessing a particular contract or project, they are inward-looking and too financially oriented for true customer value management. A far more effective approach is to view each customer individually and from a lifetime perspective. Follow these four steps.

Step 1: Measure customer breakeven    The starting point is to measure customer breakeven, mapping cumulative revenues from all historical contracts against cumulative costs on an individual lifetime basis. Figures should be consolidated from individual, family, household and organiza- tional groupings. Along with lifetime value, it is useful to track break- even from a fiscal year-to-date perspective or from the start/end points of current contracts.

Forecasting breakeven is an increasingly useful tool. It enables you to make better decisions about the level of interaction and direct customer investment necessary to push profitability forward. Breakeven forecasts can also support the budgeting process, for example, by indicating groups of customers in a similar breakeven position as a target for marketing. Some examples of these metrics: percentage of customers at prebreak- even, prebreakeven value over time including variances, prebreakeven by value segment, by product, and by distribution channel.

**Step 2: Build a weighted customer value index**    While breakeven is a good mechanism for measuring customer contribution and lifetime position, it is still financially focused. Nonfinancial aspects of customer value should be scored, such as product usage, loyalty, payment methods and habits, level of dialog and satisfaction, and marketing response. Nonfinancial measures can be related to financial measures (breakeven, lifetime value, monthly revenues, and capital cost of prebreakeven) and these can also be scored. The resulting array of "value scores" can then be weighted to generate a single index that measures the overall value of the customer.

*As competition intensifies, monitoring and responding to customer value measures will become a focal point for management throughout the company.*

Such a weighted customer value index is among the most useful tools for improving customer-centric processes and activities. In particular, call centers will have a quick and easy measure to assess the value of the customer they are dealing with. The weighted customer value index can also be used to consolidate all management information, so that results are presented by customer value segments.

**Step 3: Profile the customer**    In addition to scoring based on value, a customer profile is essential. Profiling captures and analyzes a customer's attributes—products and services purchased, product usage patterns, payment profile, interactions with the company, linkages to individuals, organizations, households, family groups and associations—as well as geodemographics and sociodemographics.

**Step 4: Manage customer value**    Once you've reached this stage, many revenue-building possibilities will emerge. Marketing can now be targeted directly at individual customers, tailoring messages and best-fit product propositions based on their profiles. New products can be based on the requirements of customer segments or even individual customers. Re-investment in the customer base can be planned for maximum impact. Web sites can be personalized and products or services priced to exploit lifetime value.

As competition intensifies, monitoring and responding to customer value measures will become a focal point for management throughout the company. Customer value principles are likely to reshape how products are priced and services are offered, and to define new techniques for managing customer relationships.

## FOCUSING ON BRAND EQUITY

Just how important are brands in the e-business world? Incredibly so, according to analysts, particularly in the business-to-consumer sector, where market valuations can dramatically exceed current annual sales revenue. Yahoo!'s valuation, for example, has been as high as 52 times sales. All the old issues around branding are reopened with fresh urgency in the new economy, where a customer base and a brand (often in that order) may be the only assets a company has. As Warren Jenson of Amazon.com emphasizes in his introduction to this chapter, customers and brands are two sides of the same coin. Brands are a huge and growing factor in e-business because:

- Internet-based companies have direct contact with their customers.

- Trade is customer driven and customers search by brand names.

- There is a level playing field for small and large companies.

- Search engines allow easy comparison among companies and products.

- Global reach offsets the importance of local brand initiatives.

Early e-players have played these cards to such good effect that in just four or five years, new brands are challenging established market leaders. Amazon has only a slightly lower recognition among Internet users than the old-economy market leader, Barnes & Noble. E*TRADE has higher recognition than the financial giant Merrill Lynch. Yahoo!, AOL, and Amazon now rank among the top 50 most valuable global brands. Sir Richard Branson, chairman of Virgin, makes this observation: "If you look at the values of companies on the Internet with strong brands, they tend to be ten times higher than companies on the Internet that have no brand."

All this explains why leading companies are devoting board-level attention to managing this key asset by quantifying brand value and identifying the value drivers that underpin brand equity. Investors now expect to see evidence that companies are managing brand equity effectively and, in the future, will require more detailed disclosure of information. Of UK analysts surveyed recently, 71% believed that public companies should publish more information on brand values.

Increasingly, companies are coming to realize that brand valuation serves a number of key management purposes, both externally and internally. *Externally*, UK companies now may value acquired brands and undertake annual reviews to confirm that their value has been maintained, bringing the UK broadly in line with the US, although amortization policies vary. These valuations serve as the basis for external and internal licensing agreements, and can be used as security for securitized borrowing. From a stakeholder perspective, they provide important substance for briefings to the investment community and in annual reports.

*Internally*, brand valuation exercises form the basis for portfolio strategy decisions, whether the upshot is rationalization by disposal such as Diageo's disposal of a number of country-specific or regional brands to concentrate on those with global reach, or some other outcome such as rebranding or concentration of scarce resources to advertise an umbrella brand. Brand valuation exercises also inform planning and resource allocation for advertising and marketing budgets, as well as providing a baseline for ongoing monitoring, performance management and accountability for brand equity, again as at Diageo. Likewise, brand valuations form a critical and growing element in M&A pricing and in licensing decisions.

CASE STUDY
Brand Valuation in Action

*A consumer products company made a number of major acquisitions during the late 1980s and early 1990s in which the purchase price included a significant amount of goodwill. Writing off this cumulative goodwill left it with depleted reserves and low book value. This prevented the company from issuing shares for other deals without shareholder approval, while high gearing brought it dangerously close to breaching debt covenants.*

*To restore financial flexibility, the company decided to value the brands acquired in the period from 1985 onward and put them on the balance sheet. Since then, it has continued to capitalize the value of acquired brands. At the last financial year-end, the brand value, assessed at historical cost, represented more than 55% of total corporate assets.*

*The company quickly grasped that its early understanding of brand valuation gave it an opportunity to develop a method for effectively managing brand equity. Managers have experimented with different valuation methods to gain a comprehensive understanding of the drivers that underpin brand value. The resulting knowledge is now fully integrated into the group management process.*

*In the late 1990s, the company had embarked on a strategic program using value-based management to identify the generators of economic profit and hone strategic focus. As part of this process, it has now developed measures to track brand value drivers and brand equity through the whole performance management cycle: planning, target setting, accountability definition, reporting, action planning, and execution. Regular reports show ongoing performance management of brand value. Investment analysts have responded favorably to this initiative; one influential group recently ranked the company number one in communicating information about brand strategy and performance.*

---

Some CFOs harbor reservations about brand valuation on the grounds that there is no one standard method for making the calculation. Our experience shows that these concerns are outweighed by the value of carrying out the exercise. Absolute accuracy is less important than the learning generated by undertaking the process and understanding the drivers of brand value, trend movements over time, and how to manage them. The important thing is to benchmark the value of your brands and consistently analyze valuation differences. Brand valuation approaches fall into four main types:

- *Cost-based*: historical cost valuation includes all costs incurred in developing a brand over time. In replacement cost valuation, experts estimate the level of costs necessary to recreate the brand. Both methods have drawbacks: cost estimates are approximate (particularly for long-lived brands) and have little to say about the future.

- *Market-based*: this type assesses how much a brand could be sold for on the open market. Market-based valuations depend on identifying an equivalent brand in the marketplace for comparison, which is not always feasible.

- *Income-based*: these approaches involve determining future net revenues directly attributable to the brand and then discounting to net present value using an appropriate discount rate. Various methods can be used to determine net revenue. One method, royalty relief, involves estimating what a brand owner could expect in licensing revenues from the use of its name. Like market-based calculations, the method has the disadvantage of lack of comparability. It is unlikely that a comparable brand is being licensed from a trademark owner in the same market.

- *Economic-based*: these methodologies have been developed by consultancy organizations such as Interbrand and Brand Finance. Their attraction lies in a comprehensive assessment of all factors that could affect a brand's ability to generate value for its owner. Market analysis and brand financial analysis are combined to derive the brand value. This is the preferred approach for brand valuation.

Although economic-based techniques differ, the steps in the valuation process are similar. The calculations we describe here are based on the method used by Brand Finance.[2]

Step 1: Calculate economic value added   Theoretically, this approach should use forecast cash flows from future brand sales. However, it is more straightforward to use an adjusted profit and loss number. The earnings figure captures the fully absorbed earnings of the brand after the allocation of central overhead costs, typically on a 5–10 year horizon. Profits attributable to own-label sales volumes should be excluded. A fair charge needs to be deducted for the use of tangible assets (fixed and working capital such as the distribution system, manufacturing plant, and stock). The charge for capital is normally at a risk-free borrowing rate on the principle that the capital is included at its real market value and therefore no risk is involved in ownership. A charge is also made for tax at a notional rate. The result is the economic value added (EVA) that is attributable to *all* intangible assets.

Step 2: Identify the brand value added   The next step is to identify the proportion of EVA attributable to the brand. A quantitative and qualitative research-based approach enables managers to understand and model the drivers of demand and estimate the brand's contribution to the business, using a form of trade-off or conjoint analysis with a large sample of consumers and some modeling of business drivers. The result is a factor to be applied to EVA to determine brand value added (BVA).

Step 3: Calculate the discount rate   The discount rate must factor in economic, market and brand risks. The starting point is to identify the risk-free borrowing rate for the geographic area in which the valuation is being completed, then the appropriate equity risk premium. The composite discount rate can then be adjusted for the specific risks associated with the market sector in which the brand operates. This information is readily available for most worldwide stock markets. Finally, the average market risk rate is either increased or decreased by reference to the risk profile of the individual brand to be valued.

> *Assess your brand portfolio. Establish a performance management system to track the development and execution of strategies for generating brand value.*

This is done by scoring all brands in the sector relative to each other against 10 key indicators of historic and current brand performance: time in the market, distribution, market share, market position, sales growth rate, price premium, price elasticity, marketing spend/support, advertising awareness/effect, and brand awareness/loyalty.

Scores on a scale of 0 to 10 are added for a final score between 0 and 100. A score of 50 attracts the average equity risk premium, a brand scoring 100 is theoretically risk-free and attracts no equity risk premium, and one that scores 0 attracts the highest discount rate with a doubling of the premium. Note that the adjustment for risk is applied only to the equity risk premium and not the risk-free borrowing rate.

Step 4: Calculate brand value   Work out the brand value by applying the risk-adjusted discount rate to the brand value added cash flows. On the assumption that the brand continues beyond the forecast period, effectively in perpetuity, you should also calculate an annuity based on the final year's earnings.

Step 5: Manage brand value   The CFO should confirm stewardship of brand value as a strategic priority for the board, with clear ownership and accountability. Brand valuation enables you to assess your brand portfolio and overall brand strategy. An important part of any assessment is investigating the impact and risks of e-business on brand strategy; for example, the threat of specific e-brands or whether to launch an Internet-only brand.

Establish a performance management system to track the development and execution of strategies for generating brand value. It should be developed jointly with a marketing team. Use the results to measure marketing effectiveness. Give strong emphasis to communicating strategies and outcomes to the investment community.

## ASSESSING AND MANAGING THE VALUE OF R&D

Before a company can proactively manage R&D assets, it must reach an internal consensus on what its R&D portfolio may be worth and why. This involves understanding the market valuation of the portfolio, reviewing the underlying expectations, and then comparing the market's view to internally generated assessments of future value. Many leading pharmaceutical companies have dramatically improved their management of R&D investment. The lessons they've learned can be applied by other companies with large investments in R&D intangibles.

CASE STUDY
Shareholder Value in the R&D Portfolio of a
Major Pharmaceutical Company

*The R&D function of a global pharmaceutical company was facing a number of major challenges common to the industry and specific to its own portfolio. In a postmerger situation, the company was eager to deliver the demanding expectations set by Wall Street and concerned about the risk of nondelivery. Preparation of a strategic plan for the respiratory therapy area identified a large value gap in the portfolio and raised the possibility of value gaps in other therapy areas.*

*The company undertook a comprehensive revaluation of its portfolio, valuing each therapy area and identifying value gaps between external expectations and its internal strategy. Management concluded that even if current strategic plans were achieved in full, there would still be a value gap against market forecasts that had to be closed.*

*Shareholder value models were built to assess the relative importance of each major value driver. The company estimated that, at one end of the spectrum, a 10% increase in sales revenue would contribute to a 22% increase in value, while a 10% decrease in working capital requirements would have a negligible impact on value.*

*Importantly, the company was able to estimate the contribution that intangible assets in its R&D portfolio made to market value, approximately 37%. With an understanding of its business model and how the market valued its tangible and intangible assets, management was able to take corrective action.*

---

Just as traditional accounting principles fail to value intangible R&D assets, we frequently find that management accounting, planning, and reporting practices fail to allocate investment adequately to the R&D portfolio. Too often, functional calendar-based processes and procedures are twisted and squeezed to become resource allocation mechanisms. In the worst examples, next year's R&D budget is calculated as a percentage of next year's sales forecast and the total divided up among different projects in different stages in the R&D pipeline. In such cases, no real attempt is made to:

- Link investment in R&D intangibles to the target market value of the company.

- Align the key operational decision making processes in R&D with shareholder value.

- Measure and track the performance of investments in R&D intangibles.

We believe that managing the value of R&D intangibles requires an organization to commit to all three of these points. The following guidance draws on learning from experience in the pharmaceutical industry.

Linking R&D investment to market value    Building computer-based models of the portfolio helps to clarify how key R&D pipeline variables (e.g., phase cost, elapsed phase time, attrition, time to peak sales, peak sales and market exclusivity period) increase or decrease shareholder value. Known as dynamic pipeline simulation models, they reflect the flow of a company's projects and products through defined pipeline and market phases. Associated costs and sales lines are established and used to drive calculation of profit and loss, balance sheet and cash flow statements themselves linked to a calculation of shareholder value.

Dynamic pipeline simulation modeling may hold the key to improving the target-setting process for investing in R&D. By understanding how changes in key R&D variables impact shareholder value, and by performing sensitivity analysis on these variables, it is possible to forecast the levels of performance necessary to achieve target market value. R&D investments are then focused on the gap between current and targeted performance levels. Instead of being driven by next year's sales line, the annual budget for R&D is driven by an appraisal of what must be improved to achieve the level of shareholder value expected by the market. In short, understanding how R&D variables affect shareholder returns helps you to map out alternative strategies for sustaining and managing market value.

Improving operational R&D decision making    Valuation decisions for R&D projects usually combine learning and compound options. Learning options are those where the holder pays to learn about an uncertain quantity or technology. Compound options are those which, when exercised, generate other options as well as cash flow. Typical pharmaceuticals R&D projects encompass both development and marketing uncertainties. Will a drug meet safety and efficacy requirements? Is there a sufficient unmet medical need to guarantee future revenue streams? Real options valuation recognizes both kinds of uncertainty and the possibility of a flexible response, typically by staging investments (Chapter 5).

Measuring the performance of R&D investments    Whatever measures you use, five rigorous requirements should come into play. First, R&D investments must be firmly linked to bottom-line performance and returns. Second, the measures must allow meaningful comparisons between categories of R&D candidates. Third, they must highlight the costs of failure within R&D. Fourth, they must monitor R&D's contribution to postlaunch product successes and failures. And finally, they must reflect the responsibility that R&D shoulders for overall portfolio strategy.

Assessing and managing the value of R&D is not easy, but companies facing up to the challenge have derived enormous benefit. Clearly, the advent of Internet-enabled reporting tools, and the spread of enterprise resource planning and data warehouse systems, have combined to make a complex process easier.

## LEVERAGING INTELLECTUAL PROPERTY

Until recently, intellectual property—an organization's codified and protectable knowledge in the shape of copyrights and content, patents, proprietary software and trademarks—was of interest only to lawyers and researchers. But in the age of intangibles it has become a central concern of the CFO. Knowledge is power and the value of know-how as an option is increasing constantly. In the case of many dotcoms, intellectual property is the only thing they have to manage (or sell). Little wonder, then, that companies like Amazon and Priceline are attempting to patent their unique business methods.

But even in many traditional firms, intellectual property is an unexploited treasure trove. In a dusty folder BT recently discovered it had a patent relating to hypertext. When Dow Chemical audited its patent archive, it scored a double coup: instantly saving several million dollars a year in maintenance by selling or disposing of patents *and* generating valuable new revenue streams through a program of vigorous licensing. Patents are worth $1 billion a year to IBM, and account for 20% of profits at chipmaker Texas Instruments, which has 10,000 of them.

Identifying corporate intellectual property assets through a rigorous internal audit should be a CFO priority. The Internet brings fresh urgency to this task because of the wholesale disaggregation and reaggregration that e-business is triggering. The shake-up is happening at all levels as, first, individual processes such as procurement or sales migrate to the Web, then whole companies, progressing to e-integration within industries as firms merge or acquire. AOL's takeover of Netscape and subsequent merger with Time Warner are good examples. In this flurry of structural change, the traffic in intellectual property has vastly increased. The logo, software or other content once taken for granted within a monolithic company suddenly takes on tradable value as the company disaggregates its value chain. The greater the changes, the more mobile it becomes, and the greater the potential for reuse in many different forms.

This makes intellectual property a prize asset. But beware: as traditional boundaries between businesses and industries erode, such assets are becoming increasingly vulnerable. If you don't manage them, someone else will. As intangibles escalate in importance, leveraging intellectual property is moving center stage as a strategic discipline. A systematic approach is emerging based on four interrelated steps:

1. *Strategic assessment*: the first step is taking inventory, identifying what you truly own. An inventory can start with patents or copyrights and then advance into the area of know-how. Central to a strategic assessment is analyzing the intellectual property position of key competitors and your industry in general.

2. *Competency development*: viewing intellectual property from a strategic perspective means involving more than just legal staff; operations, finance, and marketing must all contribute. Systems must be in place that allow these diverse groups to access and share relevant information.

3. *Acquisition and asset development*: based on its strategic assessment, a company can make informed decisions about what forms of intellectual assets it needs to develop internally or acquire in order to meet its business objectives.

4. *Value extraction*: according to our recent survey, only 26% of companies believe they fully utilize their intellectual assets. Most organizations with robust intellectual property portfolios are not fully exploiting them. Extracting value may mean selling a patent that is being maintained and not used, or perhaps donating it. It may mean taking a hard look at whether licensing fees are high enough or adequately monitored. Or it could mean using intellectual assets as collateral to reduce cost of capital.

Although managing intellectual assets may be unfamiliar territory for most CFOs, techniques for doing so are available in both the traditional economy and e-business. For relatively stable intellectual assets, including patents and copyrights, a royalty-based measurement may be appropriate.

CASE STUDY
Valuing Proprietary Software to Help Shape
a Joint Venture

*A UK software manufacturer had set up a joint venture with a US company to sell logistics services to the motor industry. The issue: estimating the market value of the proprietary logistics software that the UK firm proposed to sell to the joint venture. No records had been kept of the cost of developing the software. But the company estimated that to develop it today would cost around $1.5 million.*

*The companies began by agreeing on market value as the basis for valuation, arrived at by using the royalty relief (or royalties foregone) method. This first requires estimation of the royalty rate to which both parties to a licensing arrangement could agree. The after-tax royalty stream is then discounted at cost of capital to yield its net present value (NPV). The process unfolded as follows:*

- *Estimation of the required rate of return or cost of capital as the basis of the discount rate to be applied to projected license fees.*

- *Estimation of the initial range of royalties and values that would allow each party to earn the required rate of return.*

- *Estimation of the cost to the joint venture of developing equivalent software, including the loss of profit resulting from the delayed start of operations (it would refuse to pay top prices if it could do the same for less).*

- *Estimation of the license fee which would provide the same internal rate of return (IRR) to both parties, taking into account development and start-up costs for the joint venture.*

- *Calculation of the NPV of the estimated royalties at the required rate of return: $6 million.*

- *Estimation of the price which the joint venture would be prepared to pay up front in cash instead of licensing the software. The figure $6 million was too* *high; to do as well in IRR terms, it would need to pay not more than $1.5 million. So an equitable price was somewhere between $1.5 million and $6 million.*

- *Arrival at a figure that both sides could agree on: a midpoint value of some $4 million. This gave the joint venture an IRR of 18.7% and the software company a substantial profit.*

*The approach used required several iterations to arrive at an agreed royalty fee and value. But the resulting arrangement was viewed as reasonable and fair by both parties.*

## Online Intellectual Assets

When it comes to the Internet, valuing intellectual property is far more complex. Take, for instance, the Web's destabilizing impact on the traditional music and entertainment business. Today, unresolved legal issues outnumber clear rules of intellectual property engagement. At the same time, business models are in flux as the market disintermediates and consumers connect directly to sources of production. Several artists have released material directly on the Internet.

As traditional single/album economics are disrupted, many people predict that the currency of creativity, the song itself, will become the dominant unit of value. In sharp contrast to the music industry's history of rigidly fixed price conventions, there is now uncertainty about pricing copyright at every stage of the value chain, from setting royalties for composers and recording artists to setting retail prices for consumers. What is a song worth? With a customer-led, on-demand approach, there is potential for higher profit per unit.

Clearly, for content holders, the Internet holds enormous opportunity as well as risk. But they cannot afford to remain locked in traditional paradigms. Online intellectual property problems are more acute; they preclude any one solution or quick fix. Rights holders should focus on limiting, not eliminating, the issues they face by valuing their intellectual assets according to durability (shelf life) and perceived value to the customer (Figure 4.3). Then they must prioritize and manage those assets accordingly.

Legalistic control of an asset is almost impossible on the Net. Setting

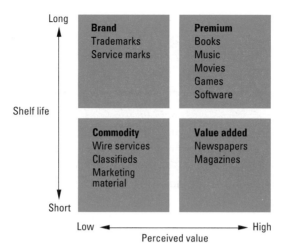

**Figure 4.3** *A value matrix for media assets*

priorities for intellectual property management allows you to shift your focus from control to usage. A use-based approach founded on business priorities can remove complexity in three ways:

- Privileging up-front flat fees (at the expense of licensing and royalties) as assets are repurposed into multiple products to encourage different kinds of use. This kind of innovation is hindered by the existing patchwork quilt of rights and payments.

- Focusing attention on the most important issues. With priorities established, companies can monitor their key assets and, where necessary, target infringements.

- Building safe havens—communities of interest which blend business objectives with intellectual property management. For instance, Ancestry.com makes much of its genealogical data available free with the goal of fueling its e-business via subscriptions to its magazine and databases.

The Internet is reshaping whole industries as it detaches content from original providers and becomes the delivery vehicle of choice for whatever can be digitized—newspaper articles, books, television shows, music, cinema. This trend will only intensify as the bandwith of the Internet pipe increases. As with other "free" content such as news or games, the issue is not that the content becomes valueless (far from it), but who controls it, and how best to distribute it and charge for it.

## VALUING REPUTATION

The investment guru Warren Buffett once remarked, "It takes 20 years to build a reputation and five minutes to ruin it." Damage to a company's reputation can lead to significant financial losses in profits and shareholder value. A well-known recent example is Nike. Despite its code of conduct defining global supplier obligations, Nike was hit by accusations of using child labor and low wages, among others. Spurred by public concern, Nike invested substantially in programs to demonstrate its corporate responsibility as a global industry leader.

*Every major strategic and operational decision can boost or harm a corporate reputation and affect market value, since reputation is closely linked to share price.*

Plenty of other examples drive home the same point. According to official figures, the mismanagement of pension sales in the UK cost the pensions industry up to £10 billion in compensation. What can't be calculated is the lost revenues from future sales to disillusioned customers who took their business elsewhere, or damage to shareholder returns. Computer Associates International shares sank nearly 31% on July 22, 1998. The cause: perceived excessive executive compensation. In its first-quarter returns, a $675 million after-tax charge was taken to pay bonuses to three top executives. Precharge earnings of $194 million became a postcharge loss of $481 million and shareholder confidence fell.

Every major strategic and operational decision can boost or harm a corporate reputation and affect market value, since reputation is closely linked to share price. Figure 4.4 lists some indicators of reputational value, both financial and nonfinancial. The nonfinancial indicators are best organized by stakeholder group; they have a strong influence on the sustainability of corporate reputation and value performance.

For the twenty-first century corporation, reputation has become a major corporate asset, to be husbanded as carefully as physical or human resources. As with any other important asset, it is incumbent on the CFO to manage, monitor and value reputation by:

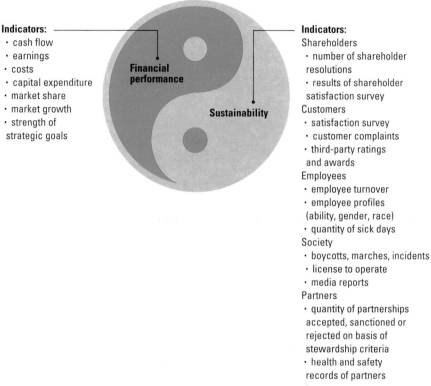

**Indicators:**
- cash flow
- earnings
- costs
- capital expenditure
- market share
- market growth
- strength of
  strategic goals

**Financial performance**

**Sustainability**

**Indicators:**
Shareholders
- number of shareholder
  resolutions
- results of shareholder
  satisfaction survey
Customers
- satisfaction survey
- customer complaints
- third-party ratings
  and awards
Employees
- employee turnover
- employee profiles
  (ability, gender, race)
- quantity of sick days
Society
- boycotts, marches, incidents
- license to operate
- media reports
Partners
- quantity of partnerships
  accepted, sanctioned or
  rejected on basis of
  stewardship criteria
- health and safety
  records of partners

Figure 4.4  *Indicators of reputational value*

- Defining the relationship between reputation and shareholder value

- Creating a reputation management process embracing all the business functions

- Monitoring effectiveness and risk, and reporting on them to the CEO

- Developing strategies to protect and enhance reputation as a corporate asset

Companies need to adopt a balanced scorecard approach. Managing reputation depends on the CFO's ability to manage all the elements of this scorecard, whether they are based on truth or perception. How does this work in practice?

CASE STUDY
Leveraging Reputation to Extend
Market Reach

*A multinational telecommunications company wanting to penetrate a fast-growing market used its corporate reputation program to help. The company was new in the market which was only recently liberalized and opened up to foreign competition. Both product and labor markets were highly competitive. Local customers and the parent corporation had shared expectations for high corporate standards.*

*The company conducted a stakeholder analysis and identified critical success factors (CSFs) for meeting business targets. To maximize shareholder value from its efforts, the company determined that it must meet the expectations of local stakeholders without compromising those of the corporate stakeholders. The main CSFs were demonstrating commitment to the local market, adapting to local economic conditions, differentiating its products, and hiring the best employees. Apart from flexibility, all the CSFs depended, to some degree, on the company's reputation.*

*The next step was to identify reputation drivers for each high-priority CSF. This involved pinpointing principles of corporate responsibility and establishing key performance indicators and business results for each reputation driver. For example, the CSF of demonstrating local commitment involved contributing to the national economy, respecting societal concerns and protecting the environment. The company used this analysis to map CSFs to shareholder value drivers and investigate options for action. For the local commitment CSF, the company was perceived as having only mid-range performance. The study results led to a series of strategic recommendations, ranging from obtaining a local stock market listing to creating jobs.*

*The final step was to prioritize stakeholders then develop a strategy and communications program to target key stakeholders. The company found that it needed to convey key messages to different stakeholders via a range of media. One important finding: the group's current marketing campaign was counterproductive. Conceived in North America, it highlighted the company's multinational credentials at the expense of its local credibility.*

Although traditionally considered a "soft" asset, this case study underlines how reputation is increasingly important to hard business success. It can be systematically managed for shareholder value by:

- Identifying stakeholders' concerns

- Measuring truth versus perception

- Competitive positioning

- Implementing strategy and monitoring effectiveness

- Communicating stakeholder value

## NURTURING HUMAN CAPITAL

As one expert noted, "People are the one factor of production . . . that animates all the others. Whatever value a company creates is a function of the way its people apply their energy and ideas to capital and the raw materials that others want. And how people do their jobs is determined by the way you treat and pay them." Of all the variables under top management's control, people offer the greatest value-building potential. Little wonder then that the system of rewards and incentives designed to attract and motivate this most precious intangible asset, employees, has by far the biggest impact on a company's performance.

Clearly, e-business has made compensation a major strategic issue in attracting and retaining talented professionals. In the Internet economy, the most important of all customer–supplier relationships is that between employer and employee. The most intense competition in global business today is not the kind that CFOs are used to, fighting for capital or market share. It is the battle for talent: where finance meets HR.

CASE STUDY
Energizing New and Old HR Initiatives

*An ambitious public publishing company, like many other media firms, has been hard hit by defections of staff to trendy dotcoms. At the same time, its traditional print operations need an injection of online entrepreneurial spirit.*

*Keen to rekindle its growth image, the company has launched a wide-ranging restructuring program, removing commercial activities such as marketing and advertising from individual publishers and centralizing them in a group-wide function. It recently announced an ambitious digital strategy and has set up a dotcom division to expand its online presence.*

*To attract new talent to the dotcom division, the firm has adopted a radical and aggressive new compensation policy. For online employees, it has stripped away benefits like company cars and standard hiring practices. Instead, it is offering potentially lucrative share options and a notice period of two weeks. On the whole, this policy has been well received by shareholders.*

*However, it leaves the company facing some urgent unresolved issues:*

- *How can it use its incentives to motivate people in the traditional print divisions (which make all the profits) who now see themselves as second-class citizens, particularly publishers contemplating the abolition of their traditional power bases and career structure?*

- *Can an incentive plan be instituted that consistently and fairly rewards managers in the group's dotcom ventures and its offline businesses? Where do the international businesses fit in?*

- *How can the company find a group-wide performance measurement and reporting system that encourages units to share across the business, rather than exaggerate their own figures at the expense of others?*

---

This case study crystallizes some of the complex HR issues that companies grapple on a daily basis. Chief among them are how effectively to motivate employees in the old economy and the new, how to tailor incentive programs without sacrificing fairness, and how to use compensation to reward cooperation and defuse internal competition. Along with these challenges, companies face another harsh reality: today's skilled employees view themselves as free agents. Taught in the hard school of downsizing and rationalization to take responsibility for their own careers, they are doing so with a vengeance. In this opportunistic, anything-goes climate, attracting and retaining talent is a relentless challenge.

What then are the components of an innovative package for the e-business era, a dynamic pay system that is both compelling to the individual and contributes to the corporate bottom line? Incentives are designed to achieve three results: attract talent, motivate it to create shareholder value, and retain star performers. It's hard for any system to succeed consistently in doing all three.

> *The stock option frenzy of recent years has thrown into sharp relief the inadequacies of standard incentive plans. All too often, the stock option tail has been allowed to wag the corporate dog.*

Traditional incentive plans, based on profitability, return on assets or equity, can weaken initiative by limiting the upside from outstanding gains and the downside of poor performance. They may also encourage quick fixes by settling for easily achievable targets that fail to tap full corporate potential. The stock option frenzy of recent years, in particular, has thrown into sharp relief the inadequacies of standard incentive plans. All too often, the stock option tail has been allowed to wag the corporate dog.

Consider the example of a major technology company, where options are at the heart of both its compensation and finance systems. Since it first went public, the company's stock price has been appreciating by 60% a year. Generous with this treasure, it has become a popular employer and its options a prized perk. The result has been a win-win situation: employees feel valued and well rewarded while its stock options strategy enables the company to keep regular salaries relatively low and reported earnings high.

But that's not all. The ability to charge employees' realized options against tax gives the company's finances a second boost. In a year when employees cash in $2 billion in options (not unusual with $25 billion in shares outstanding), the benefits to cash flow and the balance sheet will be around $500 million. Of course, doling out options on this scale creates dilution, which would normally show up in lower earnings per share, but the company offsets that by making regular share buybacks from its cash pile. Option-fueled finance boosts and buybacks help keep the stock price up, and this increases the value of the options and their popularity.

This is what the company's treasurer once termed the "virtuous cycle" of stock options. However, the magic only works when the share price is going up. When a company's share price falls, this cycle can quickly become vicious rather than virtuous. Fewer options realizations mean a smaller tax boost to reported profits, so fewer buybacks to support the share price; this erodes corporate reputation, which triggers higher salary demands; earnings take it on the chin. In the form that most boards grant them, it's clear that stock options suffer from other serious disadvantages:

- *They're expensive*: conventional option programs begin rewarding managers long before they create any wealth for shareholders. With a fixed exercise price (typically the market price on the day they are granted), options reward executives for any price appreciation, including increments too small to provide shareholders with rewards on their investments.

- *They're divisive*: options offered by a parent company to managers charged with launching e-ventures can be divisive and, equally important, they don't always promote entrepreneurial behavior. Many traditional firms, even in the IT industry, have struggled to justify to loyal offline managers the purchase of dotcom enterprises whose young founders stood to make astronomical sums from soaring stock options.

- *They give poor line of sight*: share options are a blunt instrument. They are not very effective at motivating specific types of behavior. Options can often fail to distinguish between superior and average performance. The long-running bull market of the 1990s lifted all boats, ensuring that all executives with fixed-price options reaped huge gains.

- *They create dilution*: some companies now have a huge "overhang" of shares earmarked for unrealized and future option grants—25% or more in some cases. If a business grows rapidly, this may not be a problem. But when the music stops, the silence can become uncomfortable. Even in high-growth firms, options may be unfair to paid-up stockholders.

Now that the bloom is off the Internet rose, investors are insisting that ventures demonstrate cash flow sources that will support a high rating in a much more cautious market. The same goes for individual managers, who are once again being asked to justify pay with performance. In other words, although e-business may have altered the language of incentives, the underlying economic grammar remains unchanged. As in the past, an effective incentive compensation plan answers yes to four questions:

- Is it aligned with the interests of shareholders?

- Does it provide executives with significant opportunities to share in wealth generation?

- Does it prescribe definite awards for specific performance results?

- Can managers evaluate the impact of day-to-day business performance on their incentive pay?

To encourage risk taking and nurture creativity, you need to take a disciplined approach to setting incentives. The solution that best meets the acid test for all incentives—aligning the interests of managers with shareholders, rewarding both at reasonable cost, and retaining talent over the long haul—is to tie management rewards to an aggressive, value-based bonus plan based on continuous performance improvement. To avoid pitfalls and focus all employees on the key opportunities to increase shareholder value, most companies can benefit from a systematic, three-step approach to introducing an economic-value-based incentive plan:[3]

1. *Analyze where and how your company generates economic value.* The first step is to unbundle the company's economic value in order to determine the macroeconomic drivers of total shareholder return, identify the strategic and operational drivers of value, and isolate the leverage points where action will have the greatest impact.

2. *Mobilize individuals by establishing clear lines of sight.* This second step focuses on making individuals and teams accountable for the value drivers they can influence in their work by directly linking individual jobs to the company's overall objectives. The best way to do this is to use a value chain approach.

3. *Align accountability with an incentive system that rewards value-creating behavior at all levels.* After linking economic value to the firm's competitive drivers and assigning accountabilities to the value chain, set short, intermediate and long-term performance targets.

To ensure this approach generates strong, sustainable results, be sure that all incentive programs are carefully aligned. Incentives for departments such as R&D, production, sales and marketing, all of them should focus on driving economic value; they should share accountability for drivers, where necessary, and they should pull in the same direction. At the same time, incentives should differ by organizational level and impact (Figure 4.5). Top managers who make big-ticket investment decisions should be paid directly on the shareholder value results generated by those decisions. In contrast, incentives for business unit managers who produce returns directly through operations should be based primarily on strategic and operational drivers of economic value. Time frames, degrees of accountability, and incentive designs will differ widely by level, but they must all contribute to the same goal.

Only three to five key economic value drivers hould be used for incentive purposes. More than this confuses and fragments the desired performance message instead of focusing it. Other rewards (spot awards, noncash recognition) and management processes (e.g., regular management reporting) can be used to reinforce other drivers.

Integrating incentives with the existing pay system is not important for the majority of companies, which have existing incentive frameworks that can absorb economic value measures and accountabilities without too much trouble, but it is for those in start-up situations where incentives added to already competitive packages, while gladly accepted, will have no motivational impact.

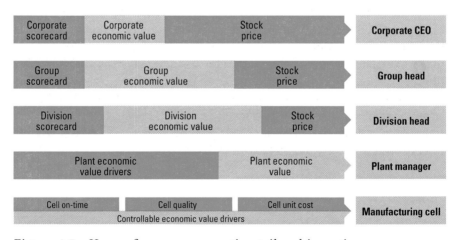

Figure 4.5  *Horses for courses: creating tailored incentives programs*

CFOs should remember that any successful initiative to improve performance includes a comprehensive communications strategy:

- Set a clear vision going forward (this is not where we need to be, something better exists and we can get there).

- Engage all employees by articulating the incentive strategy's goals; let everyone know why their performance is being measured and how their efforts contribute to corporate goals.

- Link measures and targets to reward processes; recognize the performance of individuals, teams and business units at all levels.

- Reward the right values and behaviors; goals cannot be set in a vacuum. To encourage outstanding performance, devise award and appraisal processes that recognize cultural differences both within and across borders.

## INTANGIBLE ASSETS: A MOVING TARGET

Intangible assets increasingly drive shareholder value. To perform the finance function's central role of allocating capital, the CFO must be able to measure and manage the company's intangible assets. This is a fast-changing area and techniques are currently being developed. When choosing among them, bear in mind that the essential issue is not accuracy in the accounting sense. The goal is building a comprehensive view of assets, both tangible and intangible, that your company can use to create shareholder value and then managing the relationships among them.

For the CFO, getting a grip on intangibles raises many issues, including the role of incentives, behavior, ownership and compensation. However, the most important priority is aligning business strategy with intellectual strategy. This means working closely with other functions to identify intellectual assets in their sphere of operation, assess their contribution to corporate strategy, and help them release their full value.

# eCFO CHECKLIST

IDENTIFY YOUR INTANGIBLE ASSETS AND UNDERSTAND
WHAT THEY CONTRIBUTE TO YOUR BUSINESS
Shareholders value them; they are reflected in the market's
perception of corporate value, if not on your balance sheet.
Measure and actively manage your portfolio of intangible assets.

REVISIT YOUR INTANGIBLE ASSETS IN THE LIGHT OF
e-BUSINESS
Assess the balance between your investment in online and offline
assets. In new ventures, do not assume that your intangible
investments should match those of your existing business.

UNDERSTAND, MANAGE AND GROW THE VALUE OF
YOUR BRANDS
In an age of commodity production and information overload,
brands are a key differentiator and bring hard benefits in terms of
customer acquisition and a platform for new services.

VALUE CUSTOMERS AND TREAT THEM AS AN ASSET IN
THEIR OWN RIGHT
The lesson of the Internet is that brand development is
inextricably tied to customer service. The value of the brand is
created by first creating value for the customer. Brand
development and customer value go together.

KNOW THE VALUE OF R&D AND USE IT TO MANAGE
THE FUTURE
R&D options are among your most important hidden assets. As the
CFO of Amazon puts it, "Share value is driven by the options we
have in front of us, some of which we don't even know about
today." This applies to R&D.

AUDIT YOUR INTELLECTUAL PROPERTY
Understand its place in the fragmenting value chain and decide on a strategy for managing it. In the age of the Internet, content is king; control it yourself or run the risk of having its value appropriated by others.

NURTURE YOUR REPUTATION AND YOUR PEOPLE
These precious assets can be squandered or mined for gold. Be sure you invest your energy and resources in the right direction.

# CHAPTER 5

# Allo-traction: From Resource Allocation to Resource Attraction

## MANAGING RESOURCES IN THE NEW ECONOMY
*John Coombe, CFO*
GlaxoSmithKline

*Pharmaceuticals is an industry driven by science. Technology, in this case the emerging knowledge of genetics and its application to new medicines, is a huge driver of change, as it is in so many other industries. These changes are creating enormous demand for investments to support the development of many new product techniques and technologies.*

*GlaxoSmithKline has been created from the merger of Glaxo Wellcome and SmithKline Beecham, both leaders in total shareholder return (TSR) and economic value added (EVA). To maintain our position, we are significantly reshaping and improving the way we do business. In this endeavor, focus is the key.*

*Only a few candidates identified during the drug creation process will hit the target and demonstrate efficacy; even fewer will successfully complete the stringent drug approval process. Overall the odds on failure are high. Despite this reality, the top 10 pharmaceutical companies worldwide average a TSR of 35%. Recently these returns have toned down, reflecting the threats of competition, technology, and genetics developments. The end of the millennium saw unprecedented merger activity—almost every major firm was in play.*

*Risks have to be spread and a portfolio management approach must be taken. The increasing scale of risk is too great for many individual companies to support, resulting in major industry restructuring: mergers and acquisitions (including the creation of GlaxoSmithKline), strategic alliances and divestment of noncore businesses to generate cash for reinvestment. Each day the financial pages report new deals and plans. Joint ventures are becoming commonplace: in discovery with biotech partners, in development with "in licensing" of products, in sales and marketing with comarketing deals. Outsourcing has increased, with contract research organizations for drug development and specialist providers in distribution. All these initiatives are designed to spread risk and share reward.*

### How do we gauge R&D efficiency? How does the CFO advise boardroom colleagues on which investments to back and which to drop?

*Pharmaceutical industry growth is fueled by investment in research and development. In GlaxoSmithKline we will invest well in excess of £2 billion per year in R&D; we are the biggest investor in R&D in the UK and among the largest worldwide. The key to shareholder return is success in R&D, but evaluating potential returns is highly subjective. Market potential, likelihood of scientific success, patient value, and the price government and healthcare providers are willing to pay, all must be assessed many years before products come to market. The pharmaceutical industry typically spends 15% of sales in R&D. Scientists relentlessly demand more money to fund the explosion of opportunities created by new technology while uncertainty of returns grows day by day. There are always more projects than resources. This inevitably results in rationing based upon portfolio optimization techniques.*

*The challenges facing pharmaceuticals are, I believe, identical to those facing other high-tech industries especially in e-business and the Internet: how to make investment decisions at Internet speed, how to select technologies in an ever-changing world, how to evaluate propositions ranging from straightforward extensions of existing businesses to completely new opportunities. More new ideas than ever before, high failure rates, massive investments in infrastructure and technology. In all, the similarities between pharmaceuticals and the new e-technologies are striking.*

*The pharmaceutical industry requires new planning tools and processes to meet these challenges. New processes encompass preappraisal, the development of new ideas, investment appraisal, the allocation of resources based on business priority, and performance management. Without such processes, it is impossible to position successfully the increasing number of products coming through the R&D pipeline.*

*Finance plays a key role in the management of resource allocation. Theoretically, because our industry is highly profitable, it has infinite ability to raise cash. But we still have to manage profit and loss and deliver shareholder returns. At GlaxoSmithKline finance ensures that proper funds are available and the bottom line remains viable, while meeting the needs of internal and external stakeholders.*

*Conventional discounted cash flow (DCF) analysis helps in investment appraisal but has limitations in risky situations. Real options valuation is increasingly used in the pharmaceutical industry to supplement conventional net present value (NPV) analysis, highlighting the value of options to proceed during R&D as more information becomes available. Finance is very involved in all commercial aspects of the business, helping to marry and reconcile the often conflicting financial and resource priorities of R&D and marketing/sales.*

*For the finance function, all this means using more complex project evaluation techniques, involving real options valuation, Monte Carlo simulations, and so on—always plagued by the need to estimate market size. It means dealing with more complex budget processes and resource allocation activity. How do we gauge R&D efficiency? How do we measure the effectiveness of marketing and sales budgets? Above all, how does the CFO advise boardroom colleagues on which investments to back and which to drop?*

---

When we interviewed leading CFOs like John Coombe and asked them what finance process troubles them the most, the answer was virtually unanimous—resource allocation. Resources are the lifeblood of an enterprise, and resource allocation is the one management process that can energize an organization to achieve superior returns. But getting it wrong can lead to a lack of motivation and an irretrievable decline. Not surprisingly, today's CFOs are wrestling with some tough questions:

- *Why does R&D keep asking for more money?*

  R&D routinely claims that previous investments are creating massive improvements in efficiency and innovation, but then presses for budget increases to keep up with new technologies. CFOs must decide which technologies will truly enhance shareholder value and how well equipped their companies are to exploit them.

- *The number of new opportunities is exploding, how do I cope?*

  The Internet, communications, genome research, new materials, molecular-scale engineering, and other advances are spawning huge numbers of business options. Existing approaches to capital allocation are slow and cumbersome; they can only assess a static situation in which an opportunity is either pursued or not at the time of evaluation. Faster, more flexible tools are needed.

- *Should we invest in strategic products that don't meet our hurdle rate?*

  Hurdle rates of return represent a rigid view of the future; using history as a predictor, an initiative may be rejected because its projected rate of return falls below an arbitrary benchmark. This approach has always been an imperfect assessment tool; the current pace of change makes it irrelevant. Today the concept of strategy as a portfolio of options is central to balancing risk. Since you cannot predict the future, it pays to keep open as many options as possible.

This chapter examines why and how resource management is changing, and the implications for the finance function. It argues that, to ensure effective investment, the CFO must maintain two resource management cycles: *resource allocation*, which exploits existing traditional business models, and *resource attraction*, which fosters new-economy business models.

## WHY CHANGE RESOURCE MANAGEMENT?

Make no mistake, it is getting more difficult to allocate successfully the resources of a large, complex organization. Quite simply, there are more opportunities than ever before, they emerge more quickly, and their life cycles are shorter. As a result, there are more decisions to be made and less time in which to make them, just as their impact on business success is increasing.

As CFO what is your role in this brave new world? How can you make investment decisions at Internet speed? How can you increase your responsiveness and flexibility of thought when evaluating opportunities? How can you keep pace with today's technology-driven economy, which yields more promising, and more disruptive, ideas than ever before?

One solution is to view strategy as a series of options. In a rapidly changing world the organizations that hold the most options, while fully understanding their cost and value, will be the long-term winners. What this means for CFOs is that, when it comes to resource management, they are evolving from gatekeeper to opportunity-seeker.

In short, you need to think like a venture capitalist, managing risks and options dynamically. Finance's traditional focus on hurdle rates, cost control, and go/no-go decisions is being superseded by the need to manage innovation using new valuation methods like real options valuation (ROV), and techniques like staged financing and hedging. These tools enable you to keep your options open, to incubate ideas through creative investment strategies, and to exploit promising new business models.

> *The winning organizations of the future will be those*
> *that successfully harmonize their management of*
> *resource allocation and resource attraction, to attain the*
> *powerful benefits of resource allo-traction.*

Traditional *resource allocation* focuses on generating optimal value from existing business models. In contrast, *resource attraction* focuses on challenging the status quo, nurturing new business models, and exploring new value-creating dynamics. The winning organizations of the future will be those that successfully harmonize their management of resource allocation and resource attraction, to attain the powerful benefits of *resource allo-traction*. As CFO, balancing these two investment cycles will be one of your major challenges.

What resources are we talking about? As discussed in previous chapters, resources are rapidly becoming less tangible. Traditionally, resource management focused on capital rationing—how to deploy most effectively limited amounts of investment capital. In many industries today, capital

| Resource group | Flexibility | Liquidity | Durability |
|---|---|---|---|
| Financial resources | high | high | high |
| People and competencies | medium | medium | low |
| Assets and technology | low | medium | low |
| Business processes and systems | low | low | medium |
| Physical infrastructure | low | sector specific | sector specific |
| Knowledge | medium | sector specific | low |
| Raw materials | medium | high | low |

**Figure 5.1** *Different resources have different characteristics*

is readily available and relatively inexpensive. Why then is resource management becoming more challenging?

The answer lies in the relative scarcity of other resources such as skills, knowledge and capability. These nonfinancial resources have differing characteristics. Figure 5.1 shows how some resources are more flexible than others; the tap can be turned on and off as needed. Some are more easily converted to cash (liquidity). Resources also differ in their durability, how quickly or slowly they are depleted.

Let's look at the importance of resources in three nonfinancial groups:

- *People and competencies*: a pharmaceutical company may have a list of 15 drug candidates for development into prescription medicines. However, it may be able to pursue only five of these because it lacks highly skilled people who can successfully develop and commercialize each product.

- *Assets and technology*: a CD producer may recognize opportunities in DVD but since DVD is new, there are relatively few suppliers building the technology and capital equipment. Can the CD producer obtain enough equipment to enter the DVD market, and deliver product quickly enough to outsell the competition?

- *Physical infrastructure*: an incumbent telecom provider may want to compete with fiber-optic cable television companies by providing video on demand through its existing network. However, if the bandwidth of its current system is too narrow to deliver the service it envisions, its infrastructure must be upgraded or expanded, or its bandwidth needs must be reduced.

Every market opportunity involves a number of resource constraints, and as soon as a shortage of one is addressed, another becomes a limiting factor. To optimize investment decisions, today's CFO must install systems and processes that can trade off among these conflicting constraints.

## RESOURCE ALLOCATION: TODAY'S BEST PRACTICES

CFOs today face major shifts in their role as resource managers (Figure 5.2). Although general trends are apparent, specific best practices differ from industry to industry; they are largely driven by a repertoire of new valuation techniques. A prime example is real options valuation (ROV). ROV was originally used in financial services, but it is now being employed to assess R&D portfolios in pharmaceuticals. We also see economic value added (EVA) being used in capital-intensive industries, such as industrials and telecommunications, to optimize capital planning. And we see high-tech and Internet start-ups making resource allocation decisions based on anticipated growth in brand and customer value, often in the absence of near-term profit expectations. What is the impact of best practices like these on traditional business models?

| FROM | TO |
|---|---|
| Treating the maximization of capital returns as the highest priority | Pursuing all opportunities which exceed the cost of capital |
| Short-term, often annual investment cycles | Long-term multiyear investment cycles which vary in length |
| Treating capital as limited and subject to rationing | Treating the source and volume of funding required as secondary to implementing strategy |
| Focusing resource allocation on physical, fixed assets | Focusing resource management on intangible assets such as brands, R&D, intellectual property, competencies, and other business capacity constraints |
| Project management | Portfolio management |
| Evaluating relatively small, standalone, ad hoc investment projects | Managing large, interdependent, strategically fundamental investment programs |
| Traditional techniques such as payback, ROI and DCF | Shareholder value impact assessments based on EVA, CFROI, free cash flow and ROV |

**Figure 5.2** *Trends in resource management*

Case Study
Caterpillar Overseas: Managing a Portfolio
of Investments

*Caterpillar Inc., headquartered in Illinois, designs, manufactures and markets a wide variety of heavy equipment. Caterpillar's 84 manufacturing plants employ 66,000 skilled workers; it markets products through an independent dealer network spanning 200 countries. Total shareholder return yielded 29% to investors from 1993 to 1999, outpacing its competitors. Return on assets is currently in the region of 6%.*

*In the last decade, Caterpillar's major investment initiative focused on building factories of the future. This strategy positioned it as a manufacturing innovator, but created a high fixed-cost infrastructure unable to meet growing demands for flexibility. Caterpillar's challenge was to convince Wall Street that its investment programs could produce strong, sustainable growth in returns, while satisfying investor concerns regarding market responsiveness.*

*Caterpillar Overseas, a major division, oversees volatile territories such as Russia and Africa, as well as more stable markets in Europe and the Middle East. The challenge in Overseas is to move toward a more profitable distribution of resources in the face of diverse geographic needs. Its investment program must lead to increased operational flexibility, a better-balanced portfolio, and a more focused strategy.*

*Overseas traditionally allocated capital to its operating companies based on envelopes—specific budgets for capital expenditures allocated at the operating company level. While offering speed and simplicity, this capital allocation mechanism favored companies with mature markets and sales, while it starved immature companies with high growth potential.*

*So Overseas decided to manage its investments as a portfolio. Future investments were to be ranked based on their potential contribution to shareholder value for Overseas as a whole. Envelopes were abandoned; investments are now selected using value-based metrics and allocated based on potential shareholder value. The benefits of this revised resource allocation process are compelling:*

- Process simplification: *the business case for proposals is developed in short, iterative cycles as each stage of approval occurs. Both intellectual capital investment proposals (such as rolling demand management) and physical capital projects (such as a manufacturing plant) are evaluated using the same criteria and managed in the same way.*

- Accountability for value creation: *projects are combined to meet share-holder value improvement targets. These targets are supported by specific value drivers tied to management accountability, for example, shared responsibility among managers in R&D and marketing for improving product performance.*

- Portfolio returns: *returns are risk-adjusted for uncertainties such as political instability or new technologies, supporting apples-for-apples comparisons. Funds are then allocated based on highest return potential. Operating companies are no longer competing for funds; instead it is projects that compete for funds, maximizing total portfolio returns.*

- Turning strategy into action: *using value-based management techniques, management improved its line of sight, linking individual investment initiatives to shareholder value targets. It can now see how initiatives, when consolidated, contribute to closing the shareholder value gap. For example, by analyzing customer value components in a finished product, Caterpillar can determine which additional product investments will yield the greatest customer and shareholder value.*

*Since implementing its new resource allocation process, the company has achieved several quick wins, yielding some significant shareholder value improvements.*

---

As Caterpillar's experience suggests, tomorrow's best practices in resource allocation extend beyond investment appraisal. They encompass the entire resource management cycle, from idea generation to implementation and follow-up. For example, Caterpillar is innovating the use of detailed value driver trees as a source of new ideas. And management monitors portfolio implementation against four key criteria: milestones achieved, quality standards met, resource consumption levels, and most important, flexibility.

## THE SHIFT TO RESOURCE ATTRACTION

As elsewhere, e-business is dramatically redefining resource management. Traditionally, CFO investment decisions supported the creation, marketing, and sustaining of capability and capacity along a primarily *internal* value chain, with emphasis on the physical colocation of dependent parts of that value chain. Today any company of any size in any industry can provide a range of services without owning any part of the value chain. The focus is now *external*. The CFO has the freedom to decouple parts of his or her organization's value chain and mix it with another's, spreading risk and value.

In the e-business world, the goals of resource allocation are customer value propositions and customer networking. By connecting diverse parts of the value chain, e-business allows companies to outsource. Convenient and cheap connectivity with customers enables organizations increasingly to specialize by taking advantage of mass markets and mass customization through the Internet.

The disintermediated business model that is emerging offers both great benefits and great challenges. As a CFO it forces you to evaluate a much broader range of alternatives. This requires keeping an open mind about changing any or all of the elements of your business model, including product lines, customer segments, and asset deployment.

Skillfully managing the transition from traditional to disintermediated business models is essential. Companies must evolve from infrastructure-bound physical delivery mechanisms to flexible, conceptual, strategic players. As a company learns from experience to identify and exercise the broadest array of options possible, it will arrive at the point where any part of its value chain can be brought in, licensed or negotiated for.

In the e-business world, the cost of capital assumes less importance; the importance of having the people to do the work is heightened; managing input isn't as important as managing results or output; multiyear investment cycles are more meaningful than annual reporting cycles; capital rationing is less important than managing capacity constraints or bottlenecks; distributing cash flows is not the name of the game, recycling cash flows is; time is money; value is driven by customers not by asset utilization; and projects are viewed as investment options, not ends in their own right.

Current resource allocation tools are geared to existing business models. But with the rapid emergence of new business models, traditional allocation programs are no longer able to cope. In fact, these programs can actually undermine shareholder value creation by taking you in the wrong direction. To invest effectively, you need to maintain both the resource management cycles introduced earlier in this chapter: resource allocation, which fully exploits existing business models, and resource attraction, which nurtures emerging sources of innovation and growth.

Resource allocation tends to be evolutionary, reinforcing established value-creating characteristics. It fosters stewardship, preserving assets, and making incremental improvements. Incentives are extrinsic: people tend to be motivated by performing against predefined objectives. Resource attraction is revolutionary, exploring new value-creating dynamics and promoting entrepreneurial behavior rather than stewardship. Incentives are intrinsic: people are motivated by being empowered to pursue their own ideas.

Figure 5.3 shows the four stages of the resource management cycle as they relate to resource allocation. Preinvestment appraisal focuses on improving the quality and volume of ideas within the parameters of the existing business model. Then investment appraisal, traditionally the stage where CFOs have the greatest impact, focuses on averting risk rather

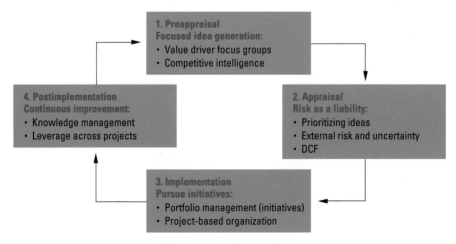

**Figure 5.3** *Resource allocation: improving existing business models*

than exploiting it. Implementation seeks to develop a portfolio of investment initiatives. Well-defined objectives, rapid execution, and a clear
endgame are the keys to success. The postimplementation stage codifies
lessons learned and redeploys resources to similar, but new, initiatives;
increased speed to market is the goal.

We contrast the stages for resource attraction, with its focus on fostering new business models, in Figure 5.4. Here preinvestment appraisal is
open-ended, unconstrained by assumptions based on current business
dynamics. Less time is spent on investment appraisal, and risk is treated
as an asset to be exploited for the creation of shareholder value. Upside
risk is maximized while limiting the downside—this requires the mindset
of a venture capitalist. The implementation stage involves continued
pursuit of all available options, and the CFO generally adopts an arm's-
length operating style. The postimplementation stage focuses on selling
off options or exercising them by scaling up a new business model.

Most companies aspire to have a robust existing business model while
building a new innovation-driven model from within. This means managing in tandem the different resource management cycles of resource
allocation and resource attraction. The following sections are designed
to help you master *resource allo-traction*: they take the four stages of
resource management in turn, examining each from the traditional perspective (resource allocation in mature offerings) and then the new-
economy perspective (resource attraction in evolving initiatives).

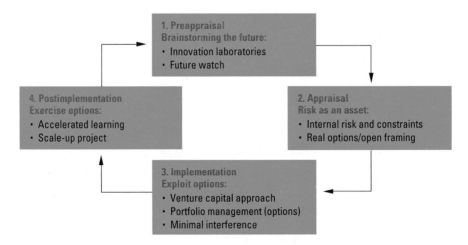

**Figure 5.4** *Resource attraction: fostering new business models*

## STAGE 1: PREINVESTMENT APPRAISAL

Following best practices today in the mature business cycle includes using value driver trees and customer value analysis. In a mature business, value-based management enables you to focus on creating shareholder value at an operational and resource allocation level. For example, you can analyze free cash flow to identify the variables that may increase cash flow and value, such as profit margin, cost of capital or growth duration. The aim is to allocate resources to the drivers most sensitive to improvement. Figure 5.5 illustrates how one manufacturing company, which distributes through dealers to end customers, consulted various

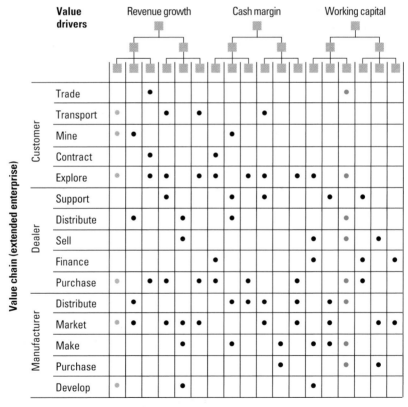

**Figure 5.5** *Stakeholder value contributions (illustrative model)*

stakeholders and assessed their contribution to specific value drivers across different parts of the value chain.

To create ideas rooted in your existing business model, you must determine its value drivers. A structured way to do this is to build value driver trees or influence diagrams. Begin by interviewing business influencers: explore potential value drivers in interviews with innovators and leaders across the company. Then draw up a shortlist of drivers, using clear criteria in selecting and ranking them. Next run workshops on specific value drivers, assembling cross-functional teams spanning the value chain. Brainstorm, draft and redraft value driver trees. Finally, create, approve and issue a value driver tree consolidating the perspectives of participating groups.

Although time-intensive, building value driver trees provides a strong basis for appraising new ideas. Here are some benefits:

- *Reaching cross-company consensus*: value driver trees provide a unified vision of key business drivers, while brainstorming clarifies intuitive concepts. Moving from intuition to articulation gives people clearly defined value drivers to focus on.

- *Developing a common language*: having major stakeholders build value driver trees promotes shared understanding and better communication.

- *Cutting waste*: having a shared understanding and focus prevents people from wasting time and effort on new ideas that don't satisfy consensus decisions.

- *Building ownership and accountability*: creating value driver trees through consensus fosters shared accountability and ignites the effort to make performance improvements happen.

- *Creating an organizational truth*: this creates a shared line of sight that keeps everyone moving in the same direction.

- *Setting the basis for performance management*: the value drivers you've identified can form the basis for your performance measures.

Caterpillar's recent experience offers an example of using value drivers to generate improvement. Functional performance of its products proved to be one of its most sensitive value drivers. Caterpillar was faced with falling sales figures in specific product/market segments of Eastern

Europe, and assumed there was a competitive product with superior functional performance. Caterpillar knew that its dealers, who work directly with its final customers, had the most intimate knowledge of what those customers truly valued. So, at its annual dealer event, the company organized its dealers into focus groups based on product/market segmentations. The dealers were asked to list the most important product performance attributes of a major Caterpillar product along with those of its direct competitors. Through this exercise it became clear that Caterpillar was at a distinct competitive disadvantage: its lifting machine was able to lift only two stories high, while a major competitor's equipment lifted three stories high. Since builders in the region were erecting higher structures, the competitor was meeting market demand and Caterpillar wasn't. Once Caterpillar closed its competitive gap, market share recovered.

*As you shift from traditional business models to emerging business models, the preinvestment appraisal process begins to change. Brainstorming and innovation become more relevant.*

By linking market observation to customer value drivers, Caterpillar generated useful new investment ideas for an existing business. In contrast, a traditional, technology-oriented investment strategy would not have identified or addressed the real customer value issue. By focusing on the most sensitive value drivers—relative product performance in the case of Caterpillar—companies can achieve superior returns. Idea generation through processes like the Caterpillar focus groups can be institutionalized using Web-enabled technology. New ideas can be expressed in real time and evaluated by a networked panel of experts who decide investment priorities in response to customer intelligence.

## Using Innovation Labs and Brainstorming to Spur Idea Generation

As you shift from traditional business models to emerging ones, the preinvestment appraisal process begins to change. Brainstorming and innovation become more relevant.

For example, Shell developed its GameChanger process to enable unconventional ideas to circumvent the usual approval gauntlet. Innovation labs bring small groups of the company's employees together, provide them with examples of radically new thinking from outside their business, and then encourage them to produce "nonlinear" ideas. Action labs then help employees develop 100-day venture plans for conducting low-cost, low-risk tests of the best ideas generated. Ideas that are approved are quickly green-lighted; they can receive as much as $600,000 within eight days. Several of the GameChanger ventures have grown into major initiatives. Indeed, of the company's five largest growth initiatives of early 1999, four had emerged through the GameChanger process.

## STAGE 2: INVESTMENT APPRAISAL

As CFO how can you help identify the best ideas and add value to them? Traditional valuation methods haven't kept pace with technology and business advances. This gap creates three major pitfalls:

- *Single scenario, dated focus*: traditional investment valuation relies on assumptions about potential investments. Future costs and revenues are based on these assumptions. Future cash flows are then projected; investments that exceed a target return are pursued. This approach ignores the many changes that occur over the life of an investment. A mere snapshot, it offers little insight or flexibility for managing an investment into the future.

- *Return-on-investment myopia*: shortsightedness may kill off projects that deliver near-term losses, yet may grow rapidly over a medium to long time frame. It also undercuts innovative initiatives that offer low revenues until a new product or service builds momentum.

- *Fixed financial hurdles*: pure financial hurdles make sense only during periods of slow, manageable change. Increasingly the assumptions underpinning a discounted cash flow (DCF) calculation, and even risk-adjusted discount rates, can change so rapidly that these approaches are becoming straitjackets.

Conventional investment appraisal uses incremental DCF analysis. Typically, the hurdle (or discount) rate used in DCF calculations is higher than a company's real weighted average cost of capital. Since the hurdle rate is high, projects that overcome it tend to be riskier. In financial services companies the capital charge against product profitability is risk-adjusted to reflect inherently uncertain cash flows. Risks are also factored into discount rates for investment appraisal. Both hurdle rates and the weighted average cost of capital reflect the risk profile of the company as a whole, not individual projects under consideration. New projects, with new risk parameters, can change the risk profile of the company as a whole (and therefore its cost of capital). Risk-adjusted discount rates reflect best practices today in traditional business models.

Consider this example. A company operated a number of retailing chains, some catering to fashionable young customers, others serving traditional older consumers. The newer, high-fashion chains offered high, rapid returns, but capital invested in this upscale retailing formula (branding, shop refurbishment and siting) was consumed in three-year cycles. The traditional retailing chains offered lower returns over longer time periods, with capital infusions required only every 10 years. The company used one hurdle rate across all the retailing chains, failing to recognize that the high-fashion chains were inherently riskier and warranted a higher cost of capital. While the company wanted a balanced portfolio, its method of capital allocation clearly favored riskier projects. Upon review, this company realized it needed to move away from a one-size-fits-all hurdle rate to risk-adjusted hurdle rates. This enabled it to allocate capital to those projects that offered the best investment opportunities.

> *The CFO should balance constraints to meet shareholder value targets. For every investment ask the key questions, What resources are available and what's the value creation potential?*

Risk-adjusted discount rates can support decisions about projects of varying risk and capital intensity, and can take account of external uncertainties (e.g., variables affecting the size and evolution of customer market segments). However, internal uncertainties (such as management availability, scarce competencies, or business interruptions) are often overlooked. External uncertainties tend to affect the size of return from new projects, while internal uncertainties put the entire return at risk.

As we shift from financial to nonfinancial constraints, why does failing to manage internal constraints jeopardize investment initiatives? It's a matter of demand and supply. On the demand side, every initiative requires specific resources. On the supply side, you must know exactly what resources are at your disposal. Once you decide which investments are likely to create shareholder value, the question becomes, Which should you undertake, given the resources available to you? This presents a number of challenges and solutions:

- Overcome bottlenecks by hiring more staff, outsourcing work to sub-contractors, hiring temporary staff, or acquiring businesses that possess the required skills and resources.

- Manage peak workloads that exceed resource capacity by redesigning projects or time-shifting work out of peak periods.

- Use joint venturing and other forms of partnering to overcome re-source shortfalls.

- Balance constraints to meet shareholder value targets; for every investment ask the key questions, What resources are available and what's the value creation potential?

## Techniques for Valuing Options and Managing Uncertainty

In the new business model, uncertainty itself has value, but only if management designs investment projects for maximum flexibility. This may mean retaining the option to switch between two distribution channels, one e-enabled and one traditional. Flexibility can also mean expansion or contraction; for example, the option to expand product range to a loyal customer base, or to contract out manufacturing rather than owning production facilities. Or flexibility can involve acceleration or delay; for example, the option to unload a noncore asset, or to delay a project in order to leverage a technology breakthrough.

Because they require predictable cash flows, traditional investment appraisal techniques undermine flexibility. In contrast to standard financial tools, a portfolio of options offers a more fluid mechanism for fueling innovation. In the e-business world, greater uncertainty about returns continues over longer time periods. New investments are valued for strategic importance, not short-term gain. Given the range of potential returns from diverse projects, management's vision and operating style must be highly flexible.

Options, arising from flexible investment structures, have value. This value resides in their upside potential, unencumbered by commitment to downside risk. A pharmaceutical company owning product patents, for example, has options to weigh up as it moves through clinical trial phases into commercialization. At every phase, the company has the right to develop the product further but without the obligation to do so. These patented products have a potential future value. The more uncertain the market, the higher the value of the options to develop them fully or abandon them.

One way of evaluating such options is to use open framing, or decision tree analysis. This approach enables the CFO to explore the assumptions, probabilities and impact of different scenarios and decisions over a project's lifetime (Figure 5.6). Open framing develops decision trees to which values and probabilities can be assigned, providing alternate scenarios. In this process, each investment proposition is broken down into a series of decisions. At every decision point, the nature, shape and size of the project can change. Advanced software can greatly facilitate the modeling and analysis of these scenarios. Probabilities as to the likely outcome at each decision point are projected, based on a combination of past experience, available data, and intuition. The power of this technique is in its decision-point approach to scoping out available options. It helps address the question, What flexibility is needed, and when?

Case Study
Building in Flexibility

*An engineering company wanted to manufacture in Russia. Initially, it acquired an option to buy land for a manufacturing facility and surrounding lots for possible expansion. It started with contract manufacturing since initial sales volumes didn't justify building a plant. The company's contract was structured flexibly, so that exit costs could be minimized if the market failed, or a factory could be built if the market grew. A key decision point: whether to continue contract manufacturing or to construct its own plant.*

*The same flexibility was sought in contracts with Russian dealers. The decision point: whether to subcontract or establish a self-owned dealer network.*

*Ultimately, the company built a plant but continued subcontracting the dealer function. Its original investment analysis had used open framing to*

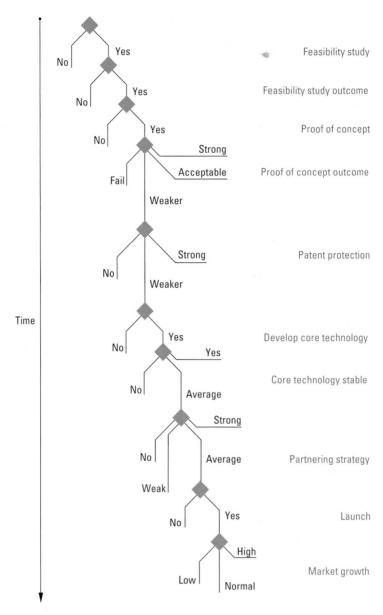

**Figure 5.6** *A decision tree for new technology investment appraisal*

*identify all key decision points over the life of the project. Critically, the analysis showed that if the company purchased a land option—acquiring the right to buy land cheaply—it would benefit from depressed land prices. Open framing also showed that if the market took off, and the probability was high, the company would need its own factory and land around it to expand. In fact, the analysis showed a strong link between market growth and land prices.*

As this case study demonstrates, open framing is especially useful in recognizing where flexibility offers the most value at critical stages in a project's life cycle. It is less powerful as a valuation tool. Open framing requires probability calculations and typically does not weigh the relative risks posed by different decision outcomes. It also assumes that decision points occur at discrete time intervals.

Real options valuation (ROV), in contrast, avoids having to determine probabilities and risk-adjusted discount rates for every part of every branch of the decision tree. It also recognizes that decision points occur continuously. The technique is based on a family of mathematical formulas, including one related to call options, applied to both tangible (real) and intangible (financial) investments. Parameters include the uncertainty of expected cash flows, net present value (NPV), the time over which options can be exercised, and investment cost (initial outlay).

ROV calculates the price worth paying for an option. Decisions to invest are rarely once and for all; even those that appear to be time-constrained, such as an acquisition, can be broken down into stages, with options at each decision point. Applying options theory to investment decisions enables you to recognize and value uncertainties in a constantly evolving environment.

When an investment can be broken into stages, with go/no-go decisions at the end of each stage, it can be managed dynamically. Each stage represents an option to proceed to the next, with the price of the option being the investment required in that stage. Options theory allows you to view investment choices as a linked set of decisions. This enables you to commit to only one step at a time, analyzing information and options at each investment stage before agreeing to the next. An option is more valuable than the underlying asset itself because it offers the flexibility to choose only the upside, not the downside. As you appraise a proposal, ROV gives you the opportunity to make the investment idea inherently more valuable by making it more flexible. Building exit options into the investment, for example, makes it easier to shut a project down.

Experience suggests some dos and don'ts. Do use the ROV framework to engineer flexibility into projects. Don't overemphasize the ROV framework to value projects. Why? Because the valuation is based on subjective judgments, and the math can become quite complex.

Do use portfolio management to raise your sights. As CFO, to maximize shareholder value, you must optimize the portfolio of options at your command. Bringing a flexible mentality to portfolio management frees you to evaluate and compare the risks and returns of projects, business units, and entire businesses. Your job becomes more strategic: like an investor, you must orchestrate financial, risk, and operational decisions. How should your company's investment portfolio be structured? How should resources be allocated? What expectations for returns should you have?

Don't underestimate the challenge of managing portfolio risk. Consider one view held by the investment community: We don't want individual companies to hedge their risks, because we can do that in our portfolio; by hedging risks, companies hold back on growth. The counterargument goes like this: If you want individual companies to assume risk, then why penalize them if they deviate from earnings projections? Consistency of earnings and growth over time do matter because investors look at a company's ability to deliver, and almost any risk can be hedged, except business intake and fulfillment.

For investors, how a CFO manages risk is crucial. That's why, at the business unit or project level, real options can be a powerful risk management tool. Using options for outsourcing or contract manufacture, allied with financial hedging instruments and insurance, can offer opportunities to add value by building in flexibility and minimizing risks.

## STAGE 3: IMPLEMENTATION

Implementing investment initiatives to improve an existing business model involves three critical success factors: speed, quality of deliverables, and efficient resource consumption. Here are some important ingredients:

- *Team structure*: subject-matter experts (or operational managers) must be teamed with project management professionals, otherwise the risks of failure are great. Time lines slip, budgets are overrun, and corners are cut, all compromising project returns. Once in place, this dedicated pool of professionals can serve as a resource for the rest of the organization.

- *Efficient process planning*: project management methodology, status-reporting standards, and project tracking should address the following four performance criteria. Progress against these criteria is reported individually for projects and aggregated for the portfolio. It is vital to achieve swift resolution of implementation issues on the critical path.

  - *Milestone compliance*: are we on track for project completion and market entry?
  - *Quality compliance*: based on interim deliverables, will all expected benefits be realized?
  - *Resource compliance*: are we consuming sufficient resources within project limits?
  - *Flexibility compliance*: are we monitoring and exercising our options at the right time?

- *Tools and techniques*: best-practice toolkits today emphasize managing the critical path, compressing delivery timetables, and monitoring scarce resources deployed across projects. From a systems viewpoint, the goal is not just capturing information at the individual project level, but aggregating it for portfolio review by the CFO.

- *Reward and compensation*: project teams are rewarded for compliance against performance criteria, but have no share in the returns from a successful project. Generally, they receive reward bonuses for their contributions to achieving project milestones.

## Setting Up an Internal Venture Capital Fund

As we shift from traditional business models, characterized by stability and predictability, to the new world of e-business, with all its rapid change and uncertainty, how do we learn from the implementation principles that served us well in the past? For new business models, speed and quality are important, but flexibility is even more so, along with creativity and entrepreneurial flair. How do you foster this flexibility? How do you reward value creation? And trickier still, how do you balance these new dynamic criteria with traditional, but still vital, execution requirements?

Silicon Valley is the ultimate entrepreneurial environment. It thrives on innovation, growth, huge rewards and the fast adoption of new business models. Successful Internet start-ups deliver shareholder value quickly for founders, staff and investors. How? Through plentiful venture capital, ownership incentives, and freedom from legacy business models.

Silicon Valley's venture capital management cycle can be replicated within organizations that wish to reinvent themselves around a new portfolio of investment options. Organizationally, this cycle is based on three building blocks: a venture capital fund, a venture capital board, and business start-up teams. The venture capital board sets and tracks financial and other critical targets that determine the value of its options as investors. The start-up teams determine their own business model and processes.

Today multinationals like Shell, Diageo, AIG, and General Motors are creating internal venture capital funds for Internet start-ups. Venture capital initiatives are seen as priming the pump for new ideas and nurturing fledgling businesses within the boundaries of existing corporate culture. These start-ups often compete with a traditional business model, such as when the Internet is used as a distribution channel in consumer goods, versus established distributors. Conventional investment appraisal criteria do not necessarily apply, the emphasis is on innovation and speed to market.

An internal venture fund generally operates on a quasi-autonomous basis, unencumbered by standard reporting lines and accountability mandates. This is especially important when a new venture presents a competitive threat to an existing business. The venture capital board should have strong, independent leadership; it sets innovation goals and reports to the CFO. The venture board is accountable for identifying bright business concepts backed by outstanding management teams, extraordinary returns, and manageable risk.

Let's explore the governance model of one of the most successful corporate venture capital programs created to date. As of March 2000 the collective market capitalization of Xerox Technology Ventures (XTV) spin-off companies exceeded Xerox's market capitalization by a factor of two or more. How did a large, traditional company encourage such innovation? Xerox committed a total of $30 million from which the XTV partners could draw $2 million at any one time without permission from its parent corporation. For larger amounts, the partners had to obtain approval from the board. Partners essentially were given full autonomy to start, build, exit or liquidate companies.

Consistent with Silicon Valley practices, XTV employees received options to buy real shares in the venture's emerging companies. This ownership had a great psychological impact on staff. XTV also used a streamlined capital structure to attract follow-up financing from outside investors. XTV and Xerox nurtured the start-ups, using the resources of the parent firm to leverage the portfolio of start-up initiatives when this kind of support made sense. This typically occurred in the areas of procurement, accounting, legal and certification. All these transactions were valued at arm's length.

Xerox used one of several funding alternatives to build XTV. A venture may be wholly owned, or it may be structured as an alliance with an external venture capitalist or technology partner. The investment vehicle depends on the nature and composition of the options portfolio.

In enterprises such as XTV, the venture capital board is tasked with selecting and backing business proposals from within the organization, and with sponsoring entrepreneurial teams to take the ideas to the next stage of development. The project sponsor for implementation might not be the person who proposed the idea; the venture board must choose an implementation manager based on drive and ability to deliver results; in other words, someone with "skin" in the game.

Team members leave behind their relatively fixed and safe salary compensation and take on highly variable risk in the form of options for equity. The entrepreneurial team generally has an ownership stake in the venture, typically through share options in the venture fund, which may operate as a separate legal entity. The venture board employs a no-interference management model. In summary, this entrepreneurial investment model differs radically from the traditional model in terms of funding, structure, business management process, and reward.

One danger of the internal venture capitalist approach is that good ideas may wither on the vine. Why? Quite simply, because idea overload can result in lack of sponsorship, lack of resources, or difficulties in business plan design. Some companies bypass these problems by setting up incubators—business development programs that nurture promising ideas to maturity.

# STAGE 4: POSTIMPLEMENTATION

How does a company leverage its wealth of learning from completed projects and speed new ideas to market? Current best practices focus on creating a knowledge management environment that gathers and analyzes project data on issues including:

- The impact on elements of the value chain such as R&D and marketing
- The impact on value drivers such as turnover growth
- The risks and uncertainties such as market size assumptions
- Geographical issues such as emerging markets

For example, Zurich Insurance's internal consultancy collects extensive data on systems projects carried out at its corporate center and business units. Its project archives include data on how system developments performed according to plan; this data is used to create performance templates for designing, executing, and tracking new projects of similar complexity. This ability to build on past experience promotes faster time to market, prevents repeating mistakes made in the past, and avoids having to reinvent the wheel.

Another global company with a substantial Internet business offers data from its intranet system to its strategic alliance partners and customers via a Web-based subscription service. This information takes many forms: benchmarking data, best-practice processes, case studies and implementation methodologies.

## Fully Exploiting Innovative Business Initiatives

For Internet start-ups and other new-economy businesses, implementation is about making options more valuable, and postimplementation is about exercising those options as they "run into the money." This happens when the value of the option, if exercised, is higher than the cost of holding on to it. In a fast-moving environment, implementation requires continuous monitoring of the value of options and *knowing when to exercise them.*

Take Amgen's large investment portfolio of biotech R&D projects based on a core technology. Implementation focused on high-volume screening—testing molecular variants against therapeutic applications. Each variant was an option; a few offered commercial potential. In the mid 1980s, Amgen identified a recombinant version of a human protein that stimulates the production of red blood cells for the treatment of anemia. At this point, the option ran into the money. Over time, Amgen exercised a number of options as the compound passed through its approval phases with the US Food and Drug Administration (FDA).

After FDA approval, Amgen held a new set of options for the commercialization phase; for example, licensing marketing and manufacturing to established pharmaceutical companies. Amgen also developed further options by moving the compound into other therapeutic areas such as oncology and acute treatments, a classic case of scaling up as new generations of options are exercised. In 10 years Amgen's share price rose from $2 to $74.

In the postimplementation stage, scaling up is the name of the game, driving exponential growth by exercising emerging options with the goal of maximizing total shareholder return. By scaling up, we mean both escalating option value and, more traditionally, strengthening infrastructures to meet the operational demands of exercising options. In particular, companies with innovative business formats that can be mass-marketed quickly—including Internet auction houses such as eBay and QXL, and biotechnology companies such as Amgen, Affymetrix and Genset—have options that offer powerful scale-up potential.

Consider Amazon.com. In three years the company rapidly scaled up to serve 16 million customers. Customer responsiveness and reliability proved critical to the company's ability to retain its newly acquired customer base. Instead of relying on third parties to fulfill orders, Amazon chose to invest heavily in warehousing and distribution centers.

What does all this mean for the CFO? Not only do you face key challenges in framing your options, you must also know how and when to exercise those options before scaling up. Timing is key. For example, in pharmaceuticals, the go/no-go decision in phase 2 of the FDA approval process is driven by two conflicting forces: first-mover advantage versus learning more before committing. Speeding a drug to market may be more important than the risk of abortive, expensive clinical trials. When exercising options, such timing issues affect all fast-moving industry sectors, from financial services to information technology.

# IMPLICATIONS FOR THE FINANCE FUNCTION

Combining the resource allocation cycle (designed primarily for traditional business models) with the resource attraction cycle (designed for new-economy business models), that's the pivotal challenge for the CFO and the finance team. In most large companies today, old and new business models run side by side. CFOs must strike a difficult balance: refraining from killing old business models which may be generating major revenues, while promoting innovative initiatives which may or may not succeed. This means supporting the existing business model, while simultaneously reviewing hard data on the viability of new business models, and remaining unswayed by euphoric projections.

There are no hard and fast rules for managing this process, but three organizational options do exist:

- *Coexistence*: serving the old world while building the new. American Express operates an e-business travel service in parallel with its traditional operation.

- *Autonomy*: keeping the new business model completely separate from the old. When First Chicago set up its Internet bank, it did so in direct competition with the traditional one.

- *Reinvention*: the new revolutionary model completely replaces the old one. Nokia's move into mobile phones completely eclipsed its previous businesses.

With one foot in each camp, the CFO must weigh the benefits of switching from the old business model to the new one. There are some key questions to address. What is the residual life of the old business model? How much value is it likely to generate? When should the new business model take over and how? If any project is failing, when should you take the exit decision?

Wal-Mart and Tesco are currently experimenting with Internet shopping alongside their existing retail channels. The potential gains of the new e-enabled model are huge. If successful, massive networks of staff-intensive supermarkets sited in costly areas could be replaced with skeletal staffing and warehousing in cheap locations. However, there are too many uncertainties for this changeover to be clear-cut. For instance, the buying patterns of Internet supermarket shoppers are still evolving.

To keep their options open, the supermarket chains must bear the additional short-term cost of running their new e-ventures through their existing infrastructures.

This may be inefficient in the short term, but it offers enormous options flexibility. It allows e-business and traditional retail operations to coexist indefinitely, permits rapid exit from the e-business ventures if they should fail, and allows for a retreat from traditional retailing channels should the e-business experiment prove spectacularly successful.

As ideas mature in the resource attraction cycle, new value creation strategies must be explored to ensure superior performance. Essentially, you can pursue one of three paths in order fully to develop promising ventures (Figure 5.7). Two of these involve developing the venture inside the corporation and the third takes it outside the coporation via out-sourcing or some other release strategy.

Spin-in   In this situation the corporation is best positioned to drive maximum value from a venture; it has access to both the capital and intangible resources required. To move forward, it will spin the project into the resource allocation cycle, replacing or reenergizing its existing business model. The switchover point from resource attraction to resource allocation occurs when a company decides to commit resources to scaling up its infrastructure. Why would a resource attraction initiative

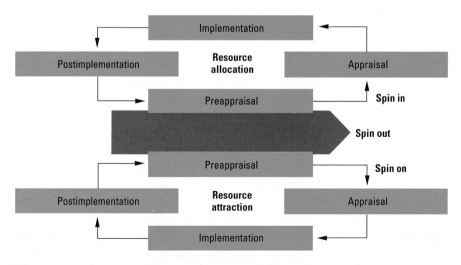

**Figure 5.7** *Resource allo-traction: sustaining value creation*

enter the resource allocation cycle? Because once the initiative matures, its management dynamic changes from innovation to execution. At this point, best practice project management in a traditional environment applies.

Spin-on    Here an idea has successfully navigated critical risk milestones during its start-up phase. In order to develop the venture further, you need it to advance, or spin on, to the next round of financing. Once it achieves critical growth targets, it will be primed either to spin in and enter the resource allocation cycle, or to spin out.

Spin-out    The new business model will generate opportunities for exit options such as outsourcing, IPOs or trade sale. If other corporations are better positioned to drive maximum value from the venture, it will be released from internal corporate development and allowed to spin out of the attraction cycle.

## What Will Distinguish Top CFOs?

The issues around resource allo-traction illustrate how radically the role of the CFO has changed. In the past, the CFO had responsibility for the accounting system, for capital and liability management, and for cost control. In the future, he or she will be responsible for proposing new business models and for explaining how different elements of the models relate to each other. The CFO will also be expected to scope the uncertainty of initiatives, develop strategies to deal with them, and then sell the value proposition to external investors.

Managing these multiple roles won't be easy. First, you must relentlessly pursue innovation and combat corporate inertia so that promising ideas don't get lost in the system. Next, you must take advantage of alternatives, using techniques like hedging and real options to manage uncertainty more effectively. Equally important, you must foster flexibility, shaking off the mindset that your existing business model is cast in concrete or that the projects in your portfolio have permanently fixed relationships. Otherwise you risk losing value and missing the new business model that may deliver sustained growth for your company. Finally, you must be prepared to *really* manage according to a portfolio, cutting free of the physical and emotional baggage of individual initiatives when it is time to let go.

# eCFO CHECKLIST

## CHANGE YOUR MINDSET ABOUT MANAGING RESOURCES

In today's dynamic business climate, yesterday's approach to resource management is inadequate and outmoded. New best practices are required to exploit existing business models, and new valuation tools are needed to assess the opportunities created by e-business and other technology advances.

## THINK LIKE A VENTURE CAPITALIST WHEN PLANNING INVESTMENTS

The traditional CFO focus on hurdle rates and cost control is being superseded by the need to foster innovation through creative investment strategies. Forward-thinking CFOs are promoting corporate venture funds, innovation labs, and other idea generators.

## LEVERAGE RESOURCE ATTRACTION TO TAP IN TO THE NEW ECONOMY

Traditional *resource allocation* focuses on generating value from and improving existing business models. In contrast, *resource attraction* focuses on challenging the status quo, nurturing new business models, identifying new value-creating opportunities. As CFO, managing both these processes is one of your most challenging jobs.

## KEEP YOUR OPTIONS OPEN FOR MAXIMUM FLEXIBILITY

In today's marketplace, flexibility is the name of the game. Remember, the organizations that hold the most options, while fully understanding their cost and value, will be the long-term winners.

## EMBRACE NEW VALUATION TECHNIQUES TO MANAGE UNCERTAINTY

Opportunities and risks are constantly evolving. To keep pace, your investment strategies must be equally dynamic. Sophisticated techniques like hedging, open framing and real options valuation will help you turn risk into an asset.

## OPERATE YOUR BUSINESS MODELS IN PARALLEL TO MAXIMIZE RETURNS

To build shareholder value in today's marketplace, you must generate optimal value from your traditional business model by applying best practices, while simultaneously exploiting opportunities in the new economy. In short, *resource allo-traction* delivers powerful benefits.

## KNOW WHEN TO SWITCH MODELS TO SUSTAIN MOMENTUM

As opportunities are harvested through the resource attraction process, the most promising among them may evolve into vibrant, profitable businesses. Over time, these businesses will begin to mature. At this stage, traditional resource allocation techniques are called for. Knowing when to switch between the two investment cycles is pivotal.

## SPIN IN, SPIN ON, OR SPIN OUT FOR SUPERIOR PERFORMANCE

Once a venture takes shape, there are three avenues open to develop it fully. Through the spin-on approach, the venture advances to the next round of financing, priming it for spin-in or spin-out. Using the spin-in approach, the venture is nurtured internally. When spin-out is most desirable, the venture will complete the resource attraction cycle via an MBO, IPO or trade sale.

# CHAPTER 6

# Blowing Up the Budget

## BEYOND BUDGETING

*Nick Rose, CFO*
**Diageo**

*Diageo is the enterprise that was created out of the Guinness/GrandMet FMCG (fast-moving consumer goods) merger in 1997. We're the world's largest branded-spirits producer, and our original holdings included Burger King and Pillsbury. After the merger, we gathered together 60 people from our predecessor finance departments and asked them, How can we best serve our shareholders going forward? Their overwhelming response was: Let's blow up the budget!*

*We all knew that budgeting consumed tremendous resources, occupied people over most of the year and, worst of all, it was one size fits all. Whether it was a business in one of our major markets, like the UK, or a smaller one in Asia, the budgeting requirements were the same. Yet all that effort was out of synch with the value produced.*

*The question became, If this is such a wasteful process, why are we still going through it? Certainly not for the shareholders' sake. They didn't care how well we were doing against arbitrarily negotiated budget targets. What shareholders care about is whether the company is worth more this year than last year.*

We knew from research by CAM-I (the Consortium for Advanced Manufacturing, International) that some companies had successfully implemented processes involving rolling forecasts and performance measures without annual budgets at all. That sounded terrific to us; we wanted to install a performance management system that would concentrate more on input than output.

We wanted to identify value levers that drive the business forward and cascade them down to a level as basic as consumer response to specific advertising campaigns. When you understand your business that precisely, you can make well-informed decisions about the future, rather than guessing based on outdated figures.

We formed a team from the individual businesses and headquarters to consider our options. Going in, their views ranged from "the current approach doesn't work, but it's comfortable, so let's leave it alone," to "wouldn't it be wonderful to have a fully automated, totally hands-off planning and budgeting system?"

> **Have we abandoned budgeting altogether? No. In certain parts of the organization it's still relevant. But we've removed much of the wasteful interaction between headquarters and the business units.**

Everyone knew something had to be done—we were wasting too much time and money. We began streamlining the current system's workload and progressed to creating an integrated strategic and annual planning process built around key performance indicators (KPIs) and rolling forecasts. We saw that if we took the world-class approach, we could reap real benefits. That motivated us.

It soon became apparent that unless we divided the task into manageable chunks, it would overwhelm us. Using an individual workstreams approach propelled us from concept to implementation without bogging us down in extraneous details.

The most important workstreams focused on developing strategy-driven KPIs that were interconnected up and down the organization. This ensured that people at every level and position had relevant metrics, while giving the board *the right information to plan with. The same data, slightly modified, enabled business units to operate most productively.*

*We moved from internally focused historical reporting to externally focused, forward-looking KPIs such as leading market indicators and brand equity. Ensuring that the businesses could collect and pass on that data was extremely important. So we formed a workstream around piloting ideas to guarantee they were workable, particularly from a data collection perspective. Also, creating consistent scorecards within the organization was difficult. How does corporate headquarters rate itself versus principal brands within business units?*

*Don't underestimate how long it will take you to design and implement a rigorous piloting process. After a couple of days, many people have sketched out what they think are the basics of a great new beyond-budgeting process, including their KPI pack. But turning that concept into reality requires significant effort and rigor.*

*Of course, we had a workstream around systems to build the capabilities we needed. It became very evident that, to achieve an automatic and less interventionist budgeting process, we needed to really improve our systems resources. This is where technology—making valuable information available in a timely and relevant fashion—really becomes crucial. Across Diageo, we are moving toward common systems platforms and data warehousing to give us real-time access to data.*

*Our other workstream focused on our "blow up the budget" initiative. From the start, we knew this was a large-scale change project and assigned a special team to oversee it. A program this big must be adequately sourced and staffed. It can't be done part-time.*

*While we're very optimistic and enthusiastic about what's happened so far, we know we're just beginning. We're already making modifications. I think it's extremely important to be prepared to make changes on the run, because no amount of analysis will get it completely right the first time around. You will miss some KPIs. You will include KPIs that you'll find can't be measured. You have to be willing to stand up and say, "We're not quite finished yet."*

*Fine-tuning sometimes catches business units off guard. If you say, "We want you to be able to spend less time worrying about budgeting and reporting," everybody replies, "Absolutely!" They don't realize that there will still be performance measures.*

*Have we abandoned budgeting altogether? No. In certain parts of the organization it's still relevant for expenditure control and cash management. But we have removed much of the wasteful interaction between corporate headquarters and the business units.*

*We no longer tally the numbers from 130 business units to create a management report; instead, we focus on the seven key business areas and manage the other 123 by exception. Our management meetings don't dwell on presentations of how well we are doing at the moment, but focus on knotty strategy problems and preparing for the future.*

*Increasingly, our discussions about the future revolve around the Internet. Diageo isn't being left behind there. We believe we'll save millions of dollars in costs by blowing up the budget; we'll use some of those funds to create business-to-business portals, both for internal purposes and to form value-added communities related to our lines of business. These are cutting-edge, highly competitive arenas. We're going to need quick forecasts and accurate performance measures to compete, and we believe our revised financial processes will provide them.*

*We weren't so open to change back when we were budget-driven; we were always too busy looking over our shoulders, watching what had happened in the past. We don't do that any longer. That's made us a more dynamic and positive organization. We're busy creating value now—that's what our shareholders want.*

---

One of the mainstays of finance, the traditional budget, is becoming more anachronistic every day. Like Nick Rose, CFOs are discovering that they have more productive things to do with their time. While budgets are likely to pass away from natural causes, their demise will be greatly accelerated by the advent of e-business. Revolutionary new approaches to business demand new financial management tools with four important attributes:

- *Flexible* enough to respond rapidly to unforeseen change; unlike budgets, which discourage variation from established norms.

- *Multidimensional* to encourage synergistic and collaborative approaches, rather than cast-iron categorization.

- *Up-to-date* to enable rapid and confident decision making about market opportunities or mergers and acquisitions, instead of relying on lagging indicators.

- *Entrepreneurial* in nature, to accommodate reasonable-risk opportunities and replace the defeatist thinking that suggests, If it isn't in the budget, we can't do it.

This chapter examines the case for blowing up your budget. It explores how better to connect strategy with operational performance; it shows what new-world budgeting options look like; and it deals with commonly faced implementation issues. We examine the feasibility of moving from the endless budget iterations to the steady-state collaboration of rolling forecasts (Figure 6.1).

Twenty-first century financial management tools must be endlessly adaptable, a characteristic seldom associated with budgeting. Diageo removed its budget obstructions by substituting KPIs reinforced by EVA metrics. And Diageo is only one of many successful budget streamliners.

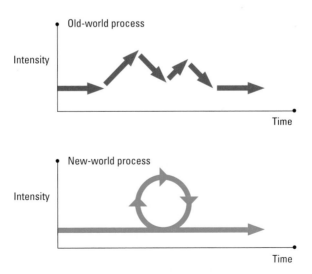

Figure 6.1 *From intensive peaks and troughs to a continuous process*

## WHAT'S WRONG WITH BUDGETS?

"The budget is the bane of corporate America. It should never have existed. Making a budget is an exercise in minimization, i.e., showing how little you can do." Jack Welch, the CEO of GE isn't the only one who has a problem with budgeting. Bob Lutz, a former vice-chairman of Chrysler, called the budget a "tool of repression." To Jan Wallander, a budget revolutionary and the former CEO of Svenska Handelsbanken, it was an "unnecessary evil."

Here are the results from a survey of CFOs:

- Only 12% believed that budgets added a lot of value to their organization.

- Some 79% said that a move to abandon budgeting was a top five priority (44% said top three).

- And 65% considered themselves responsible for leading any prospective move towards this abandonment.

In another survey, just 10% of CFOs thought their budgeting process was completely efficient, while 90% said it was cumbersome. But many corporations haven't taken even the first step toward escaping the budget's constraints—acknowledging its limitations. Consider this case study.

CASE STUDY
The Budgeting Dilemma

*After a major reorganization, a multinational consumer products corporation held a retreat for its top executives to explore alternative management approaches. Attendees were encouraged to record their views on display boards. On the board for budget complaints, here is what people wrote:*

- *The budgeting process is too detailed, too slow, and adds too little value.*

- *We need radical change—lots of people are engaged in crunching numbers against a budget that's out of date.*

- *Many of our big value-creating initiatives are intangible and difficult to manage with the traditional budgeting process.*

- *The planning and reporting requirements of corporate headquarters are burdensome.*

- *Too strong a traditional data approach forces us down a predetermined path.*

*The parent organization's CEO was surprised that there was so much dissatisfaction with budgeting, which he regarded as an innocuous, if distracting, yearly ritual. And he was completely taken aback by the CFO's contention that the corporation could decrease costs by close to 10% by eliminating the budgeting process.*

*The CEO raised this at a session the next morning. He said to the finance people, "The budget is owned and driven by your departments, yet you hate it. I don't get it." The finance people stated that budgets were wasteful, but they oversaw the process as a service to management, whom they thought couldn't function without it. After each side disowned the budget, the people from strategy were called in. Surely the budget was critical to them, ventured the CEO.*

*But the strategy people also hated the budget. They saw themselves competing with finance over whose projections were more accurate and were sick of hearing that strategy was theoretical while the budget was real. In fact, they said, strategy and finance barely spoke to each other. What strategy really wanted was to cooperate with finance and the business units so that forecasts would be more accurate and useful.*

*After hearing all this, the CEO appointed a committee, headed by the CFO, to investigate and implement budget alternatives. Given the CEO's strong public support, change came quickly.*

*In the beginning, there were constant questions about what budgeting procedures would be retained and how forecasts and strategic plans would be affected. Within two months the business units and CFO were designing KPIs. Three months later the first KPIs were being installed and the CEO announced that he wanted most of the operation in place within two years, a deadline that was met.*

*The failings of the old approach became glaringly apparent as the new measures came online. And although some business unit managers kept their own budget figures during the early stages, that passed in time. Eventually everyone acknowledged what had long been suspected: the only good budget is a blown-up budget.*

---

The question facing CFOs is not whether to change but how—incrementally or radically? The answer depends on the corporation, its markets and its employees. Traditional budgets are universal. Their new-world replacements must be tailor-made.

Before CFOs can construct improved planning, forecasting and resource allocation tools to replace outdated budgets—and win the support of their organizations for this revamping—they must understand how the budgeting process spiraled of control; and how the budget's function came to be overshadowed by more contemporary concerns.

In the beginning budgets were a by-product of the manufacturing era, when acquiring and protecting capital were the primary value drivers of most enterprises. During the early twentieth century, industrials introduced organization-wide budgeting to ration out and protect their assets. By mid-century, budgeting became a tool for setting financial targets, controlling costs, measuring business unit performance and forming strategy.

In established industries the need for substantial capital before launching a corporation also provided a buffer against unforeseen competition. Markets were steady, business cycles predictable, management was hierarchical, and assets were physical. Under these conditions an annual reporting period made good sense. It also corresponded with the filing requirements of financial oversight and tax authorities.

Over the years, the budget routine grew until it permeated the entire corporate structure. Companies began using the budget for purposes it wasn't designed to address, such as:

- An annual internal benchmark of financial performance

- A means of setting comparative production targets for business units, independent of market forces

- A tool for measuring costs, often expressed as a percentage of another metric

- A tool for evaluating job performance

- A device for forecasting future sales performance and operational profitability

Figure 6.2 shows how the budget process soon consumed the better part of the year, as business units submitted figures for headquarters consideration, only to have them returned with clichéd instructions to cut costs and improve revenues.

Applied indiscriminately and inappropriately, budgeting spawned its own set of behaviors, many of them dysfunctional. The process came to be seen as property of the organization's financial police, whose intention it was to squeeze out every loose penny while ignoring market demands and expecting continuing increases in revenues. This scenario generated many budget-inspired problems:

- Rewarding performance against budget led to gaming by employees, who were only concerned with meeting fixed goals; this resulted in incremental thinking and less than optimal target setting.

- Admonishing those who missed budget targets did nothing to identify or remediate the factors that created the shortfall, thereby alienating employees.

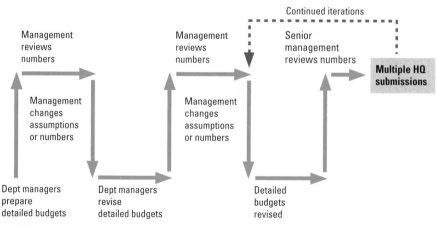

**Figure 6.2**  *A typical traditional bottom-up approach to budgeting*

- Relying on annual targets that were dated even before the budget was completed was misleading and demoralizing. After the inevitable unforeseen changes occurred, some managers achieved their targets easily, while others couldn't meet them at all.

- Budget targets have always been delineated by function or department, which tends to promote internal conflicts, turf wars and missed opportunities for synergy.

- Establishing goals pegged to past performance sustained the status quo and blinded executives to new opportunities. Once in the budget, functions had eternal life, consuming funds that might have been better spent on new programs.

- Finance departments wielded absolute control while ensconced in often distant corporate headquarters. This caused them to be viewed with suspicion, rather than as helpful business partners.

And there's another factor that is certain to amplify these budget-driven problems: the ascendance of intellectual capital as a key value driver in many organizations.

## The Rise of the Intangible

Perhaps the greatest shortcoming of the traditional budget is its increasingly dated orientation toward tangibles, such as fixed assets. As we saw in Chapter 4, most shareholder value is in virtual assets such as management processes and learning, and intangibles such as brands and R&D. Yet many underperforming corporations devote substantial resources to budgeting, which focuses on non-value-adding capital assets while overlooking the intangibles that power growth (Figure 6.3).

Leadership in the new era requires the CFO to encourage fluid performance measures, and discourage the endless collection and recitation of yesterday's data. CFOs must explain to their colleagues that, instead of linking resource allocation to what happened last year, they should base funding requests on what will happen during the next four quarters and beyond. Rather than discussing return on investment as frequently as the weather, they should begin arguing for dynamic goals such as stretch, rolling and value-based targets.

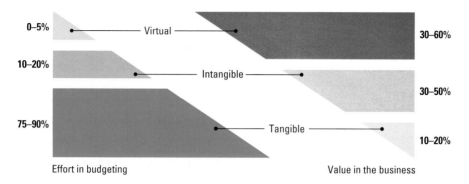

**Figure 6.3** *Effort in the budgeting process is typically not directed at greatest value*

## MAKING THE CASE FOR CHANGE

A Beyond Budget Round Table of 33 mostly large European companies joined in examining why budgets are barriers to organizational change. Since then the organization has concluded that budgets shouldn't be improved—they should be replaced.

One attempt at building a better budget was *zero-based budgeting.* This process was developed in the 1980s to remedy a serious defect: when the previous year's budget is used as the basis for the current year, existing errors are compounded. Since it began with a clean sheet each year, the zero-based process avoided this error compounding, but it required substantial amounts of work. While it became the standard point of reference for the following four quarters, it still looked backward.

Another approach was *activity-based budgeting.* This was developed to consider costs from the perspective of their relationship with activities and throughputs. By introducing metrics that used cost per unit of output, activity-based budgets moved dynamically with the work performed. This approach had the advantage of allowing volume-related overheads and flexibility, which facilitated changing the cost base. But in the end, it was comparing actuals against budget and still looking backward.

The strongest argument against improved budgets is that they are still budgets. As the following case study shows, it is becoming increasingly difficult to make a business case that supports their use.

CASE STUDY
The Real Costs of Budgets

*A retail electronics conglomerate was facing waves of new competition from Internet start-up operations, which were undercutting the organization's prices due to lower overhead. The company had formed a business-to-business procurement division to counteract this cost differential, but other savings still had to be found.*

*The CFO decided to perform a complete cost analysis of the budgeting process, unearthing all the expenses that were hidden by the cascading of budget-related functions throughout the enterprise. The results showed that, excluding the finance department, the organization had expended 6,122 person-days of work on the current year's budget, at a cost of over $750,000. The ratio of nonfinance to finance time spent on the budget approached 4:1.*

*While the finance department specified the processes and tools required to complete the budget, it was nonfinance employees who actually did the work. That meant that staff members with only cursory budget training were carrying most of the load.*

*The CFO commissioned a study to uncover the value of activities that employees were unable to perform while engaged in budget-related tasks. He also conducted personal interviews with selected nonfinance employees at various levels. He wanted to know how they regarded the budget, and whether the finance department was communicating the corporation's goals through target setting.*

*The CFO wasn't surprised when the report showed $6 million in lost activities. However, he was shocked by what he heard during staff discussions. Throughout his organization, which earned 40% of its revenues during the Christmas season, people had come to regard the budget as their real work, as opposed to keeping them from their work. They were neglecting revenue-producing activities during times of peak consumer demand to meet their budgetary obligations.*

*This promoted a culture in which people gave presentations praising their departments for having met budgetary targets, even as the organization's market valuation was falling, and those of its new competitors were rising.*

*Armed with these facts and figures, the CFO went to see the CEO. It was time, he said, for a new approach to financial management.*

---

In addition to releasing employees to perform value-adding activities, adopting a budget alternative pays a second major dividend—it gets people focused on the future so they can anticipate market changes and respond to them. By carefully selecting a budget alternative that corresponds with a corporation's maturity, performance and resources, organizations can begin to construct early warning systems that enable them to act in advance of changes and so capitalize on them.

## CHOOSING AMONG OPTIONS

As Nick Rose noted earlier, there are a variety of options available to those exploring budget alternatives. All of them recognize the demands of e-business by reducing reported data to what is essential for business operation, thus speeding up the decision-making process. Under the traditional approach, when profits fall, a great deal of time is wasted trying to identify the causes. Fingers are pointed, defenses are prepared, and weeks pass before corrections are made. When an organization employs metrics that provide a more transparent measure of its health, it can more rapidly diagnose its problems.

> *Under the traditional approach, when profits fall, a great deal of time is wasted trying to identify the causes. Fingers are pointed, defenses are prepared, and weeks pass before corrections are made.*

What characteristics should CFOs look for in selecting new-economy financial management measures? Best practices indicate they should choose tools that:

- Encourage a stakeholder value mindset throughout the business.
- Shift perspectives from traditional profit and loss metrics to those emphasizing the financial and nonfinancial targets that drive long-term value.

- Provide the right level of detail for decision-making and control.

- Emphasize the rhythms of the business cycle instead of the calendar year.

- Benchmark the organization's unique strengths and weakness.

- Highlight corporate strategy, and link it with corresponding value drivers that can be recognized at all levels of the organization.

- Employ metrics that mesh with key internal and external processes.

These attributes should be packaged in a mechanism that is more focused and less time- and data-intensive than traditional budgets. It should be exceptions-oriented, so people don't waste time discovering that everything is normal, and it should be clearly linked to the work of the appropriate people. All of this should allow for financial management that:

- Evaluates costs according to the value they add, rather than merely comparing them with expenditures for the previous reporting period.

- Controls investments to yield maximum returns over their lifetimes, instead of milking them to inflate quarterly statistics.

Although many companies want to change their budgeting processes, they can't decide how far to take the changes. They see obvious value in reducing budgeting expenses, but worry about where to draw the line. They tend to have multiple initiatives at work at any given time, and wish it were easier to link them to existing performance measures. The corporation may be moving in the direction of using KPIs and rolling forecasts, while the CFO still worries about abandoning the security of the budget. For the company in this case study, the best solution was staged changes.

CASE STUDY
Easing Out of the Budget

*An old-economy industrial products company was faced with daunting market changes. The large, centralized corporations it used to supply were being displaced by lower-cost boutique manufacturers, who were in turn buying their materials from smaller suppliers, many of which were located in developing nations. To preserve its market share, the company purchased several of these suppliers, which it planned to operate as subsidiaries. The challenge for the CFO was to develop an integrated financial and performance management system that would encompass the entire organization's needs as it consolidated.*

*As much as he disliked budgets, the CFO instituted a strict budgeting regimen at the newly acquired subsidiaries, some of which had recently been privatized. He realized that budgets bring an entire business model with them, which he believed the fledgling companies required at this stage. He needed to be sure the salespeople could sell what they projected, the production line would turn out what was promised, and the supply chain was as solid as the logistics people claimed. The budget would monitor the efficacy of these assertions.*

*At the same time, the CFO planned to meet  the parent corporation's cost reduction initiative by reducing budget expenses at his more mature operations by 50%. This was to be the first stage of a budget replacement program. After consulting with the business units, the CFO held a reconciliation conference where new standards were installed. Henceforth each unit would report exactly the same 12 pages of data; this would be looked at but it would not be reproduced in monthly management reports—no exceptions.*

*The new measures were a combination of traditional data and KPIs, which everyone acknowledged had been hastily prepared. The CFO believed that the first step would be weaning business units that didn't need them from using budgets. As the program progressed, he was prepared to implement more precise KPIs, along with advanced reporting and forecasting measures.*

*The organization didn't spend a lot of time or money developing complex options. But they made significant changes, and reaped immediate benefits, using an approach that would be passed on to their new subsidiaries as they matured.*

*Other than cost savings, the program to reduce budgeting expenses by 50% had no appreciable impact on operations. This demonstrated to everyone that, in most circumstances, full-scale budgeting was counterproductive.*

| Option / Process | Do nothing | Time line/data compression | Strategy lock/ KPI reporting | Full value-based management | Hands-off corp. center |
|---|---|---|---|---|---|
| **Target setting** | Economic profit based<br>Detailed financials<br>Annual operating plan separate from strategic plan<br>Monthly phasing | Economic profit based<br>Topline financials<br>Single planning process<br>6 1/2 month phasing | Balanced scorecard<br>Cascaded KPIs<br>Single planning process<br>6 1/2 month phasing | Balanced scorecard<br>Cascaded KPIs<br>Single planning process<br>6 1/2 month phasing<br>Extensive use of scenario models | Corporate scorecard |
| **Performance measurement** | Economic profit based<br>Detailed financials | Economic profit based<br>Topline financials<br>Focus on initiatives | Balanced scorecard<br>External benchmarks<br>Focus on initiatives<br>Internal benchmarks | Balanced scorecard<br>External benchmarks<br>Focus on initiatives<br>Internal benchmarks | Corporate scorecard |
| **Reporting and control** | Monthly, detailed<br>Versus budget | Monthly, streamlined<br>Versus last year | Monthly, balanced, trend based<br>Versus last year<br>Versus projections | Monthly, balanced, trend based, automated<br>Versus last year<br>Versus projections | By exception, major issues only |
| **Forecasting** | Detailed latest estimates | Streamlined latest estimates<br>6 1/2 month bal. of year | Balanced KPIs<br>Focus on initiatives<br>6 1/2 month bal. of year | Balanced KPIs<br>Remodel initiatives<br>6 1/2 month bal. of year | Economic profit projections only |
| **Systems** | Single stream<br>Hyperion based | Single stream<br>Hyperion based | Offline reporting<br>Modeling tools | Integrated ERP, modeling, data warehouse, scorecard | Executive information tools<br>Analyst based |
| **Culture** | Center directs and monitors | Center directs and monitors | Center sets high-level strategic direction | Center sets high-level strategic direction | Businesses are empowered |

**Figure 6.4**  *Abandoning budgeting: change options*

Corporations still using the traditional approach have five budgeting options to choose from (Figure 6.4). They range from doing nothing, with headquarters continuing to exercise rigid control, to becoming a fully devolved enterprise, where headquarters merely acts as a merchant bank for its businesses.

Selecting an approach requires a clear understanding of where the organization stands in relation to the six processes listed in the figure, a vision of where the organization would like to be, and an assessment of the CFO's prospects for winning support of the required changes. Although many mix-and-match alternatives are available, most enterprises select a combination of items from the third and fourth options. The strategy lock/KPI reporting option provides quick hits, with a smaller initial investment and a faster payback; the full value-based management option is the long-term solution, with a more costly front end and an extended earn-out period.

With the abundance of business tools and metrics that are available today, consulting a budget report to assess the state of an enterprise is analogous to taking someone's temperature: it tells only whether or not a fever is present. CFOs need to construct measurements that give more precise readings. This begins with the selection of KPIs, in consultation with the managers who will be required to live with these measures.

## DEVELOPING METRICS FOR LINE OF SIGHT

An intractable problem with traditional budgets is the lack of regard that nonfinance employees sometimes have for them, because they are often perceived as owned by the CFO. This is especially true in operating divisions, where budget-based targets can be viewed as something over which employees have little control, but for which they are held responsible. For rectifying that situation, nothing beats the development of KPIs.

In the e-business world, financial management must become part of everyone's job, while the finance department takes the lead in identifying the business's true value drivers. Most often that process begins with getting finance personnel out of their offices and into the field, where they can work alongside staff members to create key performance indicators. Here are some data-related strategic issues to consider in constructing KPIs:

- What is the authoritative definition or calculation for the measure?

- How will it be measured, with what frequency and with what reliability?

- Who owns or controls access to the information involved?

- If the factor being measured is duplicated in other areas of the organization, how discretely will it be reported?

- If it is to be consolidated, how compatible are the operations and reporting procedures involved?

- Will the measure change over time, and how will such a change be detected and adjusted for?

The essence of every KPI is *economic profit*. While one business unit may achieve that profit through asset improvement, another may focus on better cost management or greater market share. The automobile manufacturer Volvo uses KPIs that encompass market share, order intake, customer satisfaction, product costs, dealer profitability, warranty costs, fault frequency, and total ownership costs, all benchmarked against the competition whenever possible.

The following case study shows how the process of identifying KPIs can launch a dialog between corporate headquarters and its business units, a dialog that yields far more than improved metrics.

CASE STUDY
Taking KPIs on the Road

*The CFO of a food products conglomerate was leading an ambitious beyond-budgets program that was scheduled to be completely in place within three years. He had overcome senior management's initial resistance, which was due to worries that they would lose touch with their global business units without regular budget reporting.*

*The CFO convinced them that few people could make sense of the flood of data pouring into headquarters, and that they had other things to do with their time. He emphasized that, instead of worrying about the incremental performance of dozens of brands, they should be attending to strategy and long-term planning.*

*With that accomplished, it was time to begin constructing KPIs to replace the budget measures that were being phased out. The CFO's research on KPIs told him that business unit managers should be heavily involved in defining the KPIs that they were accountable for. While he was in philosophical agreement with that point, he also recognized that all KPIs must ultimately support corporate-defined strategies.*

*At early planning sessions, representatives from each department came forward with two or three KPIs that, based on their experience, were essential to the organization's future. Unfortunately, these indicators were usually operations-oriented and often unrelated to strategy. But by working backward from strategic goals such as building brand loyalty, business unit managers quickly became adept at identifying measures within their control. These measures included packaging, quality control and product innovation, measures they could influence to build brand loyalty.*

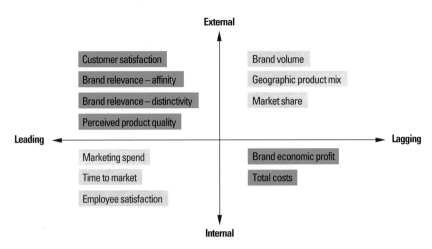

**Figure 6.5** *KPIs should be balanced*

To ensure the measures were sufficiently broad, they would apply a series of tests. They would do this by using a value driver tree to see whether the KPIs would improve economic value, constructing a mock format and populating it with historic numbers to gauge results. They also plotted KPIs on a leading/ lagging and internal/external quadrant (Figure 6.5).

As successive groups worked through this process, each improving the measures slightly, it became apparent that the more focused and clear-cut the KPIs, the easier and more successful the implementation.

After conducting similar sessions in the company's top 10 markets, the CFO and finance department took the program on the road. At each location they explained the corporate strategies and reviewed the KPIs that the larger business units had identified. This led to discussions about which indicators would work for the relevant business unit, and the adjustments needed to compensate for market variations.

These meetings, which often included a broader cross section of managers, gave the smaller units a crash course in what headquarters was trying to achieve. The CFO, whom the units embraced as someone bringing vital information from afar, also came to recognize how out of touch headquarters sometimes was with its businesses.

After completing his rounds, the CFO put a two-step plan in place. The first *step involved ending the upflow of unneeded budget data and installing KPIs. The second step grew out of meetings that discussed KPI results but not budget figures. It involved getting the business units to abandon as much internal budgeting as possible.*

*These meetings highlighted another benefit of the changes. Headquarters used to ask the business units why production was down 0.5% at a certain plant. Now they discuss a competitor's new product development and what they are going to do to address it.*

---

Three points come out of this case study:

- The encouragement of KPI ownership begins during the initial discussion of a beyond-budget program.

- The setting of KPIs must involve management and staff at all levels.

- Although headquarters sets policy, it is the business units that must implement and monitor the KPIs which will drive that policy.

The most valuable KPIs—the leading indicators—are the most difficult to identify and measure. They must often be gauged by indirect means. An organization can't continuously survey its customers about satisfaction, but it can monitor and categorize customer complaints. Once they exceed a certain level, alerts can be sounded and cascaded down to the appropriate level to identify and resolve the problem.

KPIs work best when they are tied to compensation and linked to personnel evaluations. This is especially true for general managers, who can have the greatest impact on employee behavior. Although there is often mutual resistance to this system—with headquarters fearing they are paying for something that doesn't increase profits, and employees worrying about the accuracy of new metrics—it is the strongest lever to encourage KPI ownership.

Once they have been successfully defined, agreed upon and embedded, KPIs provide improved measures of an organization's operational effectiveness, as well as the supporting data for a rolling forecast program. This program can function as a high-level corporate early warning system.

# FOCUSING ON FORECASTING

Of all the revised approaches to financial management demanded by the e-business era, perhaps none tests the CFO's adaptability as much as creating rolling forecasts. Instead of number crunching, the rolling forecast demands that the CFO coax unprecedented cooperation and collaboration out of various departments throughout the organization. This teamwork must often be won in the face of conflicting interests and orientations.

CASE STUDY
Agreeing Figures

*A medical products company that had reduced its budgeting, and was being driven largely by a 12-month sales forecast, was unhappy when its sales figures were constantly at variance with the forecasts delivered by its production divisions. Senior management wanted to combine the two measures to create a uniform, 24-month business forecast that was more accurate. The CFO was tasked with determining which of the two existing projections was more accurate, and therefore more suitable for adoption.*

*In discussions with various sales and production managers, the CFO learned that the forecasts seemed to be emanating from different companies. And, as Figure 6.6 illustrates, when these managers' outlooks were compared with those of headquarters, there were many points of contention.*

*When forecasting product demand, production tended to inflate numbers so it could function at capacity, keeping its workforce employed and being seen as having efficient facilities. The salespeople also wanted big numbers, so they would always have a large supply of products available. Headquarters was conflicted on supply. On the one hand, it wanted to build as many products as it could sell. On the other, it didn't want excess production capacity or inventory, which could destroy profitability.*

*Headquarters wanted sales targets set as high as possible, so the salespeople would be motivated to work hard. Conversely, the salespeople wanted low sales quotas that they could easily exceed, earning them bonuses and bragging rights*

| Stakeholders<br><br>Forecast | Headquarters | Sales managers | Production managers |
|---|---|---|---|
| Production | ▼ | ▲ | ▲ |
| Sales | ▲ | ▼ | ▣ |
| Finished inventory | ▣ | ▲ | ▼ |

▲ Set upside forecast  ▼ Set downside forecast  ▣ Neutral

**Figure 6.6** *Conflicts in forecasting*

for their excellent performance. The production people were neutral on this issue.

In forecasting delivery schedules for completed products, the salespeople wanted the products built and sitting in inventory as quickly as possible, so customers wouldn't wait for delivery. Production, however, favored a steady and predictable workflow through its factories, so that it wouldn't have to deal with scheduling or raw materials problems. Headquarters could see the points on both sides and it remained neutral.

As he was examining the results, the CFO realized that the greatest problem with the existing forecasts was that they were driven by the needs of the departments, rather than by headquarters. And nowhere in the process were the projections informed by market trends or corporate strategies.

The answer to the original question put to the CFO was that neither the sales nor the production forecast offered a reliable basis on which to project financials. If forecasting was to be the primary mechanism by which performance would be managed, and through which opportunities for improvement could be identified, the company had to create one overall forecast that linked all departments. This forecast must be neither unduly optimistic nor overly pessimistic.

The CFO's solution was twofold. First, the company would implement KPIs to generate the data appropriate to targets that were independent of the day-to-day needs of the sales and production departments. Second, it would create an *independent, rolling 24-month business forecast that would be informed by strategy as defined by senior management. As an initial step in this direction, the board combined manufacturing, sales and logistics and placed them under one senior manager to reduce potential forecasting conflicts.*

---

As this case study shows, organizations wanting to move to a 24-month rolling forecast must begin by building sales forecasts that focus on strategic goals and supply requirements. The aim is to produce a workable game plan, not a wish list. It isn't a logistics exercise to determine earnings, but a definition of what the corporation is going to be doing for the next 24 months. Specifically, CFOs need to do four things:

- Develop rolling business forecasts that are continuously informed by sales forecasts and key events.

- Install continuous, forward-looking exception reporting that provides recommendations to management based on achievable objectives and action plans.

- Stop building sales forecasts primarily on the basis of near-term supply requirements.

- Separate target-setting processes from operational forecasts.

Creating rolling forecasts is not about managing numbers, or hitting an endpoint like a budget target. It's about promoting collaboration between business units and facilitating business issue management. CFOs must ask more questions, be more creative, and have a more strategic day-to-day outlook. In other words, they must be less concerned with the trees and more concerned with the forest.

Many benefits are gained when forecasting is separated from budgeting, if it is done properly. After a major global entertainment company switched to rolling forecasts linked with a continuous planning cycle, it was able to halve its annual eight-month planning and budgeting process. This saved it 18,000 employee-hours. Here are some additional benefits of rolling forecasts:

- Linking the most sensitive value drivers directly to future business performance and the business cycle.

- Creating a forward-looking mindset that can be the basis of an early warning system.

- Extending future focus beyond year-end.

- Improving business process responsiveness and shortening reaction times to unexpected events.

But rolling forecasts are not just open-ended budgets. To be effective, they must be based on fresh data from KPIs, which themselves must be part of a streamlined planning and reporting process. Compared with the traditional approach, dynamic forecasts should have a wider and longer focus, while reflecting current conditions more accurately by using well-defined business drivers.

With rolling forecasts, the finance department stops functioning as a consolidator of raw numbers fed to it from the field. Instead, it starts functioning as an analyst of the trends reflected in rolling forecast reports. When they find that the actual figures are at variance with those forecast, CFOs need to work with their businesses to identify causes, plan remediation and revise future forecasts. Because it highlights areas that need attention, exception reporting facilitates the accomplishment of these tasks on a continuous basis.

Furthermore, an e-business approach, which handles forecasting collaboratively over the Internet, can make quantum improvements in both the quality of data and the accuracy of projections.

## Collaborative e-Forecasting

Collaborative forecasting is one of the most attractive e-business budgeting alternatives. As we saw in Chapter 2, the possibilities of real-time collaboration are immense, particularly in industries involving retail operations. Rather than headquarters' receiving 500 e-mails containing daily, weekly, or monthly results, they can leverage the Internet, which offers a single file, available to all. This file provides data in highly malleable form, virtually as soon as it is reported. The CFO's office then becomes the nerve center through which dynamic collaboration can take place.

It's not just the speed of the Internet that encourages collaborative dialogue. Previously, when retail units submitted their data, it seemed to disappear into a black hole. This deprived employees of the feeling that they were making a useful contribution. Now they can see the results of their contributions and change their data, forecasts or strategy on the spot.

Using supply chain enabling technology, producers of middleware programs are making it possible for two or more parties to share and analyze proprietary information simultaneously. Instead of simply transmitting orders or invoices, these services facilitate the interchange of planning and performance information over the Internet.

Pharmaceutical and other long-lead-time manufacturers are using e-collaboration forecasting to detect early warning signals in their markets. In the case of drug companies, this involves analysis of illness dynamics, and linking customer data and disease patterns more closely to product distribution.

Whether operated through the Internet or in more traditional ways, rolling forecasts have reduced work, simplified processes and improved planning. But for optimum functionality, they require considerable delegation of responsibility, plus management's firm support. This support is necessary if the organization is to move away from a focus on operating profits and toward embracing KPIs. Businesses must adopt a more decentralized approach, with headquarters setting high-level targets and operations managers handling the details. The process of blowing up the budget naturally leads to a gradual decentralization. And by the time rolling forecasts have been installed, decentralization should be firmly established.

## WHEN STRATEGY MEETS OPERATIONS

Using the finance department as an example, imagine a budget replacement procedure that begins at the top, with headquarters benchmarking itself against the competition, rather than just the previous year. In this case the CFO determines that the cost of running a finance department in a multinational organization sits between 0.5% and 2% of revenues. If the corporation's finance costs exceed 0.5%, it isn't pursuing best practices, period.

Working top-down, the CFO meets with staff to develop a strategy that will reduce spending to 0.5% of revenue over time, up to five years if necessary. As a first step, the staff are told to identify the methods used by the best-practice firms. If the staff discover that other firms have automated transaction processing while they are spending excessive time on it, the staff would investigate alternatives such as outsourcing, shared services or upgrading IT.

This means budgeting, strategic planning, performance management, and resource allocation can be linked in a way that encourages senior managers to set goals and empower their staff to achieve them.

New-world planning and budgeting differ from the traditional approach because they focus on maximizing the organization's key value drivers. Senior management, represented by the upper half of Figure 6.7, meets with the business units, represented by the lower half, to identify the KPIs of the business group in question. These drivers may be financial or non-financial, long-term or short-term, and linked directly or indirectly to increased profitability.

These discussions lead to target setting and forecasting, which is represented by the intersection of the upper and lower halves of the figure. Headquarters works with the business units on a strategy to achieve the defined goals, and allocates resources for plan implementation. The business unit then executes a plan that it anticipates will produce the desired results. At the same time, strategy and execution are continuously revised in response to market conditions, business opportunities or internal changes, as information is exchanged routinely between the two halves of Figure 6.7.

Top-down budget replacements are most effective when senior management works with staff to set clear targets, manage against these targets, and reward everyone fairly for achieving them. Communication is the vital link between strategy and execution, and it keeps everyone working together to maximize shareholder value.


## TOOLS OF THE TRADE

Technology can play a major role in creating a custom-tailored budget replacement. Financial oversight and performance management are often a matter of intelligently handling large amounts of information. Technology facilitates this tremendously by linking multiple sites, managing massive data, and blending input in unique ways. It can produce forward-looking programs able to anticipate trends—maybe signaling a rise or fall in raw material prices greater than a preselected percentage—something the traditional approach can never accomplish. Technology can be used most effectively in three areas: visualization, modeling, and data management.

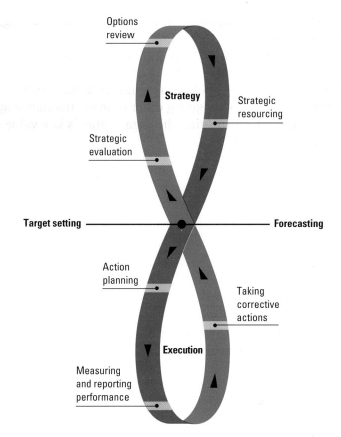

**Figure 6.7** *A new model for dynamic target setting*

Visualization   Visualization enables the finance department to use what used to be seen as other people's data in new ways that benefit everyone. Although KPIs, rolling forecasts, and other measures will generate ample data, much of it will be of limited interest. Like utility companies that have wall displays showing their power delivery in real time, finance departments should construct displays of information on company intranets or Web sites by applying to KPIs the skills once used in extracting profit and loss figures, with emphasis on presenting the most essential results in a visually appealing way. This doesn't yield new data, but it does display core indicators in a manner that encourages all employees to focus on events as they are unfolding, rather than on the past.

Modeling   Like pilots training on a flight simulator, CFOs can use modeling to work through positive and negative scenarios to put the appropriate performance management models in place. This enables senior management to reallocate resources quickly, either to resolve an emergency or to capitalize on an opportunity.

Data management   Although data management is largely IT's domain, CFOs should be involved in system construction to ensure the data meets financial management needs and supports decision making. Supermarkets and other organizations receiving mountains of data on customers' buying patterns often aren't able to analyze it effectively. Any budget program should be replaced with analytic applications to enable decision-makers to mine thoroughly all the rich new data streams being generated.

## Implementing the Vision

Strawman process modeling is an effective way to display the reversal of performance management that takes place after blowing up the budget (Figure 6.8). Today, all processes are incremental. The literal bottom line is monthly reporting, which is reconciled in detail against a profit and loss report. By the time the process is completed, however, it's too late to do anything about it.

The 24-month rolling sales forecast runs parallel to, but never intersects, the budget. The sales forecast exists largely for logistical reasons, such as scheduling, supply and distribution. Since it is budget-driven, it focuses on past performance, rather than strategic opportunities or resource reallocation in line with market forces. Performance is managed based on what has happened, not on what will be happening in three to five years.

*During the early stages of blowing up the budget, system misfires can occur because employees haven't adjusted to the new approach. Prepare everyone for upcoming changes in financial and performance management.*

Project reviews generate requests for revised rolling sales forecasts, which are negotiated in a bottom-up fashion, and occasionally lead to a medium-term plan. This process finally works up to the top of the flow chart in the figure, where long-term strategic planning occupies the most

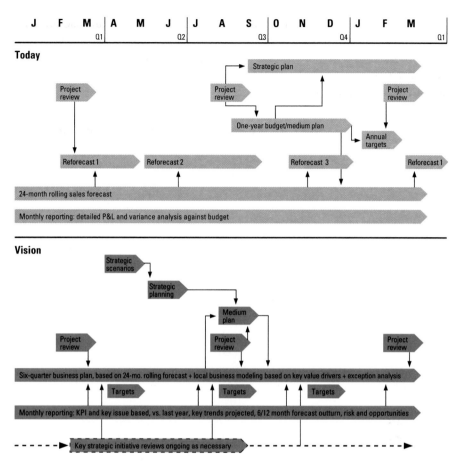

**Figure 6.8** *A visionary process approach to moving beyond budgets*

neglected and isolated place. It grows out of the medium-term plan, itself an offshoot from the seat-of-the-pants original sales forecast.

The complete inversion of this procedure is captured in the strategy-driven budget alternative model in the lower half of Figure 6.8. In this approach, strategy comes first, propelled by various strategic scenarios in the first quarter. After the most favorable options are selected, they are incorporated into long-term and medium-term plans, representing the options to be pursued. The medium-term plan informs the six-quarter forecast, causing the annual budget targets to be dropped from the flow chart.

The six-quarter rolling forecast is where the "what ifs" of strategic planning meet reality. Key strategic initiative reviews are brought into play when the forecast needs adjustment. Often this is due to changes in market forces. However, the need for repeated adjustments should sound the alarm for further investigation.

The metrics running across the bottom of the model should be examined to determine how well the organization is functioning. They include KPIs and key issues versus last year, and key trends reported 6–12 months out with risks and opportunities.

During the early stages of blowing up the budget, system misfires can occur because employees haven't adjusted to the new approach. It is especially important to prepare everyone for upcoming changes in financial and performance management. People ask what's cutting-edge about blowing up budgets, and the reply usually relates to getting KPIs right or doing rolling forecasts. But what's really cutting-edge is getting an organization to stop reporting detailed yet rearward-looking budget metrics. It requires strong leadership. Swedish bank Svenska Handelsbanken did it 30 years ago and it's never looked back.

CASE STUDY
Svenska Handelsbanken: Throwing Off the Budget

*When Jan Wallander was appointed CEO of Handelsbanken in 1970, the bank was underperforming. Rather than introduce a series of small measures and wait for results, he decided on a radical solution. Customer dissatisfaction was the most common reason for switching banks, so Wallander decided to transform his institution into one where the customer relationship prevailed, and non-customer-service costs were minimized.*

*One of his first acts was getting rid of the costly budget, based on this reasoning: either the budget will prove approximately right and it will be trite, or it will be disastrously wrong and therefore dangerous.*

*Wallander decentralized Handelsbanken and empowered its employees, 90% of whom have customer contact, to focus on pleasing their customers instead of their bosses. Headquarters set targets for the branches using key trends and internal/external benchmarking, and a handful of regional supervisors decided when and where local offices would be opened or closed. All other responsibility for managing the business was turned over to the branches.*

*The branches aim to provide products that are best for their own customers— even if they are not the most immediately profitable—to attract and retain long-term customers. The bank has a central product development office, but each branch is free to accept or reject any of its offerings. This reflects Handels- banken's stated belief that the branches are not the bank's distribution system—they are the bank. After the bank exceeds its target for return on equity, one-third of the remaining funds are allocated to the employee pension plan each year, encouraging employee retention.*

*While there are no budget criteria to meet per se, Handelsbanken does recognize outstanding achievement. Practices developed at high-performing branches, which are identified by internal benchmarking, are quickly communi- cated throughout the organization, and outstanding individual efforts are recognized with promotions.*

*How has Handelsbanken fared after 30 years of these "radical" practices? It has grown to 8,000 employees and 530 branches, which earn 80% of the bank's profit. And although there are branches throughout Sweden and other Nordic countries (with expansion to the UK in the offing), the company still has only 10 regional managers.*

*These practices give Handelsbanken one of the lowest cost to income ratios of the 30 largest universal banks in Europe. In 1996 this ratio was 39%, com- pared to most US and European banks, which had ratios in the 55–65% range. Handelsbanken's 1999 return on shareholders' equity was 18.4%, the twenty- eighth year in a row that they have accomplished a higher return than the average for other Nordic banks, while also maintaining the highest levels of customer satisfaction.*

*Handelsbanken's key metrics are the same as they were 30 years ago:*

- *Return on equity*
- *Customer-led profitability (not product-led profitability)*
- *Cost to income ratio*

*Historical analysis is low on the agenda. Customer satisfaction remains an important KPI, and it is independently verified through the Stockholm School of Economics.*

*Recently the bank moved aggressively, albeit carefully, into e-banking. Twenty percent of its transactions took place on the Internet during 1999, lowering costs another 2%. And as soon as the technology develops, it will offer customers access to their accounts via mobile phone.*

*Since the day the bank prepared its last budget, it has sent a clear message to its employees: the past is the past. While we can learn from it, and it sometimes reflects the future, it can never improve anything.*

---

# eCFO CHECKLIST

## DETERMINE IF YOUR BUDGETING PROCESS IS ADDING ANY REAL VALUE
Weigh the time taken, the resources expended, and the games played against the results achieved. Make the case for change.

## CHOOSE WHICH OPTION YOU ARE GOING TO PURSUE
Decide how best to revolutionize your budget process: timescale compression, simplification, or abandonment.

## CREATE A SET OF KPIs
Choose KPIs that reflect shareholder value goals, that measure strategically important initiatives and provide line of sight from business units to corporate headquarters.

## FOCUS MANAGEMENT'S ATTENTION ON A DEFINITIVE TWO-YEAR ROLLING FORECAST
Make it the driving force for keeping the entire business on track. Focus your finance staff on anticipating the future, not rehashing the past.

## REVIEW THE EFFECTIVENESS OF YOUR LONGER-TERM STRATEGIC PLANNING
Does it link to longer-term shareholder value goals, and shorter-term annual targets? Synchronize planning and reporting with your business cycle.

## FASHION A MINDSET OF TRUST AND OPENNESS, SO YOU CAN MANAGE THE REAL PROBLEMS OF THE BUSINESS
Abandon wasteful budget negotiations and eliminate nonproductive discussions of monthly results. Replace these with strategic planning and action-centered performance reviews. Quickly face up to the consequences of underperformance.

CAREFULLY SELECT TOOLS AND TECHNIQUES
Progressively implement those needed to support your beyond-budget requirements—for visualization, for data management and for modeling. Use the Web.

EXERCISE CAUTION
Retain those aspects of the budgeting process, at appropriate levels, that provide essential control.

# CHAPTER 7

# Delivering a New Systems Vision

## USING SYSTEMS TO TRANSFORM FINANCE

*Olli-Pekka Kallasvuo, CFO*
**Nokia**

*It is extremely important that corporations learn to live with constant change and become flexible. They need to allocate resources again and again from businesses that are starting to mature to new growth initiatives. I see my role as CFO as contributing to that process.*

*Soon every business will be Internet enabled and we'll all start dropping the e in "e-business." Everything we do is being affected: product creation, customer fulfillment, logistics, planning and, of course, finance.*

*We've implemented SAP R/3 globally—a success story so far—but now we're into e-business. As CFO I want to make sure we get the best of both worlds. We need to build on the benefits of our ERP investment and take advantage of new Internet tools to give us flexibility for growth. Every process needs to be planned and based on a new type of thinking—that's a huge task.*

*As a world leader in the mobile telephone market, our goal is connecting people, by providing innovative products and solutions, and by improving business relationships with customers, suppliers and employees. As we enter the e-business age, Nokia, like other organizations in this sector, is embracing* new technologies, particularly in the fields of customer relationship management and supply chain management. We're moving from being largely a hardware manufacturer to more of a service provider. This means our systems and business processes are under constant review.

As a first step in our finance transformation process we identified two main "services" within the finance function: basic accounting and reporting, and decision support. For basic accounting and reporting we implemented a common, global SAP system. Our SAP solution is one physical instance with globally common definitions, accounting rules and chart of accounts, and is fully integrated with SAP logistics, production and HR modules used in Nokia. This system is accessed by our finance teams in 45 countries. With our integrated solution we have eliminated our different local legacy systems and introduced a uniform finance concept. We are able to maximize the efficiency of transaction processing and core reporting, improve the quality, and minimize the cost involved. This also released resources to enhance decision-support services out in the business units.

**Our overriding aim is to enhance the role of HR as a strategic business partner by providing real-time access to people-related intelligence across our global organization.**

At Nokia we've selected i2 software for the supply chain and Siebel for customer relationship applications. The selection process was extensive because we had to be certain the software could deliver the functionality we need in mission-critical areas.

Using i2's Rhythm product, we are aiming for business-to-business integration of processes and systems with our suppliers and customers. Real-time optimization of the entire extended supply chain is what we want. Planning and scheduling will become much more collaborative via the Web, dynamically taking account of key constraints throughout the supply chain. This new system integrates with our existing SAP system, providing a decision-support layer.

*Looking ahead, Rhythm Link will help us to connect supply chain management to tools for e-commerce, including e-procurement tools for direct materials and our customer-facing tools that will allow real-time configuration. We are investing in a strategic account management system to enrich interactions via all our sales, marketing and service channels. This will give us rapid access to customer information and help us to optimize value for the customer and for Nokia. In addition, we'll be pursuing our e-marketplace strategy to explore ways of further enhancing the benefits of business-to-business e-commerce.*

*Nokia is also exploiting Internet technology to deliver direct benefits to our employees by building on our newly established SAP global HR platform using an in-house development based on BEA WebLogic. By connecting line managers and other employees with HR professionals over the Web, we can speed HR transactions and cut administration costs. We're paying particular attention to achieving seamless integration with SAP finance and controlling modules in order to allow sharing of common base data such as company codes and cost centers. The overriding aim, though, is to enhance the role of HR as a strategic business partner by providing real-time access to people-related intelligence across our global organization.*

---

Companies are increasingly turning to information technology as a source of competitive advantage. For growing numbers, it's becoming central to their customer offerings as well. With millions being spent on mission-critical applications such as enterprise resource planning (ERP) and e-business, the CFO has a prime role to play in managing risks and returns associated with systems change.

How can you reorient your systems and practices toward attracting and keeping the right customers? How can you integrate new e-business systems with existing systems? How can you link ERP applications with those of suppliers and partners? What tools will help you deliver business intelligence at Internet speed, giving managers real-time access to customized information? This chapter explores answers to these questions, drawing on the practical experience of leading companies.

# ACCELERATING BEYOND ERP

By its very nature, e-business requires installing new, high-performance hardware and software. This in turn means major investments of time and money. For CFOs—many still weighing the costs of a lengthy ERP implementation against benefits yet to be fully realized—the challenges of updating systems to enable e-business can seem daunting.

What can be learned from past experience? ERP implementations show that significant gains can be made by exploiting technology to integrate process and information flows across organizational boundaries. Designed to connect disparate back-office operations like manufacturing, finance, and HR into one system, ERP equips companies for global expansion by streamlining transaction processing and providing better, more consistent financial information.

With integrated enterprise-wide systems, companies stand to benefit from *cost savings*, for example, through reduced inventory and increased productivity resulting from improvements in planning and materials management. In addition, IT maintenance and support costs are reduced—particularly where an ERP system replaces a patchwork of legacy systems—and functional specialists are freed to work on higher value adding strategic initiatives. Forward-looking companies also aim for advantages in *revenue generation*, through enhanced ability to serve customers.

In practice, achieving the anticipated benefits of ERP has proved notoriously difficult. Early adopters of ERP packages found them cumbersome to use and often in need of complex customization. Despite product improvements, industry analysts reckon that fewer than 25% of organizations moving to ERP will generate returns that exceed the cost of implementation.

Those who benefit most treat implementation as a juggling feat, with technology representing just one of the balls in the air. While putting their new system in place, they're careful also to address associated process *and* organization *and* people changes. It was this need for integrated change management that many companies lost sight of when beginning ERP implementations under pressure of year 2000 challenges. They decided to delay the wider change process until after the system was up and running, and then some of them never began it at all.

The message for the CFO? Work with your CEO to concentrate management attention on *benefits realization* rather than simply *systems implementation*. Successful players have four strengths:

- *The skills* for modeling multidimensional change and planning priorities

- *The realism* that allows accurate estimation of resource requirements

- *The patience* to slow down IT change when this is necessary in order to synchronize change in other aspects of the organization

- *The insight* to see how best to connect results with management incentives

Above all, you must have a business case that's soundly argued and based on the value drivers of the business. It's easy to get carried away by vendor hype. Companies need to stay aware of what their ERP systems cannot do, as well as what they can do.

In its traditional form, ERP focuses on internal operations. This has led to the perception that its capabilities are irrelevant in the customer-centric scenarios of e-business. Another frequently cited shortfall is poor data access for decision support. Again, ERP packages seem unsuited to the dynamics of the new economy, where agility depends on providing real-time business intelligence to managers across the extended supply chain.

Pure ERP systems, once properly installed and stabilized, provide a foundation for e-business and other Internet-based applications. Major ERP providers are adding new functionality to give internal transaction processing engines greater external reach. Meantime, other vendors are developing sophisticated standalone products.

As a result of this activity, companies with their year 2000 concerns behind them have been able to shift attention to exploiting next-generation management systems.

- *Supply chain management (SCM) systems*: used for coordinating and optimizing all logistics, production and distribution operations, SCM lets e-businesses turn the supply chain into a demand-driven value chain. Rather than attempting to match production and inventory to expected customer behavior, the company can flex its supply chain–along with those of suppliers and partners–to respond in real time to actual sales.

- *Customer relationship management (CRM) systems*: on the Internet, comparison buying is never more than a few clicks away; long-term customer loyalty is hard won. CRM helps the company to understand and service individual customers, to cross-sell and to conduct targeted marketing.

- *Knowledge management systems*: wise companies invest in ways to make better information available to people working in key process areas *inside* the business, as well as to *outside* stakeholders. Knowledge management, maximizing performance by leveraging information assets, is one of the CFO's most important roles.

Could ERP become tomorrow's legacy system? Experience suggests that virtually all large companies need a well-functioning internal engine if they're to turn their e-business strategies into reality.[1] The key question for the CFO, then, is how to determine the relative level and timing of investment in ERP *and* e-business systems.

Figure 7.1 provides a framework to help. Assessing how advanced your ERP and e-business capabilities are now, and where you'd like them to be in the future, are important steps toward planning the necessary migration. First, determine where your company is on the path toward full ERP implementation.

- Do you have *no legacy systems*, perhaps because you are a greenfield start-up company, free to develop transaction processing capabilities from scratch?

- Do you have *nonintegrated legacy systems* for transaction processing, relying on human intervention or costly interfaces to share data between functions and business units?

- Have you implemented *single or limited function ERP*, functional applications (e.g., finance and HR) that are integrated across business units but not connected to other elements of the internal value chain (e.g., manufacturing and logistics)?

- Have you implemented *integrated business unit ERP*, a suite of applications within each business unit, but with no links or synergies across business units?

- Have you achieved *integrated enterprise ERP* by implementing a suite of linked applications across all functions and business units, company-wide?

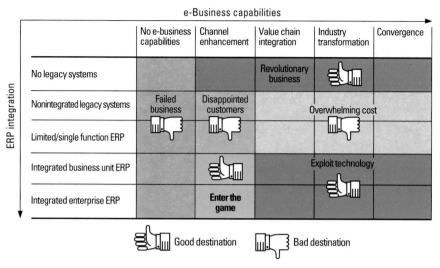

**Figure 7.1** *ERP/e-business capability matrix*

Next, determine the extent to which your company leverages e-business to generate value.

- Do you have *no e-business capabilities*?

- Do you use Web technology primarily for *channel enhancement*, by e-enabling the marketing, selling or buying of products and services?

- Have you linked your processes and systems with those of customers and suppliers to achieve extended *value chain integration*?

- Have you built e-business capabilities that drive *industry transformation*, e.g., by using the Internet to off-load noncore parts of the business?

- Are you participating in cross-industry alliance *convergence* by using Web technology to partner with others in the provision of goods and services to customers?

Map your company's current position on the ERP/e-business capability matrix in Figure 7.1 then compare it with your *desired* position. The matrix highlights stark conclusions. Any established business pursuing e-business initiatives without an integrated ERP suite is unlikely to generate long-term value for customers and shareholders. Robust internal systems are vital to handle, at speed, the volume of transactions generated by successful e-business and to share accurate information rapidly with trading partners. In short, ERP supports your Web site, letting you fulfill the promises made to the outside world.

Interestingly, while operating with *no e-business capabilities* is not an option in today's competitive environment, operating with *no ERP capabilities* might be an option for dotcom start-ups. Saving time and money on ERP, they can race ahead with exploiting advanced e-business systems, relying for internal processes on the limited functionality that such systems currently provide and/or manual and desktop effort. The risks, like the opportunities, are big: unless a technological breakthrough occurs that supersedes ERP, their lack of supporting infrastructure may limit growth and make partnering difficult.

For the company in this case study, recognition of the value of combined ERP and e-business systems drives concerted efforts to maximize the effectiveness of both.

CASE STUDY
Securing ERP Benefits

*In the early 1990s a major manufacturer of branded consumer products decided to invest in the SAP R/3 ERP solution for all 23 of its business units. In accordance with the company's management philosophy, each business unit was allowed autonomy in the way it tackled implementation. Four years on, an assessment of the status of ERP across the company spotlighted significant strategic issues.*

*With 18 separate and different SAP configurations, the total cost of ownership was high and rising. Already the company had made a substantial investment and if it continued business unit by business unit implementation, this approach would double the amount already spent. The cost of upgrades to all the systems, required every two years, was 15% of the original implementation cost. And when acquisitions or other organizational changes occurred, IT integration proved difficult.*

*The company had not exploited the full power of ERP. Achievement of benefits within business units was limited because implementation typically was proceeding without taking advantage of opportunities to improve business processes. Achievement of benefits across business units was going to be difficult unless the company moved to an integrated model. With multiple ERP installations, consistent data was unavailable on a global basis, enterprise-wide procurement initiatives relied on information from disparate sources, and systems were unable to respond to retail consolidation.*

*Moreover, the company's planned deployment of e-business solutions—requiring integration among ERP components as well as between ERP and other systems—would be complicated. Even if the company opted to use SAP rather than third-party vendors to supply its e-business applications, the business case would be hard to construct: the company would have to buy mySAP.com 18 times!*

*The CFO knew that competitors were strengthening their ERP infrastructures as a foundation for launching e-business operations. The company's global strategies for e-procurement, e-distribution with leading customers and direct customer marketing could be in jeopardy unless rapid action was taken.*

*The CFO won board approval for a global benefits realization project aimed at delivering a common IT model, based on world-class business processes. Today processes are being redesigned end-to-end into a single ERP system, represented in three regional shared service centers. For both ERP and e-business, SAP will be the core solution with, where necessary, complementary non-SAP software components to meet specific requirements and connected by enterprise application integration middleware.*

*The business case is based on growth, shared overhead costs in the centers, online stock availability, and better information on product markets and channel profitability, plus a move to full supply chain integration, from suppliers to customers. The expected returns promise a major contribution to the company's shareholder value objectives: a net risk-adjusted $750 million over three years.*

## YOUR NEW SYSTEMS VISION

Traditional companies everywhere are, like the one in the case study, positioning themselves to compete in the electronic age. As IT strategy becomes a more integral part of overall business strategy, the CFO should

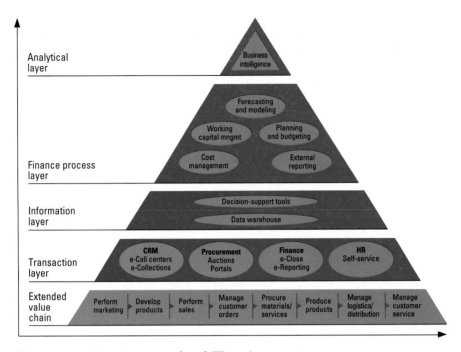

**Figure 7.2** *Creating an ordered IT environment*

work with the management team to develop a vision of the necessary systems environment.

In a less enterprise-bounded e-business world, process and information flows beyond the organization assume equal importance to flows within. An effective demand-driven value chain requires a *closed information loop* among ERP and e-business systems: front-office applications initiate back-office processes that speed a customer order through to fulfillment and, at every step along the way, provide business intelligence analysis to help the company make and deliver on the next sales.

Your twofold challenge is illustrated in Figure 7.2. You need to extend electronic connections *horizontally* across the extraprise, between the company and its customers, suppliers and partners, and *vertically* between transaction-oriented systems and higher-level financial management systems.

Both parts of your vision must be assembled simultaneously. Eager to join the e-business revolution, most companies focus IT investment on improving supply chain efficiencies and partnering, in order to boost response times to Internet pace. But unless operational processes and systems are designed for capturing valuable information—by providing real-time input to data warehouses and decision-support tools—performance enhancements are unlikely to be sustainable.

Here are some of the ways that horizontally and vertically integrated systems can enrich how companies deal with stakeholders.

- *By automating collaboration among business partners.* The company's ERP suite can communicate over the Web with the corresponding systems of suppliers, distributors and other partners, allowing for example the sharing of up-to-the-minute demand forecasts and identification of opportunities for continual interenterprise process improvement. Technology can never replace trust. But faster, more flexible data transfer, backed up by a win-win partnering philosophy, can increase value chain returns for all participants through lower overheads, quicker time to market and, ultimately, greater customer satisfaction.[2]

- *By strengthening direct links with individual customers.* A marketing manager faced with a customer complaint e-mail, for example, can use click-stream analysis to see details of the customer's Web site visits, including what was put into and taken out of shopping carts and when. Then the manager can track the history of the current transaction through order fulfillment processes, billing and payment, and product return, before determining how to manage the relationship and whether there are any systemic issues to address.

- *By turning employee desktops into self-service centers.* People across the company can access selected data, information and services, from both internal and external sources, to help them with their jobs. For example, online learning systems with collaborative features like virtual white boards can make employee training easier and more convenient; they also cut travel costs and lost work time. Product-based e-learning can also be offered to customers.

CFOs looking for new software tools to enable such connections find a host of them appearing. Faced with the urgent need to adapt their packages to e-business, ERP vendors like SAP, Oracle and PeopleSoft are pursuing targeted product development strategies.

- *Web-enabling ERP functions.* It's easier to access an ERP suite through a Web browser than through conventional ERP user interfaces. Virtually all computers have browsers installed, allowing access by much larger user groups, inside and outside the organization. While recently just 16% of the employees in ERP accounts were licensed to use the software, now many companies introduce *universal* employee access to specific functions such as HR benefits enrollment or time and expense reporting.

- *Extending ERP systems for e-business.* Simply adding a browser interface to an ERP suite does not provide e-business functionality. Vendors are modernizing their products to allow interoperability with e-business systems, or to offer e-business functionality. In particular, they are re-designing their packages to offer the same capabilities provided by CRM vendors, as well as improved SCM capabilities, with links to ERP functions.

- *Providing integrated decision-support capabilities.* Analytical applications are key to creating a closed information loop among ERP, CRM and SCM systems. As a result, vendors are adding business intelligence functionality to their packages, including data warehousing, online analytical processing (OLAP) and knowledge. High-level financial key performance indicators are being included in many products.

- *Becoming business-to-business market-makers.* ERP vendors are using their Web sites to create business-to-business communities among their customers. Participants can collaborate by integrating processes, providing access to each other's applications and carrying out e-business transactions.

For example, SAP has launched mySAP.com. This integrated solutions set includes SCM, product life cycle management, CRM, business intelligence, financials and human capital management, and it communicates with the vendor's R/3 ERP suite. In addition, mySAP.com Workplace provides a one-stop enterprise information portal (EIP) that uses Internet technology, mini-applications and personalization to let individual employees access information needed to do their jobs.

With mySAP.com Marketplace, SAP aims to facilitate opportunities for interenterprise business process integration by extending internally integrated ERP processes outward into its global customer base through the Internet and virtual private networks (VPNs). The vendor offers an array of electronic buying and selling capabilities. These include business-to-business procurement—a package that can connect buyer purchasing and supplier catalog modules from different sources—as well as dynamic pricing and the architecture to build open or closed market sites.

Despite such advances, the market for integrated systems remains immature. With many specialist as well as generalist vendors, and highly fragmented offerings, CFOs have a hard task understanding complicated functionality overlaps and gaps. Moreover, in the competitive fray of software development, vendors come and go, merge and make acquisitions, and attempt strategic alliances.

Fortunately, sourcing a complete e-business solution from a single vendor is not the only option. Increasingly, packaged applications are adopting standard component architectures, enabling companies to choose the best combination of currently available vendor offerings and to *snap on* additional functionality in the future.

If this approach is successful, it will allow companies with an ERP suite as the basis of their IT environment to continue enjoying its key advantage, functional integration that's tight and seamless to users, while opening up the system to addition of third-party components.

## e-BUSINESS SOFTWARE: SELECTION AND IMPLEMENTATION

So how can you identify the software needed to operationalize your e-business strategy? Don't expect to keep up to date with all vendors and products, the number grows at a dizzying rate. But by gaining an understanding of the main options available, perhaps with the help of advisors or experienced users, you can distill criteria that will guide selection and ultimately successful implementation. Indeed, surveying sampled software solutions may well *influence the strategy-setting process* itself, by revealing advanced capabilities that raise the company's sights. In the old world, systems usually followed strategy; in the e-business world it's often the other way round.

The major software components of e-business are applications that make it possible to link internal operations *on the sell side* to consumers or other businesses, and *on the buy side* to suppliers. The following sections concentrate on specific areas of functionality. You should also assess software products according to general technical criteria, including server compatibility and ease of configuration. Review vendor attributes too. For example, market share and company stability are two indicators of whether a vendor will be in business beyond the period of time that you'll need them.[3]

## Sell-side e-Business Software

Given the renewed focus on putting the customer at the heart of business operations, it's not surprising that CRM is today's hottest corporate applications area. Growing emphasis on managing ongoing relationships with customers—often wholly or mainly on the Internet and without face-to-face contact—sets high expectations for software in this category. The following capabilities fall beneath the CRM umbrella:

- *Sales force automation (SFA)*: applications for enhancing aspects of the sales process such as contact management, sales forecasting, order management, sales scripting and reporting for sales management.
- *Marketing automation*: applications for customer data mining, marketing campaign management, one-to-one merchandizing, customer segmentation, and management of the product mix.
- *Technology-enabled customer service*: applications that facilitate call center management, help desk management, and so on.

Here the big issue is integration. In most large and medium-sized companies, sales, marketing and service are separate divisions with strong boundaries. Integrated front-office CRM suites are increasingly in demand, especially those offering a high level of integration into back-office and other supporting systems such as order fulfillment, logistics, inventory management, and electronic bill presentment and payment. Leading providers of CRM suites include Siebel, Vantive and Clarify.

One aim is to connect all the varied experiences a customer has with the company, both *during* a transaction—including marketing, product selection, purchasing, receiving and postsale support—and *between* transactions during the customer's lifetime, from initial visitor to long-term partner. This means your system must be capable of collecting and analyzing data from the full range of sales and customer communication channels, including Web-based direct sales, traditional field sales and call centers. For the customer, the result is a seamless series of interactions that encourages loyalty. For the company, it's a source of information that managers can use to identify how and when to focus resources on key customers.

Major corporations in diverse industries are using the information and relationships created through CRM to build customer profitability, by personalizing electronic catalogs, advertisements and other content presented to customers; by running more effective pricing and promotions; or by devising more frequent opportunities for cross-selling. AT&T, Compaq, Bristol Myers Squibb, Universal Studios and Credit Suisse First Boston are among those that have begun transforming sales, marketing and service processes and systems.

Business-to-consumer and business-to-business systems are expected to respond directly to customer demand, whether for information or actual order fulfillment. To maximize their speed and responsiveness, companies must exploit technology to synchronize customer-facing processes with purchasing and other supply chain processes.

## Buy-side e-Business Software

SCM products from specialist vendors such as i2, Manugistics, Ariba and Commerce One aim to provide complete Web-based supply chain functionality either on their own or by linking up with each other or a major ERP vendor. The best products offer integration into CRM and ERP suites, as well as tools for specialist tasks including budgeting, cost accounting and financial electronic data interchange. Progressive companies use these systems to change radically the way they interact with suppliers, engaging them as partners in optimizing supply chain performance. For example, leading-edge advanced planning and scheduling (APS) capabilities can support collaboration with suppliers.

> *Progressive companies use SCM systems to change radically the way they interact with suppliers, engaging them as partners in optimizing supply chain performance.*

Consider the installation of e-procurement applications that automate, streamline and add visibility to purchasing processes from requisitioning, through ordering, to payment and performance measurement. Until recently, most e-procurement software helped manage the purchase of *indirect*, or non-production-related, goods and services (such as office and maintenance supplies). Today, using an online catalog based on prenegotiated contracts with preferred suppliers, employees across the company can find items and compare prices then access suppliers' systems for real-time information on availability and delivery dates before making purchases.

Application vendors differ in their approaches to catalog creation and management—a task that calls for ongoing cooperation between the buyer, suppliers and software experts—and in their capabilities for meeting multiple language and currency requirements. CFOs should look for a solution that's *easy to implement and use* because e-procurement, if adopted successfully, offers a quick route to massive savings:

- *Better control of spending*: many companies are surprised to discover that indirect spending amounts to some 30% of revenues and that much of this is due to *maverick* purchases from nonapproved suppliers. e-Procurement helps by reducing off-contract purchases and enforcing predetermined spending levels for individual buyers.

- *Efficiency gains*: purchasing indirect materials involves high-volume, low-value transactions and there is plenty of scope for process improvement by using automation to speed transactions and cut error rates. Some companies report reductions in processing costs per purchase order of over 80% after implementing e-procurement. Moreover, purchasing staff are freed to focus on managing supplier relationships.

- *Greater leverage of purchasing power*: e-procurement provides opportunities for consolidating enterprise-wide purchases and reducing supplier numbers. With integrated analysis and reporting tools to track purchase volumes, by supplier, product or other category, the company can monitor spending and supplier performance. This facilitates negotiation of improved pricing structures, discounts and terms.

Companies are also using emerging technologies for *direct* materials procurement. Once more, integration is key: product development teams have traditionally determined sourcing strategies with limited input from other supply chain members, including procurement, manufacturing and suppliers, even though around 70% of direct materials cost is fixed at a product's design stage. Web-enabled information sharing and collaboration during new product development lead to better design and sourcing decisions, helping to achieve aggressive time-to-market and cost objectives.[4]

## Rolling Out the New System

The experience of CFOs leading the implementation of new e-business software suggests several guidelines.

Start now and keep moving forward   Don't delay to see if something better comes along. It will—eventually. Major advances rarely happen quickly. Decide on a software solution and go for it. Provided you also invest in the necessary integration framework (discussed later) you'll be able to replace, add or upgrade components.

Don't try to do everything at once   Plan to cover end-to-end processes but implement areas of greatest potential benefit first. Divide the project into phases, each delivering user satisfaction; this will generate valuable support and enthusiasm for subsequent phases. Avoid the *tunnel effect* of a rollout that lasts months or even years.

Manage by fixed deadlines   If you try to control the *budget* first and attach only secondary importance to the *time frame*, then you probably won't succeed in managing either. Focus people's attention on delivering to agreed deadlines and resolving conflicting priorities.

Find project sponsors at all levels   For a successful CRM implementation, you need the commitment of not only the head of marketing, head of sales and the chief information officer but also the managers of local sales teams. Without this, you may find individual employees are more con-cerned about meeting their sales targets than the needs of the project.

Overcome aversion to change   Two-thirds of Fortune 500 companies be-lieve cultural resistance of managers and other employees is the biggest hurdle to implementing technology. And more than half say internal groups represent the main challenge to supply chain partner collabor-ation. What will it take to stimulate demand for the new system? You'll need a plan for communication and involvement, covering all phases of the project. For example, if you ask users to help with designing and test-ing the system, they're more likely to understand how it makes their jobs easier. Then appoint champions to help other users see how to get the most from the software.

Give users opportunities to learn the system   You can't expect users to adopt new ways of working unless it's easy for them to learn how. The ability of users to leverage the system's full capabilities is paramount. This is especially true for global companies where e-business transactions are conducted, for example, in varying payment forms and under varying regulatory requirements.

Evaluate outsourcing options    Rather than installing a popular package in-house, consider using an application service provider (ASP) integrated over the Web. You can't off-load all project challenges, particularly those of encouraging user adoption. But you can avoid setup, maintenance and upgrade costs, instead paying fees for access and usage, as well as speeding up your implementation. ASPs typically offer multiple companies the same version of a hosted application, with minimal customization of business processes and software functionality.

## Reviewing the Risks

As IT penetrates deeper and forges connections across the wider extraprise, systems security and reliability problems become bigger risks. Forward-looking CFOs take on the challenge of integrating traditional financial and business risk management with *e-business risk management.* In doing so, their role is not only to protect the interests of the company, but to safeguard customers, shareholders and other stakeholders too. Companies that fail to manage the risks of e-business face the biggest risk of all—being left out of the game.

In establishing a Web presence, companies already will have addressed some of the issues of network security. But the move to e-business presents significantly more stringent requirements. Many companies are not content to entrust to the Internet their business-critical connections with customers, suppliers and partners. Instead, they create an extranet using a channel unavailable to the public, such as a value-added network (VAN) or virtual private network (VPN).

Preventing misuse of networked systems and information requires careful consideration of security technology. The CFO must invest *before* major risks materialize; you can't retrofit protection. Dave Farber is a pioneer of the Internet and latterly chief technologist at the US Federal Communications Commission; he puts it like this: "In the world we're getting into, you're going to pay for security, one way or the other. The question is: do you want to pay to recover from the lack of it or do you want to pay to ensure it?"[5]

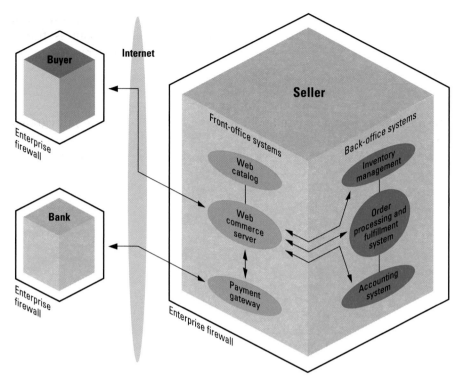

**Figure 7.3** *e-Businesses exchange large volumes of high-value data*

e-Businesses invest in firewalls, dedicated hardware and software systems designed to block unauthorized access to the internal IT environment by screening information flow between networks (Figure 7.3). Some firewalls include virus scanning, to complement desktop and other methods of guarding against computer viruses. Technological advances such as data encryption and digital signatures allow other important functions to be performed in electronic transactions, including authentication of parties, protection of confidential information and nonrepudiation of agreements.

No amount of security will prevent disruptions if applications themselves are ill-designed or misbehave. When confronting systems reliability concerns, CFOs have limited options:

● Select and install solutions robust enough to provide safeguards against failure.

- Ensure these solutions are backed up with plentiful, high-quality IT support services capable of dealing with the complexity of e-business software.

- Work with vendors to improve functionality and reliability.

At the level of the desktop PC—the main method of accessing enterprise and workgroup applications—increased reliability is promised by the operating system Windows 2000 Professional. Its IntelliMirror feature, for example, automatically copies desktop application information and settings to a networked Windows 2000 server. Not only can users access their applications and desktop configurations from any PC on the company's network, but software problems can be more quickly resolved.

## BOOSTING BUSINESS INTELLIGENCE

ERP systems alone generate huge volumes of data. e-Business expands corporate data sources and adds an important external focus to them. For example, companies are using CRM applications to create in-depth customer profiles from multiple *touchpoints*, such as Web sites, e-mail, telesales and help desks. The challenge in the new economy, as in the old, is not to *gather* potentially valuable data but to *exploit it for competitive advantage.*

So who's responsible for ensuring that the wealth of available data is used to inform business decisions? The answer is clear to Tom Meredith of Dell; the role of finance in partnering the business is to "convert data into information, into knowledge." He goes on, "And if you've reached that level, you can reach great heights in creating customer and shareholder value."

Decision support is most effective when management processes and information—strategic, financial and operational—are seamlessly integrated across functions. Figure 7.4 shows the power of such integration. The *data* from internal and external sources is consolidated and compared with targets as part of the performance measurement process, creating management *information*. Using simulation and scenario modeling, this information is transformed into *knowledge* to form the basis of strategic planning. To complete the cycle, plans are translated into targets to drive operational performance.

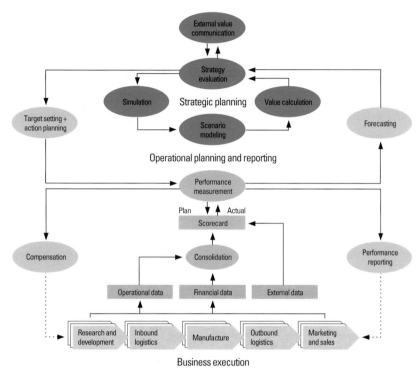

**Figure 7.4** *Decision support: a process and information view*

But as we saw in Chapter 6, this style of management remains a distant goal for many companies. Critically, they lack systems that deliver the necessary business intelligence analysis. In most cases, disparate applications serve different parts of the business without adequate connections for say accounts consolidation. By making short-term systems investments, companies like the one in the next case study stand to benefit from improved decision making, reduced costs, and lowered risk.

CASE STUDY
Introducing Integrated Enterprise-Wide
Analytical Reporting

*This company describes itself as a "highly wired" media and information group. Its interests in Europe and the Americas focus on broadcasting, consumer publishing and business services. One subsidiary, for example, provides information to the high-tech and Internet industries globally.*

*Today more than ever, the CFO needs rapid access at the corporate center to concise information on trends, profitability, out-turn results and key perform- ance indicators. He comments, "One of the issues we face is trying to under- stand the emerging dynamics of our new Internet businesses and how these should be reported to the center. But the current systems struggle to deliver this information."*

*The company's independently managed business units have standalone transaction processing systems supplied by various vendors, including People- Soft, JD Edwards and Oracle. The CFO says, "What we want is an Internet-based consolidation and reporting system that will pull not only numbers but information from subsidiaries, and allow my staff to analyze the issues. What we don't want is key staff wasting time extracting data, rekeying data and pro- ducing ad hoc reports using laborious spreadsheets and word processors."*

*The company decided on a combination of products designed to provide an integrated group reporting system that combines financial and nonfinancial information with sophisticated commentaries for executives. The company is using an online analytical processing tool and the Clime multidimensional con- solidation system, along with Internet communication technologies including Citrix Winframe and virtual private networks.*

*This solution should save time and cost while providing real-time knowledge to support critical business decisions. The CFO says, "When it comes to explain- ing business results, I want to know the why not the what. 'We see this as a vital tool to support our drive into new business-to-business and business-to- consumer opportunities. Now we can bring reasoned analysis and argument— together with supporting numbers from source—to corporate and divisional level management."*

---

In an increasingly competitive and complex market, business intelligence technology will continue providing companies with higher-performance analytical functionality, and CFOs with tougher challenges in making software selections. Gartner makes some interesting predictions: through

2003, despite falling prices, the market for business intelligence software will grow at a compound annual rate of 30%, reaching $7 billion. Access to business intelligence tools will grow to 70% of the user market, reaching employees at all levels. And at least half of Fortune 500 companies will have an *e-intelligence* strategy.

As the market stands now, business intelligence technology divides into three main interrelated groups.

- *Business intelligence stores*: by capturing, organizing, cleansing and providing multidimensional warehousing of data, business intelligence stores make information easier to access by users or by analytical applications. Some companies combine their stores with an *extraction, transformation and loading* (ETL) tool to integrate data.

- *Business intelligence platforms:* these software platforms let programmers, and sometimes end-users, create or customize their own analytical applications. According to IDC, nearly 70% of all corporate spending on business intelligence applications in the next two years will focus on building solutions, rather than buying packages.

- *Business intelligence applications*: the most advanced products, these include tools for online analytical processing (OLAP), reporting, budgeting and planning, performance management, and any other software that analyzes data for users. Some applications incorporate a small business intelligence store that performs predesignated calculations and indexes, enabling quicker information access.

Historically, many companies used decision-support applications without taking advantage of warehousing technology to enhance the underlying data. They can no longer afford to do so. Designed for the e-business world, the modern business intelligence store lets applications work much faster and smarter. Often the store comprises a combination of components. Emanating from the enterprise data warehouse, containing the granular data, there may be an operational data store (ODS) and a series of subject-specific data marts. An exploration warehouse can be added for data mining, enabling the discovery of data patterns, associations, changes and anomalies.

With an information factory like this in place, people across the company can expect virtually instantaneous help with a myriad of business-critical queries. To provide the right desktop tools, CFOs must invest in emerging capabilities. For example, new analytical capabilities are needed

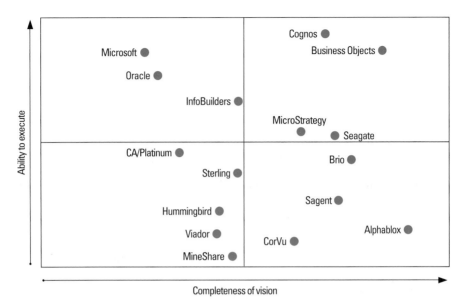

**Figure 7.5** *Business intelligence application vendors (Courtesy Gartner)*

to account for intangible assets like customers and brands (Chapter 4). Business simulation tools must be able to model the new financial and nonfinancial drivers and test new risk scenarios. Collaborative forecasting is needed to aid coordinated execution internally and among customers, suppliers and partners. Performance monitoring must be more dynamic and more tightly linked to compensation and incentive schemes. And, increasingly, exchanges of information with external stakeholders, including investors, will be Web based.

When choosing between rival analytical applications, as with other e-business applications, look first for functionality that matches your specific needs. Leading ERP vendors are developing business intelligence components of their packages, aiming to offer Web-enabled *strategic enterprise management* capabilities. SCM, CRM and best-of-breed vendors supply many more options. Best-of-breed products for financial management purposes include Hyperion, Cartesis and Comshare. Figure 7.5 shows Gartner's view of the vendor landscape for more general business intelligence applications.[6]

Whatever solution you're considering, it must have the following decision-support features:

- *Accessibility*: all the relevant information must be easily available at the point of decision making.

- *Speed of response*: the system should be dynamic and highly automated to support real-time decision making and to ensure that changing business conditions trigger appropriate, timely responses.

- *Flexibility*: it must be possible to adapt the system to reflect changes in information requirements, for example, new requirements caused by changes in organizational structures and processes.

- *Multiuser access*: the system should provide users across the company with a common repository of information, enabling them to make decisions on a consistent basis.

- *Multidimensionality*: the system must be capable of performing complex financial calculations; for example, it should allow users to decompose shareholder value by business unit, brand, channel or customer, and to compare scenarios over time.

- *Robustness and scalability*: the system must be capable of integrating large volumes of data from diverse, internal and external sources, and capable of handling simultaneous queries from large numbers of users dispersed throughout the enterprise.

- *Openness*: to ensure the company's IT environment provides all the functionality needed and to allow for future developments, it must be possible to integrate complementary third-party applications.

- *User friendliness*: as well as providing sophisticated functionality for advanced users, the system must also be easy to use for nonfinancial and non-IT-literate decision-makers, and it must be easy to configure and manage.

- *Consistency and data integrity*: all users must have confidence in the information provided.

Of course, evaluating business intelligence software to find the most appropriate solution for your company is only the first step. Success depends on using best-practice guidelines presented in earlier sections of this chapter; the most important is to manage all dimensions of systems change. Failed implementations are scarcely ever the result of the wrong technology. To get the most from new systems, pay attention to related process, organization, people, culture and communication issues.

# INVESTING IN THE INTEGRATION FRAMEWORK

Companies are discovering that e-business compels them to integrate systems at a higher level of interactivity than ever before. The ability to flex supply chains rapidly, plan and schedule collaboratively with partners, and personalize customer treatment, all this depends on tight integration between the company's own systems, both new and old, and between these systems and systems outside the company.

How can you get applications based on differing technologies and with differing business processes and data models to work together in a common way on a network? How can you integrate new systems quickly, with minimal disruption to everyday operations?

> *Companies are discovering that e-business compels them to integrate systems at a higher level of interactivity than ever before. How can you integrate new systems quickly, with minimal disruption to everyday operations?*

Components of an ERP vendor's application suite, including extensions of core functionality to support e-business, will often themselves provide integration. But for connecting applications from multiple vendors you'll need to buy third-party software. An emerging class of products called *enterprise application integration (EAI) middleware* is designed to connect applications without the need for custom programming. Like traditional middleware (such as remote procedure calls and message-oriented middleware), EAI frees developers from writing routines to handle reliable data transfer and from enforcing transactional integrity. EAI also provides business logic that links the functionality of different applications, and translation between data formats. Moreover, it enables one application to invoke functionality in another in response to business events. For example, an e-business server could prompt an ERP suite to check product availability before accepting an order over the Web.

Vendors like CrossWorlds, STC, Vitria and Tibco supply prebuilt EAI connectors for commonly used enterprise packaged applications, including ERP, CRM, SCM and database systems, as well as tools to build connectors for customized software. The aim is to achieve information sharing with little or no change to applications and data structures—good news for CFOs wanting to update their companies' systems capabilities without disrupting existing IT investment. Legacy systems that still perform valuable tasks can continue. Manual links between applications that were never designed to work together can be automated (business process automation). And a unified view of disparate applications can be created, for example, when one company acquires another with a different order entry system.

For companies rethinking their traditional business models in order to launch e-business operations, EAI can be the glue that binds the new, more virtual organization together.

CASE STUDY
Building a New Business Model Using
EAI Middleware

*A car manufacturer, with operations in the US and Europe, wanted to exploit technology in order to meet the expectations of customers no longer prepared to wait for specialized orders.*

*Its vision: customers use an Internet-based configurator to make self-service decisions on product, price and delivery options. Then they can either order the car online, bypassing traditional sales channels altogether, or find the nearest dealership that has it. Interaction between the various processes and systems involved is managed by enterprise application integration (EAI) middleware. Critically, the customer receives real-time information on inventory levels and production schedules. And their specification is communicated automatically to sales, purchasing, manufacturing, distribution, billing, finance, customer service and marketing.*

*Realizing this vision posed many challenges for the company. Its existing business model, based on mass production, standard specifications and long lead times, meant* internal *processes and systems were incompatible with the new requirement for individual customization. It also needed to strengthen* links externally, *for example with component suppliers.*

*Recognizing the need for a redesigned business model based on integrated processes and systems, the company involved customers and suppliers in a collaborative development. Vitria's BusinessWare EAI tool was chosen for its ability to support all stages, from analysis of integration needs—including system interfaces, common data formats and a workflow linking business processes—through to construction.*

*Instead of planning a direct route to implementation of the overall model, the integrated processes and systems, the company involved customers and suppliers in a collaborative development that progressed phase-by-phase. For example, it began by using the Web to provide customers with product information and prices. This approach minimized risk and enabled early delivery of benefits.*

---

Even with special middleware, the car manufacturer in the case study found linking heterogeneous applications a complex task. Like many companies that do not have the in-house expertise to set up and manage e-business systems, it hired consultants to help deliver the new vision.

The promise of future *plug-and-play* application integration is offered by the development of the extensible markup language (XML). This *meta-language*, a language for describing languages, is becoming the standard syntax for representing information so that it can be exchanged between and interpreted by different systems. XML-based e-business languages include the extensible business report language (XBRL) for financial reporting and extensible query language (XQL) for extracting XML-tagged content from databases. As XML grows in popularity, it will become much easier to enable user access to a wide range of sources, and this is the role of an enterprise information portal (EIP).

## CREATING A CFO PORTAL

EIP technology offers the CFO unprecedented opportunities for extending business intelligence to decision-makers across the distributed enterprise. Via a Web browser interface, employees can access knowledge repositories containing information drawn from internal systems, as well as from external sources including customers, suppliers, partners and competitors.

EIPs are modeled on successful Internet consumer portals, like Yahoo! and Excite, that give users a single point from which to start a search for information within an organizing structure that's simple to understand and navigate. The need for a similar access point has developed in business as the amount of information escalates. Indeed, familiarity with Internet portals means employees now *expect* corporate systems to offer comparable capabilities.

A well-designed EIP helps individuals locate, manage and use valuable information within the context of their jobs:

- It provides a common interface to data from different applications, using technologies such as EAI middleware.

- It incorporates limited-function versions of applications, allowing users to read and manipulate the appearance of a document even if they lack the full application.

- It adds a *veneer of order* over the networked IT environment, even where this has become overcomplex and unwieldy.

Rising interest in EIPs is causing an explosion in knowledge management technology and service offerings. Already, many packaged knowledge management solutions are described as EIPs. Depending on the vendor's area of expertise, these have different strengths: some provide point solutions rather than full-blown portals. Other vendors offer tools for creating custom EIPs. Portal products include TopTier, the Corporate Portal Server from Plumtree, Microsoft's Digital Dashboard Starter Kit and Oracle's Portal Framework.

For companies that prefer to have their EIPs managed and maintained by a third party, outsourcing options are increasing. Vendors such as Netscape, CoVia and Epicentric will build and host portals. Outsourced vertical portal applications, tailored to the needs of particular industries, are also appearing.

Your EIP solution should incorporate core capabilities for finding and displaying information: search and retrieval, personalization, collaborative filtering, knowledge mapping, document management and workflow.

Search and retrieval    Merely providing access to more content from more sources contributes to *information overload*, the antithesis of knowledge management. The EIP must provide effective online searching with relevance ranking of retrieved documents. Search engines that take advantage of new technologies like natural language processing, used in the consumer Web site AskJeeves, can more readily interpret user queries, even when expressed freeform in everyday language. The need to archive and search *nontextual* as well as textual data, from sources such as audio and video files, is becoming more important. Emerging solutions include Dragon Systems' AudioMining product for call centers and help desks.

In addition to answering ad hoc queries, the search engine should help users by monitoring information streams automatically. For example, software agents could be deployed to identify pertinent new competitive, market and demographic information. Interested users could be notified by e-mail or given a link to the information, accessed through the portal. Individuals need an easy way of defining what's interesting and controlling how often they receive updates—a key feature of personalization.

**Personalization**   Employees should have to deal only with information that's relevant to their activities. The EIP must provide a flexible user interface offering uniformity while allowing creation of a custom workspace with links to selected data and applications. Users can determine the type of content they want to receive, such as internal reports or external newsfeeds, and how it's presented. Other personalization features may alert people when they receive e-mail or when appointments are entered in an integrated calendaring application.

**Collaborative filtering**   Decision-makers may be unaware of the existence of valuable information or too busy to seek it out. A collaborative filtering engine identifies correlations between people's information preferences, expressed both *implicitly* by how they use the EIP and *explicitly* in response to system prompts. Then the engine predicts what information individuals or groups of users might like to receive, based on their similarity to other users, and makes recommendations accordingly. For example, salespeople in one geographic region will be notified automatically of new information that market analysts in another region rate as useful, if past choices show their interests correlate highly.

**Knowledge mapping**   Classifying data into taxonomies makes it possible to view a summary of available information resources and focus quickly on related resources. But even a well-designed taxonomy presented in traditional hierarchical fashion can be time-consuming to use. Today taxonomies can be transformed into *visual maps* that appear three-dimensional, using tools like Hyperbolic Trees from InXight. These allow users to see simultaneously many topics and subtopics, and how they interrelate. Drilling down into a selected area offers greater detail, if desired.

The more complex and dynamic the EIP's taxonomy, the greater the challenge of updating it to reflect new information sources or conceptual changes to topics. Manual reclassification is unacceptable in anything other than small-scale knowledge management efforts. If not fully automated, the system should at least make it easy to split, merge and create categories.

Document management and workflow   Increasingly, EIP software includes capabilities for organizing unstructured and semistructured data by creating *metadata* that describes document attributes. This document management component of the portal facilitates access to the mass of information available on the Internet. Most systems include processes for document life cycle management: document creation, modification, security, approval, distribution and archiving. Leading vendors, including Documentum and Hummingbird, now offer workflow capabilities for building automated business processes; these also are becoming a standard feature of EIPs.

## Delivering Business Intelligence to the Front Line

Companies that create an EIP can leverage their investment in systems by providing larger numbers of users with a desktop gateway to the information environment. The portal navigates nonexpert IT users to information more quickly and easily than if they were to connect directly to source systems. Moreover, within the same basic portal design, both content and functionality can be tailored to the needs of individuals or groups working in different business processes and communities.

Consider what the CFO of a global drinks manufacturer has done to automate dissemination of performance-related information throughout the finance organization. And how, with the new finance portal proving a big success, the company is extending its rollout to support decision-makers across the business.

 CASE STUDY
CFO Portal for Self-Service
Decision Support

*A global drinks manufacturer recently underwent a merger, leaving it with finance operations spread over 15 countries and nonstandardized processes and systems. There was little sense of community within the finance function and little opportunity for sharing knowledge and expertise. Finance staff found it difficult or often impossible to access all the information they needed to deliver value-added services to the business.*

*As head of IT and a key player in developing the company's e-business strategy, the CFO was well placed to initiate a solution: an enterprise information portal that equips each finance professional with an intelligent Web site. The portal was designed to connect the CFO and his team to useful data and tools, in accordance with four priorities:*

- Stepping up decision-support capability: *users have access to mission-critical performance data refreshed on a continuous basis, making it possible to monitor key performance indicators (KPIs) dynamically and to conduct scenario modeling.*

- Gathering intelligence from external sources: *the portal combines up-to-date corporate information drawn from internal sources with relevant industry news, economic indicators, media comment and broker views. It also supplies external benchmarks for financial management best practices.*

- Facilitating collaboration among finance staff: *bulletin boards, videoconferencing and virtual team rooms bring people together to interpret the latest results and intelligence. And the CFO uses the portal to provide regular commentaries and question-and-answer sessions.*

- Meeting personal information and communication needs: *individuals can self-generate content through searches and personalized feeds, and have links to e-mail and tools for informal use such as tracking portfolios of shares.*

*Taking advice on implementation from portal specialists, the CFO began by addressing users' most important needs, rather than trying to build in all relevant information. This led to quick wins and avoided a lengthy content management exercise. Specifically, phase 1 was aimed at improving awareness of newly devised KPIs for the merged business, in order to deliver better reporting, budgeting and forecasting.*

*The project team had the finance portal in operation in just five weeks, by taking a practical approach that limited initial functionality but captured the company's style and ethos. A snapshot of KPI data was used to road-test the solution and confirm navigability. The portal was Web-enabled from the outset, with high-quality visual presentation and an intuitive organizing structure, helping to excite demand among users.*

*A taskforce of senior finance people responsible for defining requirements for the portal continued its work in phase 2, allowing the detailed technical architecture to be designed. Critically, the portal was linked to an operational data store for real-time capture of KPI and other information from finance databases.*

*By this time, finance staff were finding it easier to work across international boundaries. And thanks to their ability to provide insights into the factors underpinning each period's results and targets, their standing with business managers was improving.*

*The CFO readily gained board approval for phase 3, expected to take 12 months. The portal will be further integrated with enterprise-wide systems beyond the finance organization, enabling use by other functional teams, including marketing and human resources, with content tailored to their specific needs.*

---

This case offers important lessons. The company's program to bring valuable information to the desktops of more employees is amply repaying the investment of resources required. The CFO puts it plainly, "An enterprise information portal is one of today's most powerful tools for enabling the kind of knowledge-based collaboration on which e-businesses will thrive."

But the notion of an EIP is deceptively simple. To gain understanding and commitment, you'll need to demonstrate the benefits using a prototype. Be prepared for testing implementation challenges; building the portal is likely to expose shortcomings and needed changes in the existing IT environment. Actively encourage a culture of information sharing so that, once connected, users everywhere work as members of the same e-business community.

# eCFO CHECKLIST

## REVIST THE BUSINESS CASE FOR ERP

Use the ERP/e-business capability matrix presented in this chapter to consider where your company is now, compared with where it needs to be for future competitive success. Pursue ERP implementation toward full integration of end-to-end process and information flows. Integrate ERP components with other transaction-oriented systems as needed.

## CONVERT YOUR e-BUSINESS STRATEGY INTO A NEW SYSTEMS VISION

Plan how you will add e-business functionality to your existing IT environment, within a closed information loop. Use technology to leverage strategy by reviewing emerging capabilities for managing Web-based interactions with customers, suppliers, partners and employees.

## UPDATE YOUR BUSINESS INTELLIGENCE REQUIREMENTS

Make sure operational processes and systems are designed for capturing valuable information, financial and nonfinancial, from both internal and external sources. Build a business intelligence store that dynamically feeds a range of analytical applications.

## INTEGRATE FINANCIAL AND e-BUSINESS RISK MANAGEMENT

Assess the risks of engaging in e-business. Look at *new risks* like Internet security, tax and legal issues, as well as *heightened existing risks* like maintaining business continuity and controlling currency transaction exposure on a $24 \times 7$ basis. Adjust your IT vision to build in protection for the company's systems and information assets.

## PUT AN INTERNET SPIN ON YOUR OUTSOURCING STRATEGY

There are strong economic arguments behind the trend away from buying new e-business software toward buying e-business software services provided over the Web. Consider using an application service provider or exploiting the potential of online trading communities, auctions and exchanges.

## TAKE FULL ADVANTAGE OF THE LATEST INTEGRATION TECHNOLOGIES

It may be years before *plug-and-play* application integration becomes easy to achieve. Get ahead of the game by using EAI middleware to help connect ERP, SCM, CRM and business intelligence systems. Favor vendors that are adopting the XML standard to enable application-to-application information sharing within and between enterprises.

## DEVELOP A CFO PORTAL

Design a gateway onto the IT environment that empowers decision-makers to get the information they need, when they need it, and displayed so they find it most useful. Build in the core capabilities of an enterprise information portal, including multimedia search and retrieval, personalization, collaborative filtering, knowledge mapping, document management and workflow.

## LET USERS TAKE OWNERSHIP OF NEW SYSTEMS

Remember that however good a software solution, the benefits accrue only by people actually using it. Communication, training and, in particular, involvement are vital. Don't compromise on usability and speed of response, especially if most users are infrequent users, as with e-procurement systems.

## PARTNER WITH YOUR VENDORS

Examine the track record of potential suppliers to find partners the company can rely on and work with flexibly over the longer term. If a vendor promises solutions that bring a competitive edge, structure the contract so you pay only as the system generates an agreed income stream.

# CHAPTER 8

# Overhauling Your Cost Base

## HOW WE SLASHED COSTS WHILE BOOSTING PRODUCTIVITY

*Jeff Henley, CFO*

**Oracle Corporation**

*We're in the business of building e-commerce software, both database tools and applications, so we have had a sense of the implications of the electronic revolution sooner than the average corporation. We started talking about transforming our internal operations into a full-blown e-business several years ago, after our success with paperless offices.*

*In the US, which represents about half of our company, we had instituted electronic expense account reporting, procurement and human resources. Transactions, from hiring to approving purchase requisitions, didn't require paper documents or large staffs of clerks whose only job was to input data. This program reduced the size of our back-office staff by 25%.*

*We had accountants and finance personnel assisting salespeople in the field. They created piles of spreadsheets and did handholding. We said, "Wait a minute, why aren't the salespeople keeping their own records—and putting the data online?" The finance department could give assistance and advice, but we* didn't need to do the work. Instead, we could start mining all the deep, rich information that would be developed, like multinational account histories, rather than rely on mere summaries.

We have global customers, and employees in 60 countries who deal with them. Yet it was really difficult for us to share information internally, because many of the regions had unique systems and ways of doing things. Eliminating these differences, and putting global data on the Internet with self-service access, had cost reduction and revenue-generating possibilities that were enormous and immediately apparent. We looked at it and said, "This is the future, when do we get on with it?"

We wanted the benefits and had to demonstrate to our customers that this was doable. It would be real-life proof that our products did what we said they would. But the initial investment was going to be large, and we knew the money was going to have to come from enterprise-wide cost reduction.

From Oracle's total revenue and expenses ($10 billion and $7 billion in FY2000), we set a goal of cutting $1 billion, or 10% of revenue. We believed this would require a 20–30% gain in productivity, and frankly such a boost would be impossible without technology. You have to address the buy side, the sell side and the inside during an e-business transformation, but for us it started with our IT infrastructure. It was the foundation of everything else to come, and it had to be modernized.

> **It took a massive effort to get everybody to embrace the cost reduction program. Our CEO, Larry Ellison, led the way. He was adamant.**

We did a massive IT transformation. With current advances in technology and communications, it's now possible for companies the size of Oracle or larger, not to mention smaller ones, to run a single global IT infrastructure. To make that work, everyone has to be on the same page. Historically, we allowed all of our divisions to modify our financial programs. The French, the Germans, the British all had different versions or releases. If we were going to optimize, that had to end. One of the hardest parts of our change process was getting 60 countries and five divisions to conform.

We've been consolidating all of our far-flung data centers into a megacenter in the US encompassing one global version of our enterprise applications such as human resources, finance, customer relationship management (CRM), supply and distribution, procurement, e-mail—everything. This will cut our global IT costs in half while providing single global databases for customer, supplier and employee information—the kind of enterprise data we've always wanted.

The biggest productivity gain by moving to an e-business model is self-service for customers, suppliers and employees. Self-service embraces three types of activities: information access, updating of records, and actual trans-actions. One of the best examples of leveraging the Internet is how we've transformed our customer support business, which generates $2.5 billion with about 6,000 employees, mainly in call centers. Until recently we added staff each year to handle rising call volumes as our business grew. For instance, our support headcount grew 35% in FY1999.

In FY2000 we added no new headcount after introducing self-service. By August 2000 some 30% of our entire call volume was going on the Internet. Customers log in and answer their own questions or leave an online message that we respond to electronically. In the near future we expect to increase call volume over the Internet to more than 50% of our total. Customers appreciate this new service because it is quicker and more efficient for simple questions and data updates that flow through our call centers. We like it because we can avoid adding thousands of support professionals.

We have also gone to shared services, which do a more efficient and more professional job than some of the small countries did on their own. These centers handle transactions for accounting and administrative functions for our 60 country subsidiaries. Besides a simple payback in less than three years, we get better quality and control. For instance, revenue recognition is a big issue in our industry, and we can assure higher quality and consistency by concentrating our talent. We don't have to do as many internal audits either, since we only have to review three centers instead of an office in each country.

It took a massive effort to get everybody to embrace this optimization program. Our CEO, Larry Ellison, led the way. He was adamant. If you don't get senior management to actively push a cost reduction program, it won't happen. When change wasn't coming fast enough, Larry began having IT, finance, *human resources, marketing, etc., all report to headquarters, instead of to their region as they had been. That wasn't a popular move, but it made the point; to be global, we needed a single set of systems and business practices.*

*When the dust settled, we had saved approximately $1 billion in the first nine months of the program. We cut our IT spend by half, to $250 million. On the sell side, where 80% of our employees are customer-facing, we saved $500 million largely through our CRM program and a 6% headcount reduction, the first in Oracle's history. On the buy side, we shaved $150 million from procurement, exchange and distribution costs. Our employee self-service programs led the way to $100 million in inside savings. Much of this recovered money dropped straight to the bottom line, allowing our profit margin to reach 30% in 1999.*

*The really exciting upside is that we now have announced a goal of saving an additional $1 billion per year over the next 12–18 months. This is possible because we are still rolling out our new CRM applications, which should drive huge self-service productivity gains as our customers voluntarily adapt to more and more self-service on the Internet.*

*While only a target, announcing our $1 billion cost reduction goal up front was extremely motivating. It put tremendous pressure on the company. There was no turning back; we were publicly committed. The target, while risky and potentially embarrassing, galvanized the company, as did linking bonuses to reduced costs and improved margins.*

*We learned that it doesn't matter if you get the detail right in the beginning of an optimization program, it's more important to have people moving in the right direction. What we went through wasn't fun, and there was anger and some mistrust at times, but all of that has disappeared now that we have transformed Oracle. The new systems are in place and functioning, and every-one is asking why we didn't do this a long time ago. Along with the improved margins, that's probably the best and most satisfying measure of our success—having people feel positive about what they do.*

---

For corporate stakeholders and shareholders to prosper in the new economy, resources must be deployed quickly as new opportunities unfold. Oracle's story demonstrates that every aspect of a successful enterprise, from employees to strategies to finances, must respond to ever-changing customer needs and market dictates. Since a corporation cannot successfully anticipate the future all (or even most) of the time, its only alternative is to fine-tune its internal processes for optimum performance so it can allocate resources quickly as new opportunities appear.

Yet few CFOs know how efficient their corporations really are. Investors pass judgment on an organization's creditworthiness and the perceived value of its stock, but not directly on its inner workings. CFOs must assume this responsibility, guaranteeing that their companies operate efficiently. To do this, they need to stop negotiating line items on departmental budgets and start monitoring the tautness of their organizations. Aside from mergers and acquisitions, this is where CFOs can have greatest impact in the new economy.

When do you need help? What are best practices? How far do you go? How do you take people with you? How do you institutionalize improvements into your corporation's culture? How do you balance cost reduction with innovation and growth? Most of all, how can e-business improve performance? And as CFO, how do you make it all happen?

This chapter is about how the dominant business tool of the 1980s, downsizing for cost reduction, has been transformed into one of the key resource allocation tools of the e-commerce world. It's about fine-tuning corporations rather than eviscerating them, about maximizing the contributions of employees instead of disposing of them. It's about deploying human and financial capital only where they add value, and how to identify where that is. Ultimately, it's about matching resources with opportunities that yield the greatest dividends.

## THE ANATOMY OF COSTS

Increasingly, the highest value-adding opportunities will flow from e-business and other Internet ventures. But e-ventures are expensive. The days of spending a few million dollars on a Web site and watching it blossom into an enterprise of immense capitalization are gone. On today's Internet you pay for what you get, and that money has to come from somewhere.

Many of these new ventures must be funded with monies from legacy old-economy operations. To free up funds without crippling existing lines of business, costs must be reduced through improved processes. New technologies provide some savings, but only when underlying processes are fundamentally sound and cost-effective.

In turn, e-investments can reduce costs by increasing process efficiencies. In the e-business world, cost control isn't about capital expenditures and headcounts. It's about managing revenues and costs—effectively deploying resources in existing business units—to free funds for corporate entrepreneurism in e-business.

Rational cost controls will become integral to the age of e-commerce. Concerns about shareholder value, pricing transparency due to the Internet, and the global drive to deregulate business, all make cost reduction a strategic imperative. Cost control must be embedded in corporate culture, not a one-time exercise in cost reduction.

Your optimization program must be ongoing and enterprise-wide. It should critically examine current ways of doing business while looking outside to identify benchmarks and best practices. The program should allow macro and micro adjustments, but not be bogged down by analysis paralysis. Its ultimate aim should be far-reaching transformation; any attempt to reduce costs without undertaking broadly based change will at best yield only short-term results. At worst, it can put an enterprise at a severe competitive disadvantage and seriously damage its long-term prospects.

Figure 8.1 shows the three phases in an optimization program: assessment, design and implementation. Each phase includes processes designed to create a common framework and achieve rapid buy-in across the organization. In this chapter we examine the framework in terms of these phases and the stages within them that lead you through the optimization process. This approach has several objectives:

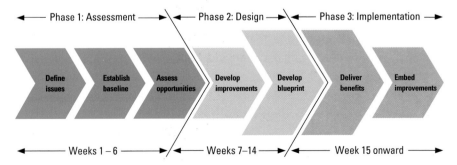

Figure 8.1 *An enterprise-wide optimization program*

- Improve processes everywhere, from production to administration to finance

- Reduce costs without diminishing capabilities

- Optimize asset allocation to maximize shareholder value

- Leverage technology to the fullest

- Create the opportunity and the mindset for growth and innovation

Momentum is crucial. While outcomes are usually overwhelmingly positive, difficult choices, and sometimes large-scale changes, are required along the way. It is human nature to resist such change. Rapid implementation provides quick wins that inspire confidence. Maintaining this *rapid drumbeat* counteracts employee resistance and is always the most productive approach.

CASE STUDY
Transformation through Cost Reduction

*A regional airline, in which a small group of associates held a controlling interest, was threatened by much larger competitors who were beginning to fly the same routes. After watching profits decline by nearly 50%, the regional airline considered two options: increase revenues by expanding its advertising budget or its route network. Each alternative required financial outlays. According to the CFO, due to its decreased profits, the airline could no longer afford either approach. Before the company could grow, it needed to control costs.*

*As a massive cost reduction program was launched, senior investors set some ground rules: no parts of the company they had so carefully nourished could be sold off and its faithful employees should be well informed throughout the reorganization. As the CFO met with business unit representatives, he found that employees had long known what the investors were just now discovering—their company was rife with waste and redundancy.*

*Each branch of the operation, which resulted from a consolidation of five commuter airlines in the 1960s, was the domain of one investor. Despite duplications, investors believed this structure created a strong local identity,*

*and built customer and employee allegiance. Employees attending cost re-
duction sessions told the CFO that the investors were wrong. The waste was
readily apparent to customers and employees, and it didn't create positive
feelings among either of them.*

*Customers, seeing too many underutilized employees, often wondered aloud
whether fares wouldn't be lower if the staff were reduced. When an out-of-
region carrier offered cheaper tickets, customers flocked to it, gladly spending a
few extra minutes at check-in to save 25%. Younger, more motivated employees left the company quickly, recognizing that excessive staff size and cost
would hinder their advancement. The remaining employees were often poorly
motivated; the light workload was a major job attraction.*

*After conducting company-wide meetings, the CFO worked with divisional
teams on a reorganization plan. He chaired the program and attended every
meeting, questioning people carefully when they resisted change. He knew that
if he left the project to others, it would fail.*

*Major investors periodically reviewed the recommendations made by the
reorganization teams with the CFO. Most proposed changes were accepted
after negotiations, including several buyouts of existing operations by managers and employees, who were then awarded outsourcing contracts.*

*As momentum built through the change program's two-year implementation,
the reconfigured airline reduced its costs by $160 million. With profitability
restored, it formed a consortium with other regional airlines, which allowed
each of them to expand globally and to compete with the larger airlines that
once threatened their existence.*

---

## ASSESSMENT PHASE: WEEKS 1 TO 6

This case study highlights the sweeping transformation that can be
achieved after underlying inefficiencies are identified and corrected. Once
change begins and early improvements are realized, the process feeds on
itself and yields unexpected gains. This starts during the diagnostic phase
of the optimization program, which uncovers the true but often hidden
processes that are driving a company (Figure 8.2).

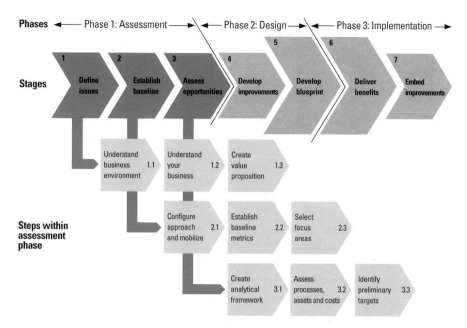

**Figure 8.2** *Enterprise-wide optimization: assessment phase*

## Stage 1: Defining the Issues

Paradoxically, any attempt to optimize internal performance should begin by looking outside at the business environment. Often overlooked by CFOs, who face more immediate operational issues, these external, big-picture factors define the parameters of what can be achieved. They also provide a real-world check on the efficacy of a change strategy.

Research your markets, suppliers, industry value drivers and financial structure, and the competitive positioning of your products and services. Questions to consider:

- Are your current products and services meeting and anticipating market needs?
- What is the industry value chain?
- Who is capturing the most value and how?
- What is your industry's financial structure?
- Have other players changed in stature and can you capitalize on that?

- How competitive is your field and is this likely to change?

- Where are the nonproduct growth drivers of your industry? Look at:

  - acquisitions

  - new markets

  - emerging technologies

  - geographical expansion

- Are more changes on the horizon?

- Is the timing right for an internal restructuring?

Next, categorize your company's financial status and performance. Do they exceed the expectations of investors, brokers, the financial markets and your board? Are you following your strategic plans and meeting imperatives? Are your value drivers widely recognized? Are there aspects of your enterprise where the need for change is glaring? If current performance is less than optimal, consider these questions:

- Do your processes and systems work smoothly on both a macro and micro level? Is continuous improvement accepted as part of everyone's job description? Are mechanisms for change in place, or does change come only after crisis? Is decision making fast and open, or slow and closed? How would you assess your organization's overall efficiency?

- Does your corporate culture encourage and support change? Are innovators recognized and rewarded, and does management model this behavior? Are internal boundaries well defined or is cross-pollination common? Is teamwork part of the culture or do people go it alone? Is cost control a way of life, recognized as normal behavior rather than something headquarters periodically goes on the warpath about?

- Are there clear and effective lines of communication? Are internal communications restricted and stilted, or direct and easy? Are the company's strategies and goals widely recognized and supported? Are problems routinely identified and dealt with?

After comparing the findings of your external and internal assessments with industry benchmarks, create a value proposition, a statement that clearly shows the total value to be created by cost reduction. Specify where savings are likely to be found, anticipated benefits, costs and time frames, and how changes will influence corporate strategy.

You need to make and communicate the case for doing things differently. After analyzing key issues, CFOs will be armed with a number of tools that will help them become organization-wide advocates for change. These include an enhanced understanding of industry dynamics and greater awareness of their competitive positions, opportunities, and vulnerabilities.

Using this knowledge, they can win support for an optimization program at the board level by articulating the need for change and crafting a credible vision of the enterprise after optimization. Then they can start cascading ownership of the program to corresponding business units, identifying stakeholders who will be affected and working to enlist their support.

## Stage 2: Establishing the Baseline

As the optimization effort spreads throughout the enterprise, the CFO, as its chief advocate, needs to involve more key people. This builds ownership and connects the process with employees who have expert knowledge of the organization's workstreams. This is especially critical in the aftermath of mergers and acquisitions, when the clash of different cultures can make joint efforts difficult.

CASE STUDY
Cross-Organization Optimization Team Identifies
Huge Savings

*A rapidly growing conglomerate in the heavily consolidated telecommunications and cable industries was producing 50% revenue growth per year. Newly merged business units were rolling out innovative products at breakneck speed, and the marketing and sales departments in those divisions were deftly supporting them. An air of accomplishment and forward motion permeated the organization, until it became apparent that, while revenues were constantly expanding, margins were spiraling downward. The promised just-around-the-corner profit improvements never materialized.*

When multiple divisions missed targets they had agreed upon with corporate headquarters in the US, the finance department began a unit-by-unit investigation. One exceptional business unit had undertaken a premerger enterprise-wide cost reduction program, and the CFO recruited members of that successful project team to work with finance.

The CFO discovered that most of the previous reengineering involved process-only initiatives. This had increased quality, but not productivity. Divisions hadn't looked at how people actually spent their time and anticipated M&A economies of scale had failed to materialize. Resource allocation had become more ad hoc than strategic.

In short, little thought was given to a company-wide value proposition. A high-level rethinking of the corporation's approach to business was mandatory, both because of the mounting pressure from investors and because e-business and new technology opportunities were reshaping its markets. The company needed to enter the mobile telephone arena and become an Internet service provider. It also had to prepare for the coming of high-definition TV, with all the new technology that would entail.

These hugely expensive investments required a steady supply of cash for the foreseeable future. No one could accurately predict what the business was going to look like in three years, but all knew that if their products and services weren't on the cutting edge of change, the battle would be lost.

The first task was to prepare a value proposition for an optimization program, with projected outcomes so accurate and striking that the board and senior management would fully embrace them and endorse the sometimes difficult steps required.

The project team knew that it could probably cut costs by 5% by increasing employee efficiency, but that to achieve the envisioned savings of 30% or more, employees would have to do things differently. The team focused on optimizing cross-organizational resources by streamlining and combining many operations through shared services, outsourcing and joint purchasing, and it also looked at redesigning work processes. Service-level changes were another focus, something that corporations traditionally resist.

Spurred by the promise of radical improvement, and by a carefully planned, well-executed optimization program, the corporation freed up $550 million *from its expenditures during the next fiscal year. The investment community showed its approval, while its employees used the reallocated funds to implement innovative programs for growth.*

---

Stage 1 of an optimization program involves high-level sketching of a value proposition that draws on the expertise of people beyond the finance department. The core resource group will grow as the baselining process unfolds.

Once senior management accepts a value proposition defining preliminary optimization, the CFO should assemble a series of panels or teams. While these should reflect the organization's operating structure, the more inclusive they are, the better. Ideally, there should be panels in four categories:

- *Subject area or business owners panels*: these teams analyze existing workstreams, functions and activities; propose changes to optimize these processes; and supervise the implementation of approved changes. Panel members should have intimate knowledge of the corporation's day-to-day functioning. Depending on organization size and the scope of the optimization program, these panels may be managed by senior subject area managers who oversee multiple panels and then report on and interpret their findings to a review panel.

- *Review panels*: as gatekeepers, these panels pass judgment on the workability and scope of changes proposed by subject area managers. They understand the processes under analysis, the corporation's over all operation, and its competitive environment. They make the final decision on which projects are funded and implemented, then they report to the steering panel (Figure 8.3).

- *Steering panel*: this panel sponsors and oversees the entire project. It is charged with winning support from top executives, clearing barriers that arise, taking corrective action when the program goes off course, and signing off on all major agreements.

- *Project management panel*: this panel is responsible for monitoring progress, managing risk, handling communication and change management with staff, and intraproject coordination. It runs the project on a day-to-day basis and trains participating staff members.

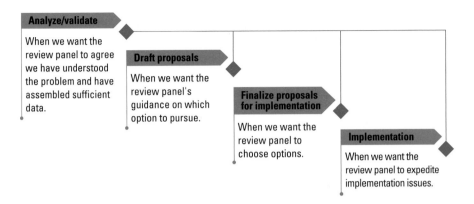

**Figure 8.3** *The checkpoints for the review panel*

In all but the smallest projects, it is mandatory that someone has full-time responsibility for the program. Figure 8.4 shows how this panel structure can operate, giving executives a clear view of both the program and its component parts. Panels that embrace employees from across the organization offer many benefits:

- They promote fairness by allowing all segments of the workforce to be heard; the perception of fairness is essential to the program's viability and success.

- They encourage innovation and employee participation while allowing senior management to provide oversight.

- They improve results by keeping everyone focused on the imperatives of the value proposition and fostering shared decision making.

- They increase vigilance against unanticipated risks that can accompany change.

- They support fast action and decisions through an interconnected panel process.

To effectively evaluate the progress of an optimization program, the CFO must assemble a detailed cost base for the organization, including budget expenditures and revenues, and headcount. This baseline data helps track where and how costs are incurred.

After baseline metrics are established, you should formulate hypotheses

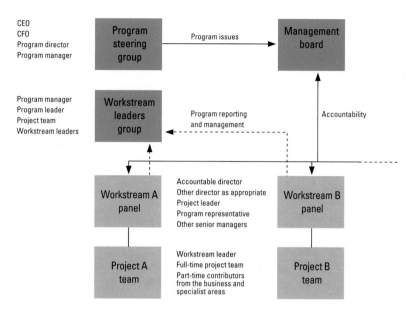

**Figure 8.4**  *Program organization and reporting lines*

about where costs can be reduced. Compare current operating perform-ance against best in class, create target environments using visioning techniques, and document assumptions for achieving proposed reductions. Ensure that resources are available to support the change.

You should prepare to handle change management. Some resistance is inevitable at the inception of any major optimization program, but the greater the effort made to involve employees, the less resistant they will be. To understand and support change, staff members need to know three fundamental things: what the compelling reason for change is, how it relates to overall corporate strategy, and how it will affect their daily lives.

In ignoring these needs, the failed corporate downsizing programs of the 1980s committed two sometimes fatal errors. They created an atmo-sphere of pervasive uncertainty, which fueled the rumor mill, lowered morale, and reduced productivity. And they never tapped the job knowl-edge of line employees, who often know better than anyone else where inefficient processes are to be found. Having performed their functions repeatedly over the years, employees could have provided vital input about restructuring processes *if only they had been asked.*

Employees' job satisfaction and sense of security will be challenged during an extensive optimization program. People are open to movement, however, when they are presented with a vision of an improved future, a reasonably solid plan for obtaining it, and the push which comes when change is accepted as necessary and inevitable.

CASE STUDY
The Delicate Process of Change

*A recently privatized government agency ($1 billion) engaged a new management team. Its first priority was to make the agency, which deals with financial transactions, self-supporting. The organization had strong prospects through its established Internet presence, highly knowledgeable staff and reputation for integrity, which was the equivalent of a brand to the marketplace. The problem was its Byzantine structure; any attempts at innovation were quickly swallowed up by a well-entrenched bureaucracy.*

*During the benchmarking stage of its optimization program, the CFO discovered that the organization had an extraordinary number of suppliers, only three employees per supervisor, and more than a dozen layers of management from top to bottom, all well out of step with industry standards. Even if the employees had unanimously supported the privatization, and they hadn't, optimization and change could not have occurred in this kind of claustrophobic setting.*

*The savings created by a streamlined procurement process, which would fully exploit the organization's Internet presence, were so self-evident that they were enacted immediately once identified. Reducing suppliers by 60% paid a quick financial dividend, and an unexpected bonus. The staff involved responded positively to the diminished drudgery attached to their jobs, and became more enthusiastic about the optimization efforts.*

*Although it was never identified as part of the privatization program, the CFO capitalized on this success by scheduling a series of lunch speakers with expertise in various aspects of the organization's domain. The management staff respected the speakers' credentials and listened carefully to their pro-*

*jections about the changes e-commerce was bringing to the world of finance. Again and again, the speakers addressed the speed and consistency of change. The message got through.*

*Resistance fell further when the value proposition for the optimization program was completed. It projected savings of nearly 30% within 18 months. Beyond the procurement process, cost savings were found by automating the audit function, adding a human resources portal to the Web site for employees, outsourcing support functions, and improving finance processes.*

*The funds freed up by the optimization program allowed the organization to become self-supporting, but growth and innovation have been slowed by entrenched employee attitudes. The CFO hopes to promote further change in the future through financial incentives, an option not currently available. The CFO remains optimistic. After vastly reducing costs and improving efficiency, he continues to work at changing outlooks, which he recognizes as a long-term proposition.*

## Stage 3: Assessing Opportunities

During this stage, subject area teams prepare detailed assessments of organizational workflows and compare them with similar processes internally and externally. The ultimate success of any optimization program depends on the accuracy of data obtained at this time. Compare today's best practices with tomorrow's as in Figure 8.5

> *You should establish how rationally assets are being employed. Assess the costs, benefits and capacity utilization of tangible assets. Likewise, survey any intangible assets: is their contribution to revenue recognized and supported adequately?*

An activity analysis is vital to understanding how people and systems use resources to transform inputs into outputs. It also enables cross-business comparisons among activities that may or may not be related. Once definitions have been completed, use them to map costs, revenue, and asset value drivers.

Figure 8.6 shows that by linking costs to activities, corporations can

| Against today's standards | Against tomorrow's possibilities |
|---|---|
| **Approach**<br>• Comparing performance to rivals and competitors<br>• Based on existing data (today's standards)<br>• Considering operational improvement | **Approach**<br>• Challenging the current business model<br>• Comparing with the optimal real-world model<br>• Considering transformational change |
| **Examples**<br>• Bad debt as a percentage of revenue<br>• Production cycle time, delivery times, time to provision<br>• Cost of customer acquisition<br>• Return rules, stockholding costs | **Examples**<br>• Application of e-business<br>• Outsourcing partnerships, exiting areas of the value chain<br>• New pricing and value models |

**Figure 8.5** *Best-practice comparisons*

tap a rich source of vision-clarifying information. In the human resources department in question, only 25% of its budget is being used to actually hire new employees; the rest is being spent on supporting activities.

Were corporate headquarters to divide the number of new employees hired into the HR budget, it would arrive at an erroneous cost per hire, perhaps causing it to outsource hiring to an employment agency. Concurrently, by identifying what it spends to provide benefits information to employees, the organization can quantify the potential savings of creating an e-employee communications program on its Web site.

You should establish how rationally assets are being employed. Assess the costs, benefits and capacity utilization of tangible assets, including offices, factories or warehouses; other fixed assets; working capital; and research and development programs. Are these operating at peak efficiency? Is there overcapacity that should be disposed of, or undercapacity that causes bottlenecks and inflates costs?

Likewise, survey any intangible assets: new product development, brands, knowledge management, strategic data, and customer lifetime value (Chapter 4). Is their contribution to revenue recognized and supported adequately? Then assess working capital and costs of funds using risk adjustment, including weighted average cost of capital (WACC). This provides a detailed understanding of the utilization of assets and identifies the gap between actual and potential performance.

| Department cost view | | Activity view | |
|---|---|---|---|
| **Costs** | **$1000** | **Activities** | **$1000** |
| Salary and wages | 1152 | Develop policy and strategy | 75 |
| Benefits | 372 | Employee communications | 314 |
| Other personnel costs | 89 | Hire employees | 471 |
| Travel, car | 38 | Write employment contracts | 105 |
| Travel, other | 2 | Determine salaries and other benefits | 115 |
| Hotel and overnight | 63 | Write reports | 218 |
| Entertainment | 8 | Maintain personnel data | 205 |
| External services, training | 4 | Correspondence | 221 |
| Premises costs allocation | 116 | Performance reviews | 85 |
| Other costs | 61 | Manage HR staff | 96 |
| **Total** | **1905** | **Total** | **1905** |

**Figure 8.6** *Activity-based cost analysis for an HR department*

Review costs, expenses and outsourced services on a category basis. Grouping purchased goods and services by category highlights the magnitude of a given expense and suggests opportunities for cost reduction. Other opportunities may be found by assessing the effectiveness of your technology structure and management. Analyze system capacity and stability, cost performance of the current platform, infrastructure and level of integration, and e-business potential. As Jeff Henley points out in his introduction to this chapter, IT can sometimes be the keystone of both cost reduction and revenue growth. Identify gaps between current IT capabilities and optimized alternatives.

Identify savings opportunities offered by e-based technologies. These might include savings in business-to-business (B2B) activities such as e-procurement and other supply chain processes, business-to-employee (B2E) savings through Web-based self-service HR benefits, and business-to-consumer (B2C) savings through reducing administrative activities in sales. Your assessment should also cover these areas:

- *Establish the productivity of your structure and people management resources.* Analyze your organizational structure for functions, layers and spans of control. Assess staff members for skills, competency and potential, while looking at the unit costs of employment, including temps, subcontractors and part-timers, according to wages and benefits. Is your payroll being spent wisely?

- *Consider the full range of product and service profitability measures.* Assess products and services by profitability and value generation according to channels, geography, production facility or process, etc. This will yield insights into their strategic importance, identify under- and overperformance and point up approaches worth duplicating or in need of optimization.

Complete your assessment of opportunities by identifying preliminary targets. Taking some quick hits out of the cost basis pays multiple dividends by establishing the potential of an optimization program, management's support for it, and the inevitability of the announced changes. Focus attention on those areas most likely to produce such outcomes. Once these opportunities are identified, sort them by risk, complexity, time frame and savings potential. Then consider constraints that would impede their realization.

Establish senior-level sponsorship and an enterprise-wide communications process. Create a program, clearly sponsored by top management, which makes the case for change and presents a high-level vision of the future. Recognize there will be questions and provide for employee dialogs in the style of town meetings.

## DESIGN PHASE: WEEKS 7 TO 14

The findings of a cost analysis can shock senior managers, even CFOs, who often learn for the first time where the true cost drivers of their businesses are hidden. It is important to move beyond this point quickly so that the real work of optimization can begin—improving existing ways of doing business to reduce costs, enhance performance and provide seed money to fund growth (Figure 8.7).

### Stage 4: Developing Improvements

Subject area panels should consider the full range of options for performing activities more efficiently or at a lower cost, including:

- *Stop it.* Is it possible to abandon the activity completely, or would that severely impact the final product or service, or the next step in the process?

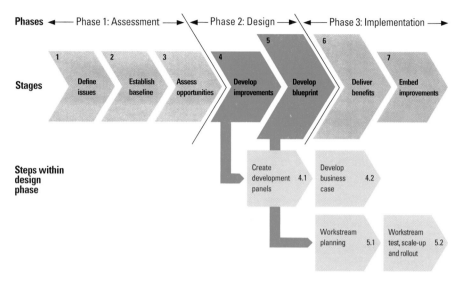

**Figure 8.7** *Enterprise-wide optimization: design phase*

- *Simplify it.* Is it possible to simplify the process without extensively reengineering it?
- *Reduce the occurrence.* Can you perform the activity less frequently?
- *Shop for suppliers.* Can you perform a process more cheaply in-house, by outsourcing, or as a shared process than you can by using current suppliers?
- *Automate or reengineer.* Can you cut costs by restructuring an activity?

CASE STUDY
Finding New Ways of Doing Business

*When an American retailing conglomerate benchmarked its costs against industry averages, it discovered they were 25% higher than best practices. The CFO assumed this was because internal processes had never been integrated as business units expanded across the US. Profits were strong, and in the press of business, there was little time to reorganize workflows and synchronize support services.*

*When board members heard the CFO's report, they agreed that reforms were needed. With the company about to get seriously involved in Internet retailing, this was the time to develop improvements. It was unthinkable at this stage to add another layer to an already highly inefficient organization.*

*The company had a dozen customer service centers in different regions, and it wanted to discover the best means of consolidating them. In preparation, subject area optimization teams reviewed workstreams and procedures. They learned that other than having the same corporate parent, these operations had almost nothing in common even though they essentially performed the same tasks. When asked to define a customer telephone inquiry, each center produced a unique answer. Each verified customer identity in a different way. But none could adjust staffing to the peaks and valleys of call volumes.*

*Initially, managers and supervisors at each location resisted change. They wanted to retain their familiar job routines, but the benchmarking data was so overwhelming that inefficiencies couldn't be denied. And the research showed that considered change could drastically alter these results. This became clear as the optimization team examined procedures that had been concocted to meet the demands of the moment and never altered.*

*In a department that dealt with designer clothing and wasn't fully automated, workers had problems keeping order forms up to date. To compensate, they attached stick-on notes to the paperwork sent to the fulfillment department. Sometimes these notes became detached, causing the wrong goods to be shipped. The problem was widely recognized by employees, but no one addressed it because their department supervisor didn't think it was critical. Of course, no one at headquarters knew business was being done this way.*

*During the workflow and best-practices review, it became clear that the company would win on every front by consolidating customer service operation. Larger centers, with better-trained and empowered employees, not only cost less to operate but also delivered superior service and adapted better to fluctuations in the business cycle.*

*By wiring all these outposts to the Internet, multiple synergies emerged. Service representatives could access far more accurate data on goods in stock; marketing and purchasing could review sales figures in real time; shipping and receiving could anticipate workloads days in advance. e-Procurement, electronic bill payment and data sharing with business partners could be easily accommodated.*

*Estimates showed that increased efficiencies would result in redundancies equivalent to 15% of the staff. After approving the changes, the company instituted an open communications program with its employees. It informed them of expected closing dates as soon as they were known, offered bonuses to workers it especially wanted to keep, and assistance to those whose positions were eliminated. Incentives were developed for workers who remained on the job until a location was closed.*

*When the program was in full swing, 13 different optimization teams were at work examining and recasting the flow of work through the organization. Within two years, $200 million had been saved, customer satisfaction was markedly higher, and revenues had increased by 10%, largely due to Internet sales.*

---

As this case study shows, when CFOs make a strong case for change, they motivate employees to develop improved approaches to business. Once the inefficiencies are exposed, alternatives can be found in virtually every instance, particularly if workers themselves are involved in developing them.

Because the different employee-led subject panels will have a range of proposals for cost optimization, it is important to develop a proposal format so that the presentations are both consistent and comprehensive enough to support equitable judgment. Content should include benefits, costs, technology requirements, time frame and risks.

Developing proposals for improved processes, activities and structures is a brainstorming step; creativity and innovation should be strongly encouraged. Unworkable proposals can be eliminated later, although panels should temper their deliberations with consideration of risk, benefit, and implementation feasibility.

Panels should also discuss reductions in service levels. Comparing the current service levels of different business units within an organization can be difficult, particularly when multinationals must contend with the varying service-level expectations of different cultures. Yet service levels can be a major cost driver, making it essential that they be measured and compared across the organization. Here are some more improvement tasks for subject area panels:

- *Develop proposals for improving asset yield.* Panels should consider reconfiguring physical structure to improve yield through improved space or capacity utilization, or process reliability; minimizing working capital requirements through altered debt/credit, treasury or inventory policy; minimizing costs of funds; and enhancing the use of intangible assets.

- *Develop proposals to reduce other costs.* Panels develop options for reducing costs of purchased goods and services, including cost/quality ratio, sourcing strategies, vendor rationalization, and vendor involvement. Other options are reducing direct and indirect cash taxes, streamlining investment projects, and redesigning the legal structure to reduce costs and reporting.

- *Develop proposals to improve technology management.* Properly applied, e-business mechanisms can yield internal savings and external revenue growth. Search for that transformational point where using technology to improve company interactions delivers major savings.

- *Develop proposals to reduce the cost of the workforce.* Of all the issues in an optimization program, this is undoubtedly the most delicate and it was handled very badly by 1980s corporate downsizes. Here are the two most glaring shortcomings of the old approach to cost management: (1) arbitrary downsizing campaigns frequently reduced costs in the short term, only to trigger falling revenues soon after due to corporate anorexia; (2) using nonselective monetary incentives to encourage early retirements or employee separations frequently caused the most highly skilled employees to defect. Salary freezes drove the same star staff members out the door; hiring freezes kept their replacements from ever coming in.

Handled correctly, the foremost concern in workforce optimization is to maximize and protect a corporation's most valuable source for cost reduction and revenue growth—the knowledge of its employees. Nothing is more counterproductive than nonselective staff reductions. Conversely, a well-planned staff optimization program delivers huge paybacks.

Given the fierce competition for superior employees, winning the war for talent means attracting, effectively deploying and retaining the right people. This requires aggressive recruitment programs *and* effective career advancement plans. At the same time, optimization programs enable management to intervene actively to improve the work of underperformers or move them out. Optimization also promotes job restructuring, which improves workflows and job satisfaction.

High performers are notoriously unforgiving of bad corporate management and poor work design. It is they, and not underperformers, who will leave if their positions aren't challenging and strong job performance isn't recognized. Top people are motivated by a company's values and culture, its management, and the exciting challenges it offers. Reallocating resources for optimum performance requires redefining jobs in old-economy operations and providing opportunities in new ventures.

> ***Develop the business case. Communicate the accepted proposals internally and externally, establishing the impact of the optimization program on shareholder value. Create performance measures and obtain sign-off.***

All the proposals submitted by the subject area teams should be examined by review panels to select those that should advance to the blueprint implementation stage. These panels should insist on detailed and realistic implementation plans while still encouraging creativity so that milestones will be met. This is where momentum is born.

Review panels, which have knowledge of the subject areas in question, should suggest alternatives to proposed changes, if appropriate. They can make important contributions by linking various workstreams, departments, or business units in joint projects that will distribute the workload evenly and multiply anticipated benefits.

The next step is to develop the business case. Communicate the accepted proposals internally and externally, establishing the impact of the optimization program on shareholder value. Create performance measures and obtain sign-off by all appropriate parties. Finalize HR plans for affected employees and then prepare a launch event, to be followed by feedback forums with employees who will be involved.

Preparing the business case for change arms the CFO with an enhanced understanding of a company's strengths and weaknesses. Building on this, project teams can move forward to prepare blueprints for implementing approved changes.

## Stage 5: Developing a Blueprint

So far, panels have prepared and reviewed recommendations for change. During the blueprint stage those efforts are shaped into an integrated program for transforming an inefficient organization into an optimized one. Here revisions must be balanced against each other, as well as integrated into larger existing business structures that aren't going to initiate change.

- *Create an integrated program structure for implementation.* Improvements proposed by subject area panels must be shaped into an integrated program. Coordinate individual proposals with other change initiatives, and with proposed time frames and resource availability. Design reporting and controlling mechanisms for implementation; define program and workstream responsibilities.

- *Develop detailed implementation plans, including predefined milestones.* Have the subject area panels prepare implementation plans for review panel approval. Emphasize predictable and measurable milestones to ensure easy program monitoring and trigger corrective actions as needed. If extensive changes are being implemented, it is especially important that guidelines remain readily visible. Program management is critical to implementation.

CASE STUDY
Seeing a Business in New Ways

*The CEO of an international media and information group took pride in fostering an entrepreneurial spirit among the senior managers of his business units. As long as they met his annual revenue figures, he told them, they could run their businesses any way they wanted. This was partly a reflection of his talent for selecting able senior executives, and partly a manifestation of his damn-the-torpedoes, full-speed-ahead business style. Much of corporate planning, he believed, was a matter of going with your gut.*

*The CEO was so adept at attracting smart and talented executives that his empire was a growing one. The European company had expanded into the US* *and other countries through a series of acquisitions. But with revenues in excess of $1.5 billion, the decentralized, highly autonomous business units weren't benefiting from economies of scale. With major e-commerce investments ahead, the CEO decided it was time to consider an optimization plan.*

*During an initial review at the business unit level, the CFO discovered wide discrepancies in the ways that managers spent money—offices in North America tended to be spacious, while those in Europe were less expansive. With everyone working to increase revenue, standards had never been set and some of the dividends that discipline can produce were being forfeited.*

*It was only after the CFO profiled the organization's spending patterns and discovered that $45 million could be cut with little risk and no diminished capacity that the CEO began to take heed. Optimization panels were formed in each business unit, and the CEO discovered that, in addition to his top people, there were many other talented and knowledgeable employees throughout his ranks. They knew their jobs and their industry, and offered many constructive suggestions for change.*

*Given what he heard during the assessment phase of an optimization program, the CFO raised his savings projection to more than $100 million, and the optimization team went into the blueprint stage, creating a plan for implementing selected programs.*

*The corporation's history of business unit autonomy meant that the implementation had to be handled with a light touch, respecting the creative nature of the businesses and the varying cultures in their far-flung geographic locations. Cohesiveness among the businesses was weak, so the CFO needed to ensure that program managers strengthened the links between the operations facing cross-organizational change.*

*At this stage, the CFO saw that the key to making the optimization process work lay in managing the process of change. Although cost reduction and process optimization could improve cash flow more than an increase in revenues, these approaches were not as inherently interesting to employees as building a new business. People had to be encouraged, and then recognized and rewarded, when they optimized an organization—just as they were when they brought in new business.*

*Many were surprised at the inefficiencies that emerged during their investi-*

*gations. The optimization teams were diligent about preventing the project from being sabotaged by agonizing, How did we ever allow things to get this bad? Staying positive and focused on the beneficial aspects of the plan kept people from shirking tasks they sometimes didn't want to perform.*

*Employees' resistance diminished as the blueprint was completed, partly because they realized that changes were inevitable, and partly because positive aspects of the new approaches were apparent, including the cost reduction incentives being offered. In the end, the optimization program produced significant savings, as well as an enterprise that was more efficient and more unified.*

---

In addition to coordinating implementation plans, the review panels also need to assess the enterprise-wide impact that revisions will have on the six levers of change:

- *Organization:* if the organizational structure must be adjusted, what will the new structure look like? How should existing interfaces be altered?

- *Customers and markets:* what will be different for the customer? Will the impact be positive or negative? How will it affect the competitive position of products or services? Have all potential e-business connections been exploited?

- *People and culture:* will the revisions affect staffing levels? Will employees involved require more or fewer skills than those currently performing the work? Will the change alter the atmosphere of the workplace?

- *Policy, products and services*: will the change conflict with existing policy? Will it require changes in current products, or in a service and/ or a support level?

- *Process*: at what stage of the process is the change being proposed, and how will it affect leading and trailing processes?

- *Technology*: how large an investment is required, how long will it take to earn out, and how will users be touched by the change?

Using a scale appropriate to proposed changes, run pilots of revised processes to allow for revisions and uncover bugs. When planning has been completed and tested, it is time to advance to the final phase.

# IMPLEMENTATION PHASE: WEEK 15 ONWARD

If blueprint development is the crunch point for identifying where budgets are going to be cut and programs curtailed, the implementation phase is where CFOs ensure that approved changes are actually carried out with dispatch. The importance of momentum cannot be underestimated.

One organization which delayed implementation until after the summer vacation period found, when it tried to resume optimization work, that everyone wanted to reopen discussion of changes already agreed to, or postpone scheduled starting dates for new procedures. All the urgency created over weeks of meetings and employee communications efforts had disappeared. Only after the CFO had staged a revival session in a large auditorium, and the project team had instituted several quick-win initiatives, did the program get back on track.

## Stage 6: Delivering Benefits

Having established momentum, ensure that responsibility for implementing the approved changes and delivering the anticipated benefits is transferred from the optimization team to the appropriate managers and staff. The baseline performance figures gathered in the assessment phase are important elements of the optimization scorecard. Comparing postimplementation outcomes with the earlier figures makes it immediately apparent how effectively changes are being made, and whether any alterations that slipped through testing are needed.

Because employees were involved from the optimization program's launch, they participated in change rather than having it inflicted on them. That process comes full circle here, as empowered staff members accept responsibility for the results of projects they helped to design.

As the following case study indicates, transferring the responsibility for optimization to workers occurs most easily when employees clearly see that the entire process has been one of fairness, one of shared responsibility and rewards.

CASE STUDY
Taking a Common Route Home

*The top management of a large and highly successful financial services firm came to grips with some unpleasant news as it prepared for upcoming presentations to market analysts, shareholders and government regulators. Although the company was highly profitable, trouble was lurking. A recent industry-wide benchmarking study had put its costs at 25% above average, just as low-overhead competitors were about to invade its primary markets. Worse yet, e-commerce was revolutionizing the way the industry interacted with its customers and sorely testing their loyalty.*

*The corporation needed to cut costs quickly, then use its savings to aggressively retain its best customers and invest heavily in Internet technology. Given its massive girth, this project needed a lot of reach to succeed in reshaping the company. Fortunately, the organization, which had completed a string of acquisitions, had a culture that was used to supporting large-scale change.*

*After exploratory consultations, the CFO assembled 10 workstream-oriented project teams that often cut across divisions. Each of these teams began with a four- or five-week analysis that established a baseline of existing practices, which were cross-checked by review panels for accuracy. The review panels then heard proposals for nearly 200 cost reduction, process improvement projects developed by the business units. Ultimately, the approved proposals accounted for $160 million of savings, or 24% of the cost base.*

*The most sweeping and broadly supported proposal called for transforming the corporation's Web site from a symbolic footprint into a major point of interchange with its customers, employees, suppliers and business partners. The Internet was to become the company's reservoir of change. Customers would visit it to pay bills, check balances and open accounts. Employees would schedule their vacations, review their pension benefits and file health insurance claims. Suppliers would bid for contracts, check inventories and schedule payments. Business partners and other interested parties would learn about new undertakings, check stock prices and review externally facing financial data that was updated continuously. All these interactions would take place, unassisted, for a pittance once start-up costs were paid.*

*The indirect returns of the Internet investment promised to be great. There was a strong silo mentality in the company. When a marketing department scheduled a promotional campaign, it seldom included anyone from customer service in the planning, even though the implications for their workload were self-evident. By enabling data warehousing, the Web site permitted people from far-flung company processes to see how seemingly isolated costs reverberated throughout the value chain.*

*As the Web site and dozens of other approved initiatives moved forward, the CFO and his steering, review and project management panels carefully monitored implementation by the workstream teams. At each milestone the teams worked to build ownership and sustainability into the process of change. Every major aspect of the program was aired publicly before the appropriate audiences. When necessary, in order to intercept watercooler gossip, open de-bate was strongly encouraged. The CFO was creating a common route home — ensuring that the program was equitable, that everyone perceived it as being fair, and that changes were implemented in the same manner corporation-wide so they would become embedded in the culture.*

*If the CFO learned anything from the implementation process, it was that you had to work at building and maintaining a coalition for change. It had to be tended to constantly. When problems or recalcitrance surfaced, they had to be dealt with instantly. Given a chance to backslide, someone would always seize it. As the process moved forward, however, and people saw their ideas being put into action, the need for such behavior diminished.*

*A visible and highly active project management team remained in place over the two years of the implementation phase. They worked to keep things moving and to foster a spirit of accomplishment that allowed the company's Web site to become a wellspring of unexpected opportunities. By developing its electronic interface with the world, the corporation established a permanent mechanism for growth and change.*

---

The processes modified or developed during optimization programs do not automatically become institutionalized. To make this happen, the employees involved must assume ownership, and new approaches must have delivered the promised benefits.

## Stage 7: Embedding Improvements

This final optimization stage involves making onsite adjustments to altered processes to ensure their continued proper functioning; and using lessons learned to reform other aspects of the corporate culture. The most important of these involve personnel.

You should develop policies that encourage higher performance by employees. While technology and improved processes can make enormous contributions to optimization, they are only tools. Achieving ongoing peak performance rests in the hands of the people who deploy the processes and operate the technology. It is the innumerable human tasks performed that represent the real work of a corporation.

To encourage their people to continuously improve their daily routines, great companies have four attributes:

- Cultures that promote individual accountability and cost awareness

- Well-defined strategic objectives that are routinely met

- Managers who coach their staff members

- Incentive systems that recognize and reward exceptional performance

Because optimization programs are about future growth and new opportunities, they give everyone something to strive for. They encourage corporations and their employees to work smarter instead of just working harder. They also create organizations that blaze their own frontiers and therefore don't have to gut their ranks at each periodic downturn in the business cycle.

## FOSTERING INNOVATION AND GROWTH

It is essential to remember that cost reduction is not its own reward. Indeed, no corporation can succeed, or even survive, by retuning its cost base alone. But with a structured approach to optimization, and after embedding lessons learned as best practices going forward, the corporation can become fit and agile for one of its most important functions—innovation.

A recent study of successful innovation in 400 companies around the globe highlights its importance.[1] The study found that innovation was the number one concern among the CEOs and board members surveyed, ranking significantly ahead of globalization and industry consolidation. Yet not all firms were equally successful in nurturing innovation. Among the surveyed companies, those with total shareholder returns of over 37% derived 60% of their turnover *from products or services that had been introduced within the previous five years.* Companies with average or below average total shareholder returns derived less than 40% of their turnover from such products.

The survey illustrates that growth and innovation seldom occur by chance. They are carefully fostered by the companies that inevitably end up at the head of the pack. These are the characteristics that put them there:

- A high degree of management trust in its employees; people believe in those they hire and show it by delegating decision making.

- A more active flow of ideas from day to day, and less hiding behind the status quo.

- Fewer organizational levels between executives and customers; managers remain in touch with their markets.

- Explicit idea management processes in place that people adhere to; unsolicited proposals don't get brushed off.

- Challenging managers who set the tone and pace for change; in these companies, motivated workers rule the day.

- Inclusiveness as part of the company's charter; staff members get to participate in the implementation of their own ideas.

- Regular attempts by managers to imagine the future, based on intimate knowledge of their markets; they aren't always right, but when they are, they win big.

- Risk taking at healthy levels seen as normal rather than dysfunctional behavior; everyone acts this way, don't they?

Likewise, companies that grow consistently have some similarities. Learning from its own behavior is a logical next step for an organization that has embedded its optimization program. Having tuned the corporation's existing processes for maximum efficiency, and empowered its work-force to maintain momentum, senior management is free to decide how it can best utilize recaptured funds.

This is especially true for corporations that aren't the market leaders. Those who are number one are intuitively doing the right thing. Those below are ranked beneath in everything, such as market share and profit-ability, and they usually have a manage-and-control approach to busi-ness. They have also gone as far as they can using their current business model.

Ultimately, innovation and growth are characteristics which blossom in organizations that nurture them. These enterprises don't allow bureau-cracy to destroy motivation, and they are too busy celebrating success to be distracted by the occasional failure.

# eCFO CHECKLIST

### CLARIFY YOUR OBJECTIVES FOR ENTERPRISE-WIDE OPTIMIZATION
Why are you doing this and what do you hope to achieve? To take advantage of new technology? To release resources? Or because inefficiencies can no longer be ignored?

### DEVELOP AN UNIMPEACHABLE VALUE PROPOSITION
Are you confident that this is going to create the most value? Are your goals high enough? What are the shareholder value payoffs? Optimization will be unpleasant at times and consume a lot of time and resources. Be sure you have it right.

### INITIATE A COALITION FOR CHANGE
Start at board level and then cascade it throughout the organization through participation and ownership.

### KNOW THE DETAILS
Make sure you are absolutely clear about what your baseline costs are and where they occur. Many organizations can't truly identify them.

### KNOW WHERE YOUR RESOURCES ARE ACTUALLY BEING DEPLOYED
Develop a firm understanding of the as-is activity/process analysis.

### MARSHAL THE BLUEPRINT FOR CHANGES
Force a review of difficult options and single out nonproductive activities. External voices can be effective in dealing with politically difficult options. Everyone must commit to change, even when it produces short-term discomfort.

### KEEP SCORE
Track actions and benefits rigorously during implementation to ensure that people are doing what they are supposed to do and that the plan is delivering the promised results. If it isn't, adjust

it. If your cost basis changes during the process, perhaps through the divestiture of a business unit, make allowances for that. March to a fast drumbeat to maintain momentum.

## SUSTAIN THE CHANGE
Institutionalize the learning that has occurred during the cost reduction process into your budgeting, planning and reporting processes. Ensure that cost controls and value creation happen automatically. You've just made a step change. What controls have you put in place to ensure that you don't have to do it again? Ask yourself why you haven't done business this way all along.

## DEVELOP A COMMON ROUTE HOME
Use a process management structure that can be applied to a variety of projects. Some teams might be looking at e-procurement, others at customer service. Use a process that enables everyone to see that the same standards are being applied and the same results achieved.

## ELEVATE INNOVATION AND GROWTH TO EXALTED STATUS IN THE HIERARCHY OF YOUR CORPORATE VALUES
When you empower people to do work that excites them, they'll control their own costs, freeing CFOs to become e-business entrepreneurs. This is the win–win.

# CHAPTER 9

# Unlocking Value from Acquisitions and Alliances

## MERGING FOR VALUE

*Howard Smith, CFO*
AIG

*At AIG we really view ourselves as a global financial services enterprise. Clearly the predominant part of our business is insurance, but more and more we are concentrating on the financial services area. We have a market cap, depending on what day it is in the stock market, of approximately $220 billion, which places us in the top 10 or 15 companies in the US. We are also one of the few companies in the world that retain a triple-A rating from the major rating agencies.*

*One of the goals of this corporation is to produce a return on equity of approximately 15% a year. We are able to achieve that because AIG is a profit-center-oriented organization. Our culture drills down to the smallest profit centers, where every manager is really charged with the responsibility for his or her bottom line. If all profit center managers meet their targets, obviously the organization can meet its own on a broader scale.*

*Clearly a big event for us over the past couple of years was the completed acquisition of SunAmerica in 1999. We had been interested in acquiring an organization like SunAmerica for some time.*

SunAmerica had built up a tradition as a retirement specialist company, but their boundaries did not extend beyond the US. With our international presence, we recognized a good fit, and with their product and management expertise, matched with our policyholders, it was just a natural merger.

We believe that the positioning and retention of SunAmerica provide us with a tremendous opportunity in the retirement savings and asset management businesses. We have literally tens of millions of policyholders throughout the world, and are actively mining our databases to determine the range of products we can sell to each individual. Mergers and acquisitions clearly have to become an important part of strategy in any organization of our size. You cannot continue to grow by only expanding individual businesses.

The SunAmerica merger came together fairly quickly. As with any acquisition of that size, we wanted to keep the due diligence process quiet and limited to as few people as possible. We basically had a contingent of people resident in a hotel in Los Angeles, not even in either company's quarters, just to keep the secrecy. And I think that over a period of about five days—and they were long days, very long days—we got to the point of being comfortable with what we saw in SunAmerica. They did the same kind of due diligence review of AIG. The deal came together very quickly.

> **Some of the most interesting transactions we're reviewing involve Internet start-up operations. We must satisfy ourselves that the opportunity is unique, well thought out, well structured.**

After the merger actually closed, the key corporate people and the people running major profit centers from both companies started working together on specific steps for the transition. Timetables were set, review and feedback processes were established. Communications have gone very smoothly.

We did not enter into this acquisition believing the combination offered huge opportunities for cost savings, because ours were two different types of organization. However, we saw the synergies clearly and we've already begun to realize rewards from those synergies.

We've been involved in a few acquisitions over the years; we don't do a lot, *though we review many. At any point in time, we probably have 50 different transactions that are on the table, but we've got some pretty high standards. It's got to be an organization that we think will give us 15% return on equity, and when you do the homework and the due diligence, there are very few that fit that mold. This one worked. And the transition has gone remarkably well.*

*Some of the most interesting transactions we're reviewing now involve Internet start-up operations, not only as investments but also from a strategic-link standpoint. We're convinced that the Internet will be a form of distribution in the insurance industry and we're going to be on the cutting edge. As we consider investing in Internet entities, we must satisfy ourselves that the opportunity is unique, well thought out, well structured. While we certainly hope that the Internet investments produce a healthy return for us, we believe their value will also lie in the strategic initiatives we can jointly sponsor.*

AIG has plenty of company. As the Internet opens up new avenues for value creation, more and more industry leaders are venturing beyond traditional mergers and acquisitions (M&A) to fuel their future growth. Like AIG, many are considering joint ventures and strategic alliances in order to capitalize on the e-business explosion and tap new revenue sources.

CFOs attach huge importance to their deal-making role, and with good reason. Most view external transactions—mergers and acquisitions, strategic alliances, joint ventures, etc.—as the most important tools they have for building shareholder value and influencing their companies' strategic direction. Many CFOs, in fact, spend about one-third of their time assessing, planning, and executing deals, often with mixed results.

How do you make a persuasive case for value creation in promoting a transaction? How do you map targets, identify synergies, and recover premiums? How do you choose between an M&A and a strategic alliance? How do you assess "cultural fit"? Why do deals go wrong so often? As a CFO, how can you increase the chances of success? And once a deal goes through, how do you merge or coordinate the finance functions most efficiently?

This chapter tackles these and other thorny issues head-on. First, it will explore new partnership models that are emerging in today's e-business world. Next, it looks at pitfalls to avoid; identifies best practices that can help guide decision making in both traditional M&A deals and in more complex strategic alliances; and addresses the all-important issue of cultural fit. Most important, this chapter focuses on value creation.

Clearly, the CFO's biggest challenge is bringing financial rigor to the practice of deal-making, whatever form it may take in today's confusing and volatile marketplace. Despite the current e-commerce feeding frenzy, the core approach to valuing M&A targets or alliance partners remains the same, whether a transaction involves an e-business or a more traditional enterprise.

In fact, experience shows that sticking to the fundamentals is *especially* important in evaluating an e-business situation, precisely because so many start-ups lack financial discipline. Granted, in an e-business venture, there may be more variables involved in assessing future expectations. Nevertheless, the principles of sound financial decision making remain the same, a comforting thought if you're feeling somewhat adrift in today's ocean of opportunities.

## MAPPING NEW RELATIONSHIP MODELS

Industry convergence, technological change, and globalization are all fueling a surge in high-impact and high-risk transactions. Over the next five to ten years, we expect a strong drive toward more and bigger acquisitions, mergers, strategic alliances, and disposals.

The number and value of deals have risen steadily. The sheer size and complexity of such transactions point to their importance. Clearly, every deal is different. Every set of potential benefits and pitfalls is unique and must be rigorously evaluated. Today the CFO's role as deal-maker is made more challenging by the number of structural options available.

Each of the options in Figure 9.1 poses different risks, offers different benefits, and demands a different degree of organizational integration. The mindset required to successfully pursue alliances, for example, is very different from the mindset which fuels growth and market share through acquisitions.

Research suggests that the decision to pursue either an M&A or a strategic alliance is dictated by a firm's market position, history, and culture.[1] The evidence indicates that wealthy, well-established companies seldom make effective and dedicated alliance partners because embedded deep within their cultures is a preference for splendid isolation. This

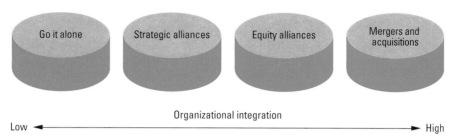

**Figure 9.1** *The four basic options*

simple but compelling explanation means acquisition is their favored tool.

In contrast, alliances are favored by competitive companies that allocate resources sparingly, seek to hedge their bets, and are willing to make major commitments only when positive results are reasonably certain. Such firms tend to reassess their options continually, asking what they've learned before taking the next step in the deal-making process.

This is not to suggest that alliances are preferable to acquisitions or vice versa. Each has its place. The choice between partnering and a formal merger is often dictated by how a company interprets its market position and the strength of its internal resources. The AOL Time Warner transaction highlights some of the issues involved.[2]

CASE STUDY
Joining Old and New:
The AOL Time Warner Merger

*The $100 billion plus deal between America Online, a 14-year-old Internet company, and Time Warner, a long-established, old-style media giant, marked the coming of age of the Internet. In many respects, it represented a leap of faith by Time Warner boss Gerald Levin, who became the first media chief to exchange his company's solid assets for the highly volatile, speculative value of an Internet company's stock—a decision that generated enormous publicity and speculation.*

*Yet the deal also vindicated the work of AOL's president, Bob Pittman. Pittman was the architect of AOL's transformation from a subscription-based company* to one deriving an increasing proportion of its revenues from advertising, marketing, and e-commerce.

## Merger versus going it alone

*Recognizing the opportunities presented by the Internet, Time Warner had been, since the early 1990s, attempting to develop an Internet strategy to strengthen its position in the interactive television market. Yet most industry analysts viewed its effort to build an Internet presence as a failure. By merging with AOL, Levin admitted he was attempting to rectify the situation: "We could have gone it alone. But I came to the conclusion that merging with AOL would accelerate our own development."*

*AOL and Time Warner share a common conviction that the two companies can grow a lot faster together than either could have individually. In fact, going it alone may no longer be an option given the pace of change in the e-enabled world. Most big media companies have faced the same problems as Time Warner and many may now find themselves impelled by similar imperatives to merge with successful Internet businesses.*

## The importance of cultural fit

*As merger talks progressed, momentum was created by the conviction of the top teams that a close cultural fit existed between the two partners. Time Warner chief Levin commented, "They have the same value system, blue-chip board, very consumer-brand-oriented, very aggressive in building market position, and they are both subscription-based companies."*

*Having the right fit kept the talks on track at a time when difficulties in valuing the two companies might have derailed the entire process. More importantly, the ability to leverage fit and mobilize the combined resources of the two companies will be the basis on which the deal's success or failure will be judged.*

## Valuation of Internet stocks

*Despite the compelling strategic rationale for the deal, both sides had to confront the valuation disparity between media and Internet companies. Indeed,* for long periods during the negotiation process, it looked as if a financial agreement might not be reached.

Ultimately, the deal was structured as a purchase rather than a pooling of interests. This means that AOL will have to write off goodwill, but it will not be limited by the conditions of pooling, which would include restrictions on big disposals, balance sheet restructuring and share buybacks. There will of course be goodwill write-offs, several billion dollars a year, which would mean that AOL paid a 70% premium for Time Warner's shares.

The price paid by AOL highlighted not just the importance of content, but also the true underlying value of AOL's stock. At the time the deal was struck, AOL's market value was twice that of Time Warner. However, the merger terms gave AOL investors only 55% of the merged firm. This suggests that the valuation of Internet stocks may need a downward adjustment, good news for bricks-and-mortar firms whose content is still in demand by consumers.

---

At this point, in order to give investors an annual return of 15% over 15 years, the new media giant's market cap will have to reach $2.4 trillion. Achieving this goal will require an ambitious accomplishment: a 15-year growth rate in profits of 22.5%. Can AOL Time Warner pull this off?

The market's initial reaction was to mark AOL shares down. Why? Most analysts may have concluded that AOL had forfeited more valuable future options in the e-business world by linking itself to Time Warner. A more positive view would hold that the deal has potential to create the first true digital media company, combining real assets with Internet speed and interactivity. These diverging market views of the AOL Time Warner merger underscore just how difficult it is to craft a value-enhancing deal. Perhaps that's why so many postmerger companies go astray.

## GETTING IT WRONG: SOME MAJOR PITFALLS

Despite the feverish pace of global deal-making, expectations continue to outstrip results. In fact, once the ink has dried, one out of every two M&A deals fails to enhance performance, market position or shareholder value. In some cases, value is actually destroyed and performance declines after a deal is completed. The same holds true for strategic alliances. The following comments from CFOs underscore the harsh reality:

- If we had known it was going to be this hard, we never would have started.

- As a result of the deal, we lost focus on our own customers.

- The consequent decline in business has left us vulnerable to takeover.

- This deal has destroyed overnight the corporate reputation it took us more than 30 years to establish.

Recent surveys reveal the extent of corporate devastation. A study of 300 of the biggest mergers of the past decade found that, in terms of total shareholder return, 57% of the merged firms lagged behind their industry peer group three years after the deal. Another survey studied 116 mergers and concluded that 61% failed to better the cost of capital. Other findings indicate that, on average, corporations subsequently divest more than 50% of their acquisitions in new industries.

Why do so many deals appear to offer powerful benefits but ultimately prove disappointing? Our research pinpoints 10 mistakes that consistently lead to poor results:

1. *Failing to achieve strategic clarity.* Strategic clarity involves rigorously and accurately evaluating an M&A candidate's or alliance partner's fit with a company's strategic goals. Experienced CFOs assess this factor on three fronts. First, they ensure that a potential deal supports their company's long-term strategy and marketplace objectives. Second, they use a rigorous screening process to identify and rank candidates or partners. And third, they objectively assess their implementation capabilities.[1]

2. *Calculating synergistic benefits retroactively.* Deal-making is usually frenzied and emotional, clouding the managerial vision of the CEO and top team. Frequently, the process is dominated by an obsession with establishing a price and deal structure that will allow a transaction to go through, rather than a focus on a price or structure that accurately reflects value.

3. *Engaging in opportunistic, reactionary deal-making.* Quite often, acquisition or alliance decisions are countermoves made in response to competitive plays or unexpected marketplace developments. In many cases, a strategy is postrationalized, with no evidence that it is realistic, robust, or even capable of being safely implemented. Seasoned deal-makers, however, are proactive rather than reactive.

4. *Using outmoded valuation tools.* The profit/earnings valuation yardstick has well-documented shortcomings. More often than not, a target company's expected economic value is derived from estimates of earning potential based on historical performance and against comparable peer-group companies in a given industry sector. The problem: profit/earnings multiples are short-term indicators that are normalized and then extrapolated into the future to predict the target's long-range performance.

5. *Relying on inadequate analysis.* Typically, acquirers or alliance partners project increased cash flows from proposed deals. But equally typically, the models they use in valuation lack analytical rigor. The result may amount to a quick, dirty guesstimate of how many people they can cut and plants they can close as the basis for moving ahead with a deal.

6. *Failing to price a deal accurately.* Accurate pricing plays a pivotal role in M&A success. A recent study we conducted shows that five concepts of value contribute to accurate pricing: *intrinsic value* (the net present value of expected future cash flows); *market value* (the intrinsic value plus any bid premium); *purchase price* (the price the bidder anticipates having to pay to win the target); the *value gap* (the difference between the intrinsic value of the target and the purchase price); and *synergy value* (the total net present value of improvements flowing from the combined companies, involving expected cost savings, revenue enhancements, and process improvements, among other factors).

7. *Overestimating market attractiveness.* Many companies pursue M&As and/or alliances in order to gain a foothold in what appear to be robust, profitable markets, only to find those markets radically redefined or even eliminated almost overnight by emerging technologies. Novell's acquisition of WordPerfect, for example, came at a time when Microsoft's domination of the desktop computer market was changing the competitive structure of the PC software business.

8. *Misjudging competitive position.* Technology changes, regulatory pressures and related factors make it extremely difficult to assess accurately the strength of an acquisition or alliance target's competitive position or what unexpected events can erode it. After PCS, the US-based prescription drug distribution company, was acquired by Eli Lilly, the US Congress ruled that PCS could not discriminate against other drug companies whose products it distributed. Forced to sell its direct competitors' products, Eli Lilly eventually wrote down the value of its investment by over $1 billion.

9. *Underestimating investment needs.* Acquirers or alliance partners often seriously underestimate the investment in management resources and capital required for implementation. BMW's acquisition of Rover for $1.2 billion in the early 1990s, for example, led to additional investments that totaled a staggering $5 billion over five years. In AT&T's acquisition of NCR, major change management obstacles and cultural differences were never overcome. NCR was subsequently divested, but only after billions of dollars had been pumped into it.

10. *Failing to manage postdeal integration or strategy implementation.* With so much emphasis placed on making the deal, all too often postdeal implementation is an afterthought. Once the announcement has been made, management typically awakens to a cold reality: *strategy* and *execution* are two different animals. Deal strategy and deal execution often become disconnected and the results are never positive. Such experiences strongly underscore the importance of striving for "accelerated transition" to achieve early momentum, early stability, and quick wins during implementation.

> **The companies involved must share a clear strategic purpose and compatible marketplace objectives, strong enough to support integration.**

Avoiding these pitfalls requires constant vigilance; indeed, they are encountered at every stage of the deal-making process. If an M&A or alliance strategy is poorly conceived, for example, its implementation is necessarily doomed. Conversely, the best strategy in the world will prove of little value if it is badly implemented.

## VALUE-ENHANCING DEALS: SIX CRITICAL SUCCESS FACTORS

Successful deals don't happen by accident. CFOs with strong track records consistently attend to the six Ps:

- *Purpose: be brutally honest about your objectives.* The companies involved must share a clear strategic purpose and compatible marketplace objectives. This clarity of purpose and direction must be strong enough to support the integration or alignment of critical resources and capabilities.

- *Planning: plan, plan, plan (do it now).* Planning is not just a predeal activity, but a continuous process. The key here is to create continuity between front-end strategic analysis and the back end of the transaction process, i.e., the postdeal transition and/or integration phase.

- *Process: rigorously manage the whole deal continuum.* All parties involved must take a disciplined, consistent approach to assessing potential business models, growth synergies, and common, or divergent, decision-making and operating styles.

- *Price: pay the price that's right for you.* There is no right price for an acquisition, but there is one right price for each potential bidder. Accurate pricing is closely linked to the market's evaluation of the company's ability to implement. In strategic alliances, "price" translates into the investment of both dollars and resources required.

- *Pace: act with incredible speed.* Speed greatly increases the chances of success of any transaction. The more quickly integration is achieved, the more rapidly a merged company or alliance can build momentum.

- *People: communicate and act with absolute integrity.* Cultural fit is a pivotal issue in any cooperative venture, regardless of structure. It is especially critical, however, in deals involving high-tech companies where true value is generated not by the product base acquired, but by the innovative capabilities of the professionals added to R&D teams.

## GETTING IT RIGHT: EMERGING BEST PRACTICES

Let's look at how the principles of the six Ps play out in both traditional M&A situations and more fluid and complex partnership options, such as strategic alliances. How can you increase the chances of generating real shareholder value?

CASE STUDY
Cisco Systems' Acquisitions Strategy

*Cisco Systems is the world's leading end-to-end networking solutions provider. It has acquired 70 companies in the past six years; in one 10-day burst in August 1999, it made moves to acquire four different companies, including the $6.9 billion purchase of the optical networking equipment maker Cerent. Few management teams understand the complexities of assessing, purchasing, and assimilating a new company as well as Cisco's. Here CFO Larry Carter outlines his company's game plan.*

*Cisco's strategy*

*When we acquire a company, we recognize that what we're acquiring is not so much its current products; it's the next generation of products through its people. If you pay $0.75–4.5 million per employee and all you're buying is the current product portfolio, then you are making a terrible investment. In the average acquisition, 40–80% of the top management and key engineers leave within two years. We measure success in our acquisitions very simply. It's the retention of people and the revenue that we generate from them two or three years later.*

*Our approach to acquisitions*

*Our approach to M&As is simple. We apply the following five key criteria. And if we don't match at least three of the five, we don't touch it:*

- Shared vision: *you have to be in agreement with where the industry is moving and what role each partner wants to play in it. If the visions are different, or the roles don't complement, then it will be impossible to make the relationship work.*

- Short-term wins for acquired employees: *new employees have to see a future. In the immediate aftermath of a takeover or merger, people can be very uncomfortable. When you're paying a premium for intellectual capital, you can't afford to disregard how people may be feeling. When we look at the potential revenue stream from an acquisition, we look two or three years out.*

- Long-term strategy wins: *the long-term strategy of potential partners is another important consideration. We focus on long-term wins for shareholders, employees, customers, and business partners.*

- Similar cultures or chemistry: *possibly the most important factor of all. This doesn't mean that one chemistry or culture is right; but if the cultures are different, they are likely to remain so. We avoid the temptation of thinking that although the cultures may be different, we can somehow make it work.*

- Geographic proximity: *if you're doing large acquisitions, you need to have geographic proximity to your current operations. Otherwise you have the head of finance in one location, the CEO in another, the head of sales in another, and you'll create politics forever.*

*Our basic approach has served us very well. People underestimate how difficult these deals are to do. If we don't meet these basic criteria, we will walk away. Indeed, we have killed as many acquisitions as we have made; it takes courage to walk.*

## On dotcom start-ups

*If you consider how fast the technology industry is growing, many start-ups are simply being realistic when they set up with a view to being taken over by ourselves, AOL or Microsoft. There is consolidation going on. Customers don't want more vendors in their network or environment; they want fewer. So you have to align based on how customers are purchasing.*

## On the future

*It's my belief that the companies who win in the future will master five things:*

- *Having a horizontal business model*
- *Having open standards*
  - *proprietary standards are history*
- *Attracting and maintaining talent*
  - *a handful of bright engineers will outproduce 1,000 average ones*
- *Moving fast to exploit opportunities through empowered employees*
- *Focusing on customers*
  - *"customer-driven" used to be a magical philosophy, but in the new Internet society, customer expectations and what they'll pay for are going to change so rapidly that any company and any industry that doesn't have its finger on the customer will get left behind*

---

Cisco's sharply focused, value-driven approach to the M&A process highlights the importance of combining strategic clarity with aggressive execution. With this in mind, how can you, as CFO, play the deal-making game better, whether you're pursuing an M&A or a strategic alliance? Here are some best-practice guidelines for CFOs that can significantly increase the chances for success:

- Examine the odds carefully
- Plan for postdeal integration
- Move from due diligence to value diligence
- Build a value staircase
- Keep pace with implementation dynamics
- Search for the parenting advantage
- Track performance using a value scorecard

## Examine the Odds Carefully

Many present-day acquisition premiums pose unrealistic challenges. The performance improvements they demand are virtually impossible to achieve, even for the best managers under the best industry conditions. It's critical to recognize that a target's share price already has built-in profitability and growth expectations. By and large, share price valuations are driven by the future discounted cash flows that the market believes current management is capable of delivering. Simply to close the value gap, you'll have to:

- Meet investors' existing performance improvement expectations, not just for the target but also for your own company.

- Lift performance above the market value of the target to that implied by the premium.

Before shifting into a deal-making mode, get beneath the numbers and establish what you must do to realize any notional synergies in the deal. An overreliance on complex valuation models, combined with poor understanding of how synergy is achieved, has led to many predictably bad acquisitions and caused destruction of billions of dollars in shareholder value. The same can be said of strategic alliances.

True synergy can be defined as an increase in competitiveness and resulting cash flows beyond what either of the two firms could have been expected to accomplish independently.[3] The easiest way to lose is by failing to evaluate synergies in terms of measurable improvements in competitive advantage. If instead you ask yourself not simply how you are going to recover the premium, but how and if the merger is going to extend or strengthen competitive advantage, you can more accurately assess whether the proposed deal holds genuine promise.

## Plan for Postdeal Integration

How will you tackle integration? How fast should you go? What changes must be made, and when? How will you make the changes stick? What can you do to ensure that key people, many of whom will not take part in a deal's formative stages, commit fully to the new venture?

Historically, acquirers have viewed proposed deals from either a strategic or a financial/economic standpoint. Organizational change has been considered only as an afterthought. The best approach links all stages of the transaction process, from predeal analysis to implementation, by continually bringing to the surface and questioning the assumption underlying any deal; namely, that you can successfully integrate the two firms involved. And it keeps the creation of shareholder value at center stage.

The CFO and his or her staff are ideally suited to act as the *glue* ensuring that proper integration teams are formed and guided by clear shareholder value objectives. Again, there should be no split in the process between predeal and postdeal. Good integration plans are created early and in sufficient detail. They are comprehensive and flexible enough to accommodate the inevitable changes required as new findings are revealed. Focus on value, start as early as possible, incorporate new priorities as they emerge, be specific on timing and responsibilities, and above all, share your plans widely and secure the buy-in of those involved.

In communicating, include all your target audiences: shareholders, bankers, suppliers, customers, employees, and sometimes regulators. As each group has different concerns, you must tailor your message to each constituency. But these messages must be consistent and without hype. Come up with a communication strategy early on in the M&A process, make the messages timely, content-rich, generally supportive of strategic objectives and, in particular, sensitive to local cultural requirements.

Fail to plan adequately for integration before the deal is done and you'll almost certainly doom your company to unpleasant surprises later on. Consider the question of corporate culture. Unless the two organizations have reasonably compatible cultures, people in the target company are likely to work hard against integration. There are countless cases where a clash of cultures could have been spotted early on and dealt with to prevent the deal from running into trouble (Figure 9.2).

For example, the merger of the two pharmaceutical companies Upjohn and Pharmacia was dragged rapidly into the shareholder value destruction zone by major cultural differences. Management recognized too late that employees in the US and Sweden had significantly different values, beliefs, behaviors, and policies. Once integration was under way, it was obvious that inherent organizational problems meant assumptions made in the valuation process could not be realized. With the deal at risk, a new CEO was appointed to turn the situation around.

## Move from Due Diligence to Value Diligence

Delivery of value after the deal has generally been viewed as a shared responsibility assumed by members of a company's top management team. Today, however, this responsibility is increasingly shifting to the

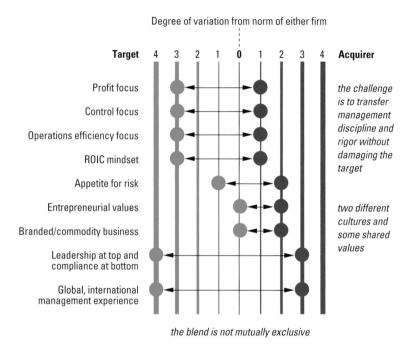

Degree of variation from norm of either firm

| Target | 4 | 3 | 2 | 1 | 0 | 1 | 2 | 3 | 4 | Acquirer |

Profit focus

Control focus

Operations efficiency focus

ROIC mindset

*the challenge is to transfer management discipline and rigor without damaging the target*

Appetite for risk

Entrepreneurial values

Branded/commodity business

*two different cultures and some shared values*

Leadership at top and compliance at bottom

Global, international management experience

*the blend is not mutually exclusive*

**Figure 9.2** *Example of a high-level cultural assessment*

CFO, who often acts as sponsor for the implementation. This sponsor-ship role is critical since it focuses on leveraging synergies and releasing value.

Most firms undertake financial due diligence. But many overlook the need to assess a target's culture, processes, and networks, even though these clearly have a fundamental impact on the drivers of cash flow and value. A more complete approach places emphasis on what happens downstream of deal consideration, through a process we can call "value diligence."

Value diligence preferably involves securing the cooperation of target management. This might seem a radical departure from traditional practice, but successful mergers down the years have proven both its feasibility and its wisdom. A target's managers are often willing to be included in the process because they're looking out for their personal interests. This was the approach adopted by successful leveraged buyout firms such as KKR, which has routinely generated investment returns of 25–40%.

Creating a role for target management at an early stage enables you to:

- Learn about risk and opportunities in the target's business that otherwise wouldn't surface until after the transaction. Clearly, an essential step in prudent investing is to uncover as much as possible about a company from the individuals familiar with it.

- Assess the quality of management in the target, which can profoundly affect the underlying value of the business.

- Forge a commitment to deliver projected results. Almost all economic value will be created postdeal, during the implementation of the integration program, through interaction among people who must be willing and able to collaborate in the transfer of strategic capabilities.

## Build a Value Staircase

Advanced diagnostic tools demystify the traditionally complex deal valuation process normally understood only by corporate financiers and economists. They help you to isolate the components of the *value staircase* you must climb if a deal is to create incremental shareholder value (Figure 9.3). You can start to construct a value staircase by determining six value components:

1. The target's intrinsic value, assuming 100% equity funding and a nonoptimal balance sheet structure.

2. The value added by adopting the optimal financial structure.

3. The value added by achieving the performance improvements assumed by investors in the target's current share price.

4. If relevant, the value added by lifting the target's performance to the level of the best-performing company in the industry sector.

5. The shortfall between the proposed purchase price (including the value gap bid premium) and the sum of value components 1 to 4; this is the aggregate value of the cost synergies and strategic growth needed to close the value gap.

6. The value of the cost synergies and additional strategic growth needed to provide an acceptable rate of return on investment for your shareholders, assuming a reasonable degree of risk.

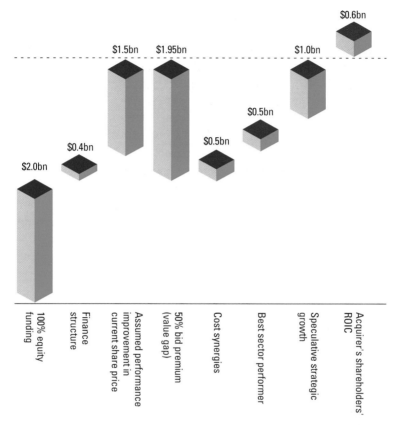

**Figure 9.3**  *Value staircase for a target with a $3.9 billion market value*

By providing an objective picture of the challenges ahead, the value staircase helps you make decisions about key strategic, tactical, and operational issues. It also makes transparent to everyone involved the assumptions on which financial and economic forecasts are founded. Only if these assumptions are reasonably accurate and realistic will value be created.

How can you judge whether projected results are attainable? First, examine the drivers of cash coming into the business, generally turnover growth and cash profit margins. Then look at the drivers of cash going out, the cash tax rate (actual tax paid), fixed-asset expenditure and working-capital expenditure. Next consider the weighted average cost of capital (WACC) or discount factor. This takes into account risk, the balance of equity to debt funding, and the capital structure of the business. Finally, examine changes to these drivers during the competitive advantage period for the merged firm. This is the time frame within which the capital markets believe that the firm is capable of maintaining returns above its cost of capital.

By comparing your findings with the performance improvements needed to close the value gap, you can gauge the scope of the implementation challenges you face, viewing them from investor, industry and competitor peer group perspectives and against the target's performance to date.

## Keep Pace with Implementation Dynamics

With the days of heavy cost-cutting generally thought to have ended, many companies are pursuing mergers and acquisitions in order to achieve strategic growth ambitions. Those that succeed pay close attention to the dynamics at work during implementation.

Speed of integration   In a recent survey, 89% of respondents said they wished they had implemented their M&A more quickly. The most common implementation mistake is moving too slowly. Time is money: the longer you delay substantial integration, the bigger the performance improvements you will have to achieve.

In two takeovers by two firms in the same industry sector, different timetables led to dramatically different results. In Figure 9.4 both merged firms are assumed to have similar financial profiles, giving them a level playing field. Competitor B, believing that revenue would remain steady, was relatively slow to begin reducing costs. Competitor A moved more quickly, protecting its resource-generating capabilities despite rapid revenue decline. A was 10 times more profitable than B at the end of the fourth year.[4]

Market and customer dynamics   Competitors react immediately once a deal is announced, and the longer it takes for your company to realize its synergies, the greater the likelihood you'll lose the game. The market begins to change along with customer dynamics.

To help management anticipate these dynamics, use a value-based decision-support system. It should combine financial and economic analysis with systemic simulation to analyze the competitive interplay in varying strategic, tactical, and operating scenarios. The system should be

| Competitor A | 0 | 1 | 2 | 3 | 4 | Cumulative |
|---|---|---|---|---|---|---|
| Revenue | 2000 | 1700 | 1400 | 1200 | 1300 | profit yrs 1–4 |
| Cost | 1600 | 1400 | 1200 | 1000 | 1000 | |
| **Profit** | **400** | **300** | **200** | **200** | **300** | 1000 |

| Competitor B | 0 | 1 | 2 | 3 | 4 | Cumulative |
|---|---|---|---|---|---|---|
| Revenue | 2000 | 1700 | 1400 | 1200 | 1000 | profit yrs 1–4 |
| Cost | 1600 | 1600 | 1400 | 1200 | 1000 | |
| **Profit** | **400** | **100** | **0** | **0** | **0** | 100 |

**Figure 9.4** *Impact of a one-year delay in cost reduction*

capable of mimicking the behavior of a multitude of variables and relationships as a given scenario unfolds. At the same time, the business process model provides a stream of valuable updates to the base case P&L, balance sheet, cash flow and balanced scorecard. Along with modeling competitor reactions, the decision-support system can be used to evaluate change proposals within the integration plan.

**Growth rates and terminal value**   Be careful about making assumptions of growth and using them as the basis of terminal valuation. Growth rates of 20% have not been uncommon in recent years, but what would happen if actual performance were 12% or less? Whatever assumptions you make, the reality is that sustained performance improvement will be needed to close the value gap. One frequent hidden assumption is that the target's performance will never fall below premerger levels.

In mergers in mature industries, or where the level of capital intensity is high, recovery of the premium is often justified in one of three ways: growth is assumed to go on forever; growth is projected to take off some time in the future, usually after the third year; or the calculation of terminal value constitutes more than 70% of the total valuation. When tested against a given sector's changing dynamics, such assumptions have often proven to be unfounded.

**Interaction between value drivers**   A one-dimensional view of any change proposal is never adequate. Take the example of a major merger between two fast-moving consumer goods companies. This is a merger of equals.

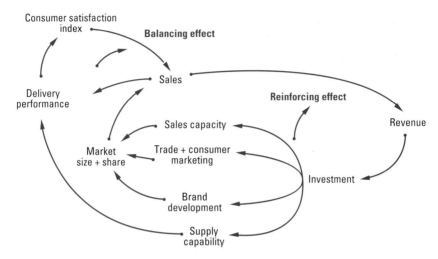

**Figure 9.5** *Trade-offs in the fast-moving consumer goods industry*

The absence of a premium in the deal increases the chance of success. But even in these circumstances, victory won't come easily. Not only do both firms' predeal share prices already reflect performance improvement targets, but the stock market generates its own premium by bidding up the stock to reflect expected merger benefits.

So here too, management is asserting that it will meet market expectations, close the value gap, create a bigger business, and absorb substantial integration costs. Figure 9.5 shows the investment trade-offs the newly merged entity has to make, built into a *cause and effect* relationship business model. Here investment in brands (through advertising) actually reduces the previous year's economic profit. But the longer-term consequence of focused investment in brands creates market share and additional sales, increasing economic value in the future. In the newly merged company, strategic trade-offs between long-term investments in intangibles, such as brands, can be weighed against the short-term benefits of improving supply through the integration of distribution channels.

## Search for the Parenting Advantage

As a new parent company, it's crucial to establish as early as possible how you can positively influence the target's business. Inevitably, you can add only limited value through cost reductions and process improvements. In most cases these steps are not enough to recover the premium paid and create a return for your shareholders.

Success depends on achieving revenue growth by, for example, increasing market share or taking the target into new markets and territories. Take time to examine the nature and degree of fit between the two organizations. What are the critical success factors driving the target's business? What opportunities exist for boosting its performance? Which of these can you best exploit?

Take the case of Diageo. When the merger between Grand Metropolitan and Guinness was announced, Diageo's CFO stated the objective of the deal: "We will be the world's leading branded spirits and wine business. This step change in scale will provide the new group with five valuable benefits which, together, will establish a platform for sustained future growth, including a complementary and broad product and brand range, greater geographic breadth, enhanced marketing capability, greater cost efficiency and financial capacity to develop businesses."

Pulling off such an ambitious growth strategy, even when justified by the available brand and channel leverage, is difficult unless the investment trade-offs are clearly understood. In other words, high-level vision statements must be translated into solid operational programs that can be executed by line managers. Ultimately, the newly constituted Diageo corporate center provided critical leverage through the sharing of brand expertise, promoting core competency on a global scale, and supporting a performance-based management culture.

Contrast Diageo's approach with the $6 billion takeover by another global consumer products company of an entertainment company with a portfolio of music, theme park, movie, theatre and merchandizing businesses. Conventional assessments were abandoned when the lack of identifiable synergies signaled that an alternative approach to integration planning was needed. Instead, the parties used value chain and core competency concepts to develop a resource-based strategy with four objectives:

- Take full advantage of the parent's ability to provide strength and expertise in sales and distribution, brand management, marketing, and financial management.

- Outsource aspects of the music business that could be performed more flexibly and at lower cost by an external service provider.

- Create a unique organizational model for managing the show-business side of the company, essential due to the differences between managing artists and branded consumer goods.

- Implement a risk management program for dealing with newly acquired high-tech products and services.

Business design is the most important determinant of competitive advantage, but in our experience it usually receives scant attention from new parents. Major options for the target include (1) retaining its standalone status, (2) retaining its standalone status but with a change of strategy, (3) becoming a division of the acquirer's operations, (4) being 100% integrated into the acquirer's structure, and (5) taking over the acquirer's existing business (reverse takeover).

Your choice of design and associated operating strategy should address how the business will become more competitive across the entire value chain. This means studying competitors' business designs along with their R&D efforts, alliances, and strategic positioning, and then acting to change the industry structure and drivers in your favor.

The rise of very large deals, $150 billion plus, such as the merger of SmithKline Beecham and Glaxo Wellcome, has fueled debate about how to structure and manage vast new enterprises for optimal value creation. But shareholder value is quite independent of the size of the two parties. Often it is smaller firms that introduce more innovative and powerful business designs, capturing most of their industry's market value and growth. Rewarded by investors and customers, such brilliant moves force industry incumbents into defensive plays.

Business design also plays a critical part. It should define the new role of the corporate center: not merely who gets what job but how the center will influence value creation (Chapter 10).

## Track Performance Using a Value Scorecard

How will you know whether you're on track for value creation? The problem with using traditional, accounting-based performance reporting is that implementation of a deal sanctioned on the basis of discrete discounted cash flow analysis is monitored on a completely different accounting basis. As a result, managers are forced to play the game blindfolded.

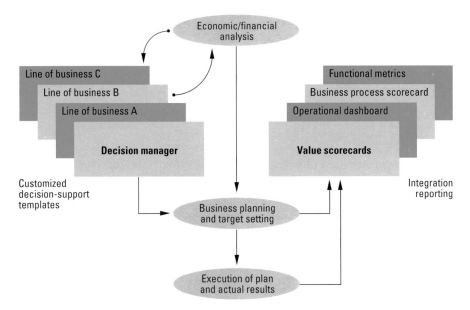

**Figure 9.6**  *Using an integrated value scorecard*

Advanced decision-support systems make it easy to link decision making, reporting, and follow-up within a shareholder value framework. Using a value scorecard, the system balances financial and nonfinancial key performance indicators, and hardwires them to the profit and loss and balance sheet (Figure 9.6). On an ongoing basis you can measure progress against your original M&A criteria. You can:

- Determine whether the speed of integration matches milestones set for closing the value gap.

- See how different functional parts of the business affect the drivers of business performance.

- Assess the impact of strategy, timing, and policy changes from multiple perspectives.

- Segment value management, by channel or brand for example, and use drilldown metrics to put this information into action in the guts of the business.

- Bridge strategy, finance and economics, and operations.

- Discover the intended and unintended consequences of decisions.

As a new parent company, you will be successful only if you extract more value from the business than its original owners could have done independently. With ever bigger proportions of managers' compensation, at all levels, being linked to the value of their companies, everyone has a personal interest in understanding how to meet performance improvement targets.

## VALUING CULTURAL FIT

Failure to bridge the culture gap during postdeal integration is the most frequently cited barrier to successful M&As and strategic alliances. Bringing two different cultures together is not as simple as trying to get everyone heading in the same direction. What appears to be a straightforward strategic fit often becomes very challenging from an implementation standpoint.

Consider the complexities of bringing two very different brands under common control, or of combining two very different operating models under a new single management. For example, the merger of the German company Daimler-Benz with US Chrysler was to create a new company with a market capitalization in excess of $100 billion. The challenges of melding the brand and realizing cost savings through joint purchasing were overshadowed by the challenge of merging German and American notions of capitalism. While the combined company continues to make inroads in the marketplace, the Daimler group has emerged as the dominant company and the combination could more accurately be characterized as an acquisition. In the following example, the cultural challenges were even more pronounced.

CASE STUDY
Planning Cultural Integration

*When a US-based hotel company wanted to buy a similar business owned by a Japanese conglomerate, cultural issues emerged early in the negotiation process. The price paid was clearly important, but addressing cultural differences ultimately proved even more so. The company was credited with success in the deal because it overcame this potential barrier by capitalizing on its previous M&A experience in Japan.*

*At the time, the acquisition boosted the company's shareholder value by* *some $3 billion. This increase was attributable to the synergies arising from expected revenue growth and cost savings from combining hotel back-office systems. But it was also dependent on bringing together two very different cultures. The company set the integration process in motion immediately after the deal was announced. Integration teams covering revenue generation, central services, systems integration, and brand awareness were launched. Implementation plans focused on combined service concepts, joint initiatives, timing, resourcing and priorities.*

*The CFO said, "We were quick off the mark in putting together an integration plan which was comprehensive in that it covered both revenue upside as well as cost reduction in the search for value. We also built a new umbrella brand which enabled us to exploit branding synergies across our entire hotel portfolio. This in itself added shareholder value.*

*"The learning points? Well, we should have started the integration planning earlier, enabling us to deliver the benefits quicker. Time is money! We've also spent an enormous amount of senior management time on employee communication, recognizing that we had a major task in bringing together two very different cultures."*

---

How does culture affect shareholder value? How do you plan for the softer benefits? How do you avoid unnecessary conflicts, but face up to the tough people decisions? How do you make people issues everybody's issues, not just HR's?

History has shown that integration initiatives can actually destroy value by damaging positive aspects of your existing culture. Conversely, your existing culture can destroy value by damaging the positive aspects of your integration initiatives. Therefore, the full value of synergies will be realized only when your integration initiatives and your culture are mutually reinforcing.

And how do you determine that point of synergy? Map integration initiatives against cultural characteristics, for *both* the target and the acquirer. Determine:

- Where your cultures need to change
- Where your cultures must not be changed
- Where your integration initiatives need to be modified or abandoned

# ASSIGNING FINANCE'S INVOLVEMENT IN M&A ACTIVITIES

Strategic activities will remain important for CFOs: analysis of the value embedded in both tangible and intangible benefits will always be vital to ensuring the underlying soundness of a proposed deal. But the shift toward postdeal completion is a necessary response from finance to the poor track record of M&As in the past and the complexity of strategic alliances as well. No longer confined to the security of its predeal silo, finance will need to take an active role in ensuring that the integration and/or alignment of partners proceeds efficiently after completion of the deal. The CFO's role in M&As should focus on four areas:

- *Strategy*: analyzing the partnering activities of competitors and evaluating targets.
- *Value*: analyzing how to structure the deal (including raising finance if needed), due diligence and a high-level, top-down assessment of synergies.
- *Transition*: assessing legal and technical issues, such as how to integrate systems and satisfy statutory reporting requirements.
- *Transformation*: releasing value and tracking benefits.

Integrated finance moves to another level of sophistication when organizations bypass the M&A route and embrace more complex and demanding forms of partnership. Nowhere is this truer than in the telecommunications industry.

CASE STUDY
One Global Venture: Two CFOs

*Two telecommunications companies came together to form a global joint venture with two main purposes:*

- *To bring complementary geographic strengths in Europe and Asia.*
- *To provide large multinational customers, who require global coverage, with a one-stop shop for all their communication needs.*

*For one company the global venture represented an important addition to its existing international investment portfolio; but for the other company it was more than a portfolio investment, it was an essential step in becoming a truly global organization. One company had a financially oriented culture that stressed financial control of operations; the other's engineering bias was geared to technical excellence. Both organizations wished to become more innovative and agile.*

*One of the key challenges in forming the joint venture was bringing together two corporations with distinctly different geographic and cultural backgrounds. The first step was to recruit a CEO, someone from within the telecommunications industry but who had no prior connection with either company. He was given free rein to appoint his senior board and select executives from both companies and the outside. These executives are empowered to get their respective functions up and running. The CEO has set a broad strategic framework within which the new organization can establish its own ways of working, effectively creating a new culture by leveraging the relative strengths of the parent organizations.*

*At the time of this writing, there are two CFOs. Their joint task has been to build a robust financial management function. The two parent organizations were to provide transaction processing operations, covered by intracompany agreements that defined levels of service and costs. The challenge for the joint CFOs was to provide sufficiently detailed management information and control when they did not have direct ownership of the basic accounting services. As the new organization matured, the financial management service would become more independent of the two parents, although some element of shared service would likely remain.*

*As far as finance is concerned, the venture has gone through three stages:*

- *Stabilization: getting control of the basics*

- *Transition: establishing accounting independence and shared services*

- *Transformation: providing strategic decision support*

*Unlike a typical acquisition (where one finance department takes over another) the joint venture had the opportunity to create, from scratch, an agile and innovative finance capability, one that is lean and mean but delivers adequate business support. One of the CFOs said, "Adopting this process enabled us to get control immediately and provided us with a platform for quickly moving to our visionary finance function. Our focus centered on providing value to the organization, not being a cost center. Finance would be embedded within the operating units of the global venture. We intended to make more and more strategic alliances—finance at the forefront in identifying partners, negotiating the deals and integrating the operations. This would have required finance to have a strong sense of purpose and a cohesive identity."*

Globalization, industry convergence and the pace of technological change are factors prompting some of the world's leading organizations to go for less conventional and more innovative ways of joining forces. The venture in the case study offers an intriguing glimpse into the future. Critical success factors for finance integration include:

- Establishing a simple high-level plan for profit and loss, balance sheet and functional cost reporting.

- Quickly establishing a common, standardized financial language.

- Embedding synergy targets in first budgets or rolling forecasts.

- Setting up a finance integration team to avoid polarization between groups from legacy firms.

- Developing a small number of understandable measures that are linked to value and the expected benefits of the merger.

- Enhancing external reporting to communicate value-generating initiatives.

- Closely tracking integration projects based on clear milestones and profitability targets.

The bottom line? Releasing transaction value is the most critical dimension of the CFO's role as strategic architect. The stakes are enormous. Synergistic value can be delivered, dissipated, even destroyed at any point in the transaction process. Effective CFOs adopt a rigorous, three-step process. First, they bring strategic clarity to identifying and valuing potential targets. Second, they broaden their deal-making repertoire to include more fluid, opportunistic partnerships, such as strategic alliances and joint ventures. And third, they apply best practices to maximize the benefits delivered.

---

# eCFO CHECKLIST

## STAY FOCUSED ON VALUE CREATION
Since value can be created or destroyed at any stage of the transaction process, be sure that value creation is the key driver behind every important strategic decision.

## AVOID COSTLY MISTAKES
Use careful planning and proactive problem solving to avoid common pitfalls you encounter throughout the deal-making cycle.

## BECOME A BUSINESS ANALYST
Rather than a market or security analyst, think of your job as *business* analyst. Will the interdependencies of external and internal value drivers lead to better margins, increased growth, and higher-yielding investment?

## ALIGN PREDEAL AND POSTDEAL PLANNING
Don't give short shrift to postdeal implementation. Those heady days of deal strategizing and negotiating are not too early to begin your implementation planning. Devise an integration plan that is comprehensive, flexible, and value-driven.

## REMEMBER: TIME IS MONEY
From a purely financial standpoint, the faster the implementation, the faster you realize returns on your investment. From a human resources viewpoint, speed reduces pain. In the investment community, analysts want quick evidence of meaningful progress against objectives.

## DON'T BE BLINDSIDED BY CULTURAL ISSUES
Identify cultural roadblocks sooner not later. Take the concept of cultural fit seriously and work overtime to make it a reality.

---

COMMUNICATE EARLY AND OFTEN
Frequent communication can help you shut down the rumor mill,
tap the full capabilities of your newly acquired management team
or alliance partner, and build momentum quickly. Failing to
communicate consistently and forthrightly may lead to an exodus
of valuable talent you can't afford to lose.

PAY ATTENTION TO FINANCE INTEGRATION ISSUES
The finance function leads the development of business design
that is so critical to postdeal integration. Plan how and where to
merge or coordinate finance resources for optimum efficiency, or
the value proposition underlying your deal can quickly unravel.

# CHAPTER 10

# Reinventing the Corporate Center

## THE VALUE-ADDED CORPORATE CENTER

*Thomas W. Horton, Senior Vice President Finance and CFO*
**AMR/American Airlines**

*American Airlines is an almost $20 billion company with a widely recognized name and product, the world's largest loyalty program and almost 100,000 employees. Our financial performance tends to be toward the top third of the industry, and we're trying to raise that even further. Toward that end, we recently launched a strategic plan called the Leadership Plan to produce the best possible outcome for shareholders, employees and customers. To do that, we've identified six areas where we must be the industry leader: safety, network, service, product, technology and culture.*

*Within the finance function, we've made a pretty dramatic step in that direction. For instance, we've reduced an organization of 1,500 people by almost half. To do that, we first outsourced much of the work to get our labor rates aligned with the skill sets and services being provided. But we didn't stop there. We also identified a lot of work that simply should have been automated. In this business we have historically dealt with a lot of paper, and in a manual way. We therefore have focused a great deal in the past several years on getting the paper out of the process, such as going with e-tickets, and on automating processes where appropriate. A side benefit of this effort was that we also identified activities we shouldn't be doing in any event, whether manually or automated. This focus has had a huge productivity impact on the finance organization. And it's allowed our employees to focus on more value-added activities, giving them greater job satisfaction.*

*In terms of financial systems, SAP has been by far our largest investment to date. Quite frankly, I think the jury's still out on whether the investment was justified. But it has allowed us to bring our systems into the twenty-first century, and to eliminate a lot of legacy systems that were badly patched together. It's also allowed us to sizably shrink the number of programmers we need on staff to support legacy systems.*

*We also implemented SAP for human resources, which has enabled self-service. This is a great result in that it eliminates paper, it relieves some administrative burden on our managers, and it provides meaningful and timely data to our employees. As our people become more technologically savvy, these types of services should really take off.*

*Creating meaningful communications with our employees is a real challenge. An airline is by its very nature an almost virtual workplace; many of our employees never come to an office. Because we want to change completely the way the company interacts with its people, we also recently funded an initiative that provides a PC for every one of our employees. I think we have a huge opportunity to create a more efficient, effective interface with our employees.*

**Some people view the Internet as an end unto itself.
At American Airlines we prefer to think of it
as a means of transforming our
business.**

*At the other end of the spectrum, American pioneered the Computer Reservation System business many, many years ago. Its outgrowth, Sabre, eventually became the leading computer reservation system around the world. It also evolved into a provider of technology and decision-support solutions to the travel industry. Sabre grew quickly and very profitably, but in ways increasingly divergent from the interests of the airline.*

*Over the years it became more and more clear that owning Sabre created a dysfunctional business model, so we thought it made sense to separate the relationship. Two other reasons highlighted the need. One was that, while owned by AMR, Sabre was hamstrung in winning major contracts with some airlines; they viewed it as doing business with a competitor. The second is that the financial markets were not crediting AMR's market cap with this technology business embedded in the company. So we made the decision to spin off Sabre, which we did successfully in early 2000.*

*Interestingly, Sabre, at the time a company of $1.5 billion in revenues, had an implied market cap greater than the airline which, without Sabre, is a $20 billion company. Shortly after the spin-off, American's stock price rose from $25 to about $37, creating well over $1 billion in market cap for our share-holders and closing the profit/earnings gap versus the rest of the industry. So the spin-off clearly achieved its desired value effect.*

*Preparing for the initial public offering meant creating standalone financial statements for Sabre. We also had to formalize most of our internal business relationships with Sabre, and create a contractual outsourcing relationship with the new company. We separated a number of the corporate center functions which were theretofore comingled, everything from asset accounting to human resources. By the time Sabre was fully spun off, there were virtually no shared services; the relationships between the two companies are now very much at arm's length, and reflect market prices, terms and conditions.*

*Going forward, my corporate development organization is devoting the major portion of its time to Internet ventures. Some people view the Internet as an end unto itself. We prefer to think of it as a means of transforming our business.*

*Business-to-business ventures are also becoming very interesting. One example is the venture we have launched with five other international airlines. We think it has great promise in terms of streamlining our procurement and supply chain processes; it could also save us some money by using techniques like reverse auctions. But we've been having some debate about what we are really trying to accomplish. Are we trying to change our business? Or are we trying to create an Internet company? Or both?*

*New ventures equity is nice, but at the end of the day, our principal mission is to improve the profit and loss equation in the airline. If we can do that, and in the process create some new venture equity value, that's great.*

Most corporations use the term "corporate headquarters" to refer to their corporate center. But the corporate center is much more than the head office with its executive suite. The corporate center is also the financial hub of the enterprise and should be its primary source of shareholder value. In some cases, as with AMR, the corporate center can actually create value. And always, the CFO is at the heart of its operating style.

This chapter shows that one of the keys to building a value-adding corporate center is fostering the right relationship between the center and its business units. For example:

- Is the corporate center a controller of cost or a growth engine? Can it be both?

- How do you sort out those activities that add value and those that don't?

- With the advent of the Internet, can the corporate center be virtual?

- What role should the center play in e-business?

## THE CFO's CHALLENGE

For better or worse, the corporate headquarters affects nearly every aspect of a company's operation and influences its most important decisions, from strategic orientation to M&As and e-business strategy. A corporate headquarters can be either a brake or an engine. It can impede success by burdening business units with costs and sluggish decision making. Or it can inspire businesses to achieve more than they could on their own.

Yet corporate centers are rarely designed with this kind of impact in mind. Instead, they evolve randomly over time, getting bigger and more set in their ways. Still more rarely does their design engage the attention of the finance function, except in relation to costs and headcount. However, corporate centers have such huge power to create or destroy shareholder value that what they do and how they work must be central concerns for the CFO.

Never has this been truer than in the Internet age. Most centers are suboptimally organized, even for existing business. How much less fit, then, are they to confront the challenges of the future, particularly those of e-business? Since the Internet fundamentally alters industry economics, the center is critical in performing evaluations:

- *How will new technologies affect operations?* e-Business offers huge opportunities for centralizing cost savings (e.g., in procurement). By the same token, it also makes such activities easier to outsource. So how far into the virtual world should the corporate center go? Is the corporate center a parent that adds value by influencing or a portal that adds value by facilitating?

- *How should the company approach e-ventures?* As established companies ponder the opportunities and threats of e-business competition, they face a number of dilemmas:

  - Does the corporate center have the skills to incubate and launch e-ventures in-house? If not, can it acquire them?

  - Is it equipped to partner with others to launch a portfolio of e-businesses?

  - Can the corporate immune system cope with a brash new venture that may cannibalize its existing business, or would a quick spin-out be better?

In today's uncertain climate, old paradigms of strategy and organization no longer apply. Change has become continuous, not episodic. Can the corporate center manage this instability? Can it make adjustments to expand business options, while building capabilities and networks to convert those options into real value? This chapter will show how the CFO can be instrumental in defining how the corporate center can add value in the e-business era and in helping the center function at Internet speed.

## WARNING: CENTERS CAN SERIOUSLY DAMAGE YOUR WEALTH

The role of the corporate center is to add value—to do something for group companies that they can't do for themselves. Otherwise it has no purpose. Many corporate centers clearly do add value, in both the old economy and the new:

- Canon's headquarters enables its businesses to recombine their skills and create entirely new divisions.
- Emerson's headquarters often helps newly acquired businesses double their profit margins with its famous strategic planning process.
- 3M maintains a technology-based culture that has made its name synonymous with innovation.
- GE, often described as the best-managed large company in the world, is now urging its businesses to embrace the Internet vigorously.

CASE STUDY
Unilever's Corporate Engine Links Diverse
Businesses around the World

*Unilever has been an international company for almost 70 years. It operates in more than 30 countries, producing fast-moving packaged goods for the mass market in four basic areas: food, personal products, detergents, and chemicals. Prior to its recent reorganization, Unilever became adept at linking its country-focused business units with one another and with the parent's centralized research, management development, and product development capabilities.*

*Though the local business units operated with a high degree of autonomy, Unilever headquarters offered them support in many areas, including research and product development, human resources management, and perhaps most importantly, coordination among international locations and product groups. The company's research laboratories were centrally controlled, but they had to persuade the individual businesses to fund them.*

*One important aspect of Unilever was its strong personnel division, which provided a pool of truly international managers and offered extensive man-agement training activity. The parent was heavily involved in recruiting, career planning, and corporate policies, including the requirement that managers have experience in more than one product area or country.*

*Another powerful value proposition was Unilever's ability to create profit-*

*able links among its countries and product areas. The central category management function was at the heart of this value creation, which was greatly facilitated by a cadre of seasoned expatriate managers, as well as a rotating group of international product managers. The category managers were former marketing directors or senior executives whose function was to help provide information, leverage best practice, and forge links among the company's far-flung operations.*

*In 2000 Unilever divided its business into two divisions: food and household. Much of the value previously added by the center is now the responsibility of the divisions. The company's decision to reorganize in this way has been widely praised, in part because the food and household product areas have some different needs and priorities. By dividing the company into two it should be possible to tailor the added value of the divisions to the specific needs of the two product areas.*

---

Unfortunately, not all centers are as good as Unilever's. Recent experience shows that underachieving corporate centers can seriously damage organizational wealth. In fact, researchers at the Ashridge Strategic Management Centre in the UK have estimated that the *mere existence* of a corporate center places an administrative burden on businesses that can reduce an organization's value by 5–10%. In some cases, Ashridge estimates that this reduction can reach as high as 50% of organizational value. In other words, all things being equal, group companies are normally at least 10% and perhaps as much as 100% better off without a corporate parent.

> ***Misdirection by a mediocre corporate center, or a mismatch between the capabilities of a center and subsidiaries, can actually threaten long-term survival.***

Damage can run even deeper than this. Consistent misdirection by a mediocre center, or a mismatch between the capabilities of a center and subsidiaries, does more than stunt development and kill creativity. It can actually threaten long-term survival. The UK-based conglomerate BTR is a good example. When BTR attempted to reinvent itself as a focused engineering concern in the 1990s, a stream of initiatives from the corporate center failed to produce meaningful results. The culprit was not incompetence or ill will. Business units that were used to a decentralized, strongly cost-oriented regime simply did not know how to respond to the new demands from the center. As profits plunged, BTR merged with rival Siebe.

For similar reasons, it is common for the managers of units spun out of larger groups to comment on the surge of energy and enthusiasm they feel when freed from parental supervision. e-Business spin-offs are a case in point. While the parent views the spin-off as a way to crystallize value, spin-off managers often tell a story of liberation and release from corporate constraints.

## Why Do Corporate Centers Underperform?

Many CFOs are already alert to the potential damage that the corporate center can do. In the survey of over 100 CFOs illustrated in Figure 10.1, more than 65% of those questioned said they were at least "somewhat dissatisfied" with the performance of their headquarters.

There are three potential sources of dissatisfaction. In the recent past, attention has (rightly) been paid to the issue of *excessive costs*. But *lost opportunities* and *damaging influences* have been largely ignored. All three issues are now being urgently brought to the surface by the demands of e-business.

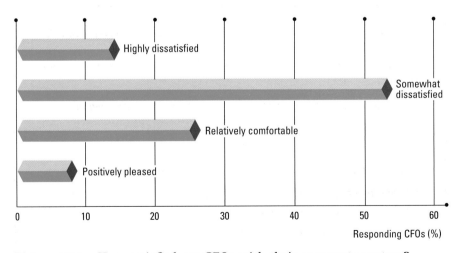

**Figure 10.1** *How satisfied are CFOs with their corporate centers?*

**Excessive costs**   Corporate centers are often larger than needed, usually because they have forgotten their purpose. Functional empire building and senior management requests for information frequently combine with history and other factors to produce a center that is two or three times its ideal size. As with junk in an attic, a center can accumulate excessive costs without regular spring cleanings. The arrival of the Internet is an ideal opportunity for such a spring cleaning, since it can reduce the cost of many corporate center activities and open up new ways for the center to add value to its portfolio of businesses. Launching an e-business is the ideal time to review the purpose of the corporate center.

**Lost opportunities**   Corporate centers create procedures, processes and criteria. Investments that meet a particular hurdle rate are approved; those that do not are rejected. These bureaucratic methods are created with the best of intentions: to raise the quality of decision making, reduce mistakes, and improve controls. But they also contribute to lost opportunities. Decisions and investments that don't fit the mold are rejected or delayed so long that the opportunity disappears. In the e-economy, the rules are changing. Investments that would have been rejected out of hand can now be financed. Business plans that would previously have been ignored are now viewed as growth options. In this environment, companies that do not review their corporate procedures may miss out.

---

## Does Your Corporate Headquarters Add or Destroy Value?

- *Do your business units have a favorable opinion about the effectiveness and style of the headquarters?*

- *Does your headquarters have clearly articulated and widely known value propositions (ways in which it creates value)?*

- *Is your headquarters regarded as an industry leader?*

- *Does your headquarters have defined roles and responsibilities?*

- *Has the company defined performance measures for headquarters and is it meeting its performance targets?*

- *Is the group worth more or less than the sum of its parts?*

**Damaging influences** Corporate center managers exercise significant influence over business units in matters ranging from culture to strategy. In some cases, guidance from the center may be inappropriate. Strategies that work in one business may be irrelevant to another; synergies that appear valuable to the center may actually distract business units from more important priorities. If the center does not fully understand the dynamics and risks of a business, it can easily push the unit off track. This danger is especially strong in e-business, where corporate centers have little or no experience. One recent survey found that 38% of companies that offered e-services had been in business for less than six months. Nearly nine out of ten respondents said that their key managers lacked the skills to make e-commerce happen.

## CORPORATE CENTERS CREATING VALUE

Corporate centers are intermediaries between investors and market-focused business units (Figure 10.2). As such, they can justify their existence only by adding shareholder value. Experience reveals that value is created when three conditions exist:

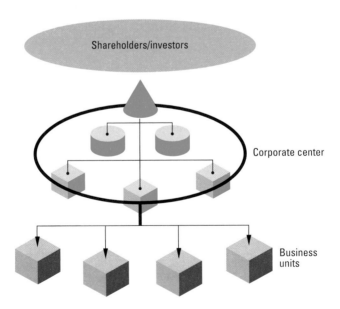

**Figure 10.2** *The corporate center as intermediary*

- The business units are clearly not fulfilling their potential because of faulty strategy or operational shortcomings. In other words, there is a "parenting opportunity" for the center to improve business unit performance.

- The center has the relevant strategic or operational resources, skills, and capabilities to enable the business units to correct their faults. In other words, it has the necessary "parenting skills" to enable them to perform better.

- Center managers understand the business units well enough to avoid influencing them in negative ways by interfering inappropriately (and thus destroying value). In other words, the center has a sufficient "feel" for its businesses.

Undeniably, in most corporate centers, one or more of these conditions are likely to be missing. For example, opportunities are far more common than the skills and resources needed to exploit them. Almost all multibusiness groups have some units that underperform. This is thrown into sharp relief by the growth of e-business. While there are clearly huge opportunities for companies to develop group e-strategies, help business units use e-technology and launch e-channels, the skills and experience to do so are frequently lacking. The fact that companies have been caught off guard by start-ups such as Amazon.com, eBay and others is compelling evidence of this.

"Feel" is also often lacking. This is not surprising, since the technical and cultural norms of e-business differ completely from those of large incumbents. Established budgeting, decision making and review processes are hopelessly inappropriate in an e-speed world where dotcom business plans are put together in days, Web sites can be bought off the shelf, and businesses are launched in weeks.

As we enter the e-business era, many corporate centers face a dilemma. Although there may be an obvious need for headquarters to add needed capital, devise an e-strategy or kick-start a venture, their capacities to do so may not be highly developed. To resolve this dilemma, corporate centers need to take a hard look at their capacities and opportunities and, in light of this analysis, develop a carefully crafted set of value propositions.

## VALUE PROPOSITIONS: THE REAL WORK OF THE CORPORATE CENTER

Each corporate center should be designed around the skills and resources needed to support and grow the businesses it oversees. This requires an eye for value and the skills to grasp it. We refer to these distinctive combinations as *value propositions*—the specific ways in which the corporate center intends to contribute to the value that business unit managers are creating.

Value propositions should be clear enough to be expressed in a single sentence. Here's an example: Because we have relationships in Southeast Asia both with governments and major corporations, and experience in hiring local managers and operating in Southeast Asia, we can help businesses unfamiliar with the region.

> *Most corporate centers will develop several value propositions that crystallize how they will contribute to organizational health and wealth.*

This statement describes the source of the added value—relationships and experience—and explains why some businesses need help—unfamiliarity with the region. It also describes the activities that are given priority in the corporate center—nurturing relationships, maintaining a pool of region-experienced managers, and ensuring that businesses already in the region welcome and support the efforts of sister units.

Most corporate centers will develop several value propositions (probably no more than four) that crystallize how they will contribute to organizational health and wealth. This enables the CFO to:

- Shape an environment that provides the conditions necessary for the creation of value.

- Ensure that the corporate center stays on purpose and remains cost-efficient.

- Ensure that the center focuses on continuous improvement and adjustment, taking every opportunity to deepen its skills and mold new value-creating options.

Centers can develop value propositions in five broad categories: build, link, stretch, leverage, and select. The CFO should review the corporate center's purpose in light of these categories and how they are affected by e-technologies.

**Build propositions**   Build propositions are about helping a business grow, improve its positioning, merge or acquire, or expand its market share, markets, or product offerings. Examples of build propositions include helping businesses globalize, or develop a cluster of related products from a single offering. Build propositions are especially helpful when industries are converging or consolidating. The role of the center is to assist with alliances and acquisitions, and ensure that unit-level managers stay focused.

e-Business opens up a number of build propositions. At GE, Jack Welch launched his destroyyourbusiness.com initiative—a wake-up call to all its businesses not to allow themselves to be "Amazoned."

By investing in appropriate businesses or e-ventures, the center can capture stakes in the new economy that can be integrated with existing businesses once the competitive terrain has become more settled. Two examples are MCI WorldCom's deals in telecommunications and Citigroup's move to become a full provider in financial services. A third example is Prudential's creation of the online bank Egg.

**Link propositions**   Many corporate headquarters define their purpose as helping their businesses create synergies by working together. Shell's far-flung business units have access to their parent's large pool of mobile international managers. Unilever's corporate headquarters provides product research and marketing information to its units around the world. Many companies pool their negotiating power to forge better deals with suppliers, customers, unions or governments; others create extra value by linking upstream and downstream operations. For example, BG Group links its gas asset businesses with its downstream businesses in countries where demand does not match supply.

Conversely, the Internet can make existing link propositions less valuable. For instance, now that communicating among business units is easier, they may no longer need the attention of central experts to share best practices or act as intermediaries. The creation of portals for sourcing components, often involving direct competitors (e.g., the proposed deal between GM, Ford, DaimlerChrysler and others; or between Sears and Carrefour) will make central purchasing functions obsolete.

Stretch propositions   Stretch is the challenge of squeezing more profit from existing operations by reducing costs and/or finding other ways to improve margins. A classic example of a stretching corporate center is Emerson, whose headquarters uses a structured strategic planning process to expand margins and drive performance.

e-Technology makes it easier for corporate centers to monitor performance and develop performance-oriented cultures. Most businesses would benefit from help in making decisions about whether to set up a purchasing portal, for example, or introducing Web-based ERP and other back-office systems. Just as self-service created a new model for companies from McDonald's to Shell, so the Internet extends the opportunity to create virtual self-service models for almost every business.

Leverage propositions   Corporate centers often possess valuable resources and assets that can be leveraged across business units. These include brands, patents, properties, licenses, and relationships with other companies. Disney is a prime example of a company that leverages its brand to create movies, related products and theme parks. Virgin has also leveraged its brand from music to airlines, to financial services, mobile phones, cola, cosmetics, and beyond. Longer term, Virgin may expand into utilities such as energy, linking them in a Virgin portal that connects customers easily to all its offerings. Amazon has also used its brand to enter other retail areas.

Leverage can also create new corporate resources. For example, alliances with leading technology players can be leveraged across a portfolio. AOL's merger with Time Warner aims to leverage Time's content across AOL's distribution capabilities.

Select propositions   Buying, selling and establishing new businesses provides further opportunities for centers to add value, as does the selection of senior managers. Almost all centers seek to create value by developing and selecting good managers. Most have an active portfolio development program, selling businesses that are worth more to others and buying attractive businesses. Some companies, such as Canon and 3M, are famous for their "intrapreneurial" ability, using in-house project teams to develop a constant stream of new companies.

Clearly, e-business technologies are creating many new select propositions. Dixons, a leading electronics retailer, launched Freeserve, Britain's leading Internet service provider. Mannesmann, the German engineering company, entered the mobile telephone market and was subsequently taken over by Vodafone AirTouch.

Other corporate centers are establishing venturing departments to buy, sell, and/or start up new businesses. Johnson & Johnson is exploring the purchase of promising biotech companies. Intel, Microsoft and Sun Microsystems have venture capital arms which invest heavily in companies with promising new technologies. Cisco has acquired more than 50 businesses in the technology area. In the last couple of years, a flood of companies have started incubators or venturing units to launch their own e-business start-ups, e.g., Reuters' Greenhouse fund. Every major corporate center should be reviewing its business development activities along these lines.

New technologies are also creating opportunities for people development and selection. Quality people are scarce in every e-business discipline. Long-term success will favor companies that can attract or develop this scarce resource. Methods of selecting managers for senior posts may also need to change. The sort of manager who has typically led an established retail format is unlikely to be the ideal person for leading a battle against new dotcom competition.

## Choosing e-Value Propositions

Once it is clear that the center is not acting as a drag on e-development, management needs to choose between alternative value propositions. The new technologies are creating so many opportunities that companies are faced with a rich agenda. The CFO plays a key role in ensuring that the right choices are made. If a center lacks the skills to support the value proposition it selects, then it reduces its prospects for exploiting the new economy. If it chooses well, the center's contribution can mean the difference between success and failure.

Will the center launch a destroyyourbusiness.com initiative? Will it focus on using the Internet to drive down costs? Will it act as a magnet for attracting good people? Will it create an e-ventures function? No center can do all of these at once; it must set priorities. It must also avoid doing anything that is better done at the business unit or division level. In many cases this means giving units and divisions more autonomy than they currently have, especially vital in turbulent times.

## Centralization vs. Decentralization

In the past, corporate centers viewed their control over businesses in terms of centralization or decentralization—how far down the hierarchy decisions can be made, at what level the center intervenes, etc. (Figure 10.3). More recently, they have aimed for the best of both worlds: the center takes the lead on the issues it deems most important (the portfolio, etc.) and devolves the rest within a risk management framework designed to ensure that the right decisions are made at the right time.

As e-business networks of interdependent firms emerge, and as companies disaggregate and processes reconfigure dynamically, it is clear that the centralization/decentralization model no longer captures all relevant choices. To succeed in the networked e-world, the center must adopt a far different approach: *loose organization* combined with *tight processes*. In this approach, the risk management framework for the network is provided not by formally delegated authority, but by firmly internalized values that dictate the right thing to do around here. This could be "bad news travels fast" (Microsoft) or "the environmental stuff goes quickly to the top" (Shell).

The center's role shifts from control to coordination, facilitating group activities, disseminating key messages, and reinforcing overarching goals. As organizations become more fluid and the pace of change increases, decisions and actions must become more instinctive. In this environment

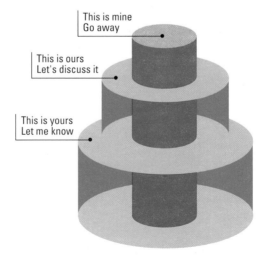

**Figure 10.3**  *Corporate center intervention levels*

the informal shapers of instinctive behavior—leadership, values and culture—become increasingly important.

The center must decide which value propositions it can master. It must develop skills that surpass those of its businesses and equal those of its external rivals. In the area of e-venturing, large corporates are normally at a disadvantage relative to dotcoms, which can move faster, attract more committed and capable talent, and form alliances more freely. Hence e-venture departments normally need to focus on leveraging corporate resources rather than acting as venture capitalists themselves. However, the opportunities are so rich that, if it lacks more important priorities, a center may want to pursue broad e-venturing activities, especially if it can ally itself with a technology incubator or other skilled partner.

The message: no value propositions are out of bounds. The challenge is choosing those that offer the biggest payoff. The danger lies in not being selective enough or in choosing the wrong propositions; the market's judgment can be harsh. When Reuters announced major corporate initiatives to boost its technology presence, its share price rose 12%. A week later, a major publisher announced a similar package and its share price fell 10%.

## RUNNING YOUR CORPORATE CENTER AT THE SPEED OF e

Whatever the value propositions selected, the Internet and related technologies offer new ways to implement them. Running the corporate center "at the speed of e" requires changes in its size, structure, and culture.

In the 1980s and 1990s, the default approach to corporate centers was limited to downsizing and cost-cutting. Indeed, for many companies, a small headquarters has become a mark of corporate health. Needless to say, this blunt instrument approach is inadequate for the emerging e-world, where the center's role is so crucial and the stakes are so high. If it is to add value in an e-world, you must take a close look at what your center does and how new technologies can improve its cost/benefit ratio.

### Structure and Size

The activities a center pursues fall into three categories (Figure 10.4). *Core*, or compliance and governance, activities are control-oriented and

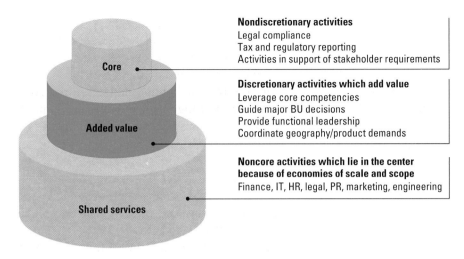

**Figure 10.4** *The corporate center's activities*

generally nondiscretionary—the minimum necessary to fulfill the organization's obligations to authorities and stakeholders. They include legal compliance; regulatory reporting and due diligence control; and the support of stakeholder requirements.

*Value-added* or parenting activities (value propositions) enable the center to contribute to organizational well-being and growth. They define what the center will do to execute its build, link, stretch, leverage or select propositions.

*Shared services* and other support activities are noncore activities carried out centrally because of economies of scope and/or scale. Much of the activity in human resources, IT, finance and marketing may fall into this category. The issues here are cost-efficiency and appropriateness. Since these activities are not central to the value that the corporate level is trying to add, it is important to consider their opportunity costs and value-destroying risks. Increasingly companies are separating these activities into shared service centers to distinguish them from value-added (parenting) activities.

e-Business technologies affect all three areas of corporate center activity. In the core areas, they provide opportunities to change the way that many activities are carried out. For example, the traditional approach of sending shareholders expensive glossy documents, hosting annual meetings, and producing press releases may already be out of date since it is now possible to communicate directly with shareholders via the Internet. Financial control will also change, as Web-based reporting systems become commonplace. In future the corporate center may pull the information it wants from a shared Web-based data center.

No responsive CFO can ignore the Internet's huge impact on the corporate center. Yet why are so few giving it high priority? "We have more important things to do," is the common answer. One global consumer products company was in the middle of a corporate center redesign when the CEO called it off: "We don't have time for this right now—it may distract us from changes needed at division level."

Such avoidance can be costly. Yet there may be even a greater danger in delaying a major overhaul. Changing the way the center works is an important opportunity for senior managers to get close to emerging technologies. If they are not required to confront the implications for their own activities, they may well under- or overestimate the challenges that their businesses face. Moreover, if the center becomes a backwater of the old economy, it will be viewed as irrelevant and quickly lose its ability to add value.

## Culture

Culture reflects the manner in which business is conducted within an organization. Companies can be formal and procedure-bound, or informal and more entrepreneurial; bureaucratic or lean in their processes; rigidly hierarchical or loosely networked in organizational design; cautious and centralized, or bolder and decentralized in their attitudes to risk, with business units empowered to make key decisions.

New technologies demand new cultural attitudes. Unless its center can lead e-business change (or at least protect those moving in the right direction), a company will be severely handicapped in the new economy. Required new attitudes include speed, a new view of senior managers, and the willingness to make mistakes.

Speed is the value most likely to be at odds with the average corporate center. The new economy will not wait for the next board meeting or for poorly presented proposals to be resubmitted. New-economy talent will not wait 10 years for a promotion or submit to three layers of budget review. Speed also requires a new attitude toward senior managers. Corporate centers can no longer be the refuges of managers who are loyal to the company but underperform in a line job.

## Design

Other changes in values may also be necessary. In general, corporate centers need to be less formal, bureaucratic, hierarchical and risk-averse. At the same time, they must not overlook the value of discipline in performance measurement, delivery, and strategic thinking. The successful center of the future must strive for balance; it must find a new way to adhere to discipline while avoiding processes or policies that stifle entrepreneurial spirit.

Figure 10.5 shows that the best centers will become role models for the news way of managing and will have a powerful ripple effect. For each company, the balance among core, value-added and shared services activities will be different. However, the definition of *effectiveness* is always the same. Where an effective parent is at work, ventures with innovative value propositions will reach the customer first. Their competitive offer is enhanced by access to lean and efficient operational

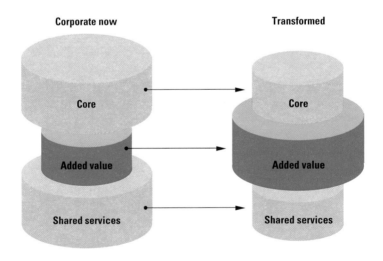

| Corporate now | Transformed |
|---|---|
| • Size result of history and events | • Fit-for-purpose design |
| • Relatively slow to respond | • Responsive/focused |
| • Expensive | • Lean, benchmarked with best |
| • No design link with leadership style | • In line with leadership style |
| • Tends to be bureaucratic | • Appropriate level of formality |
| • Weak link to value proposition | • Clear contract with business units |
| • Functionally based | • Cost controlled |

Figure 10.5  *The benefits of redesign*

structure and back-office processes. Their ideas come to fruition fueled by the collective excellence of the network and the partners within it. A "value web" connects the players, delivering vertical (parent-to-venture) synergies. Meanwhile, access to complementary services and innovations from other ventures leads to horizontal synergies, as the "white space" between them is explored.

## TRANSFORMING YOUR CORPORATE CENTER

As more non-value-adding activities are outsourced, e-business models offer tantalizing opportunities to reduce the center in size, while freeing up its entrepreneurial ambition. The choices at hand are only secondarily about technology; they are primarily about mobilizing and structuring the organization to capitalize on opportunity and risk. Agility and responsiveness are now as important to performance as good strategy, operational excellence, and customer intimacy. The transformed center must reflect this.

Aligning the corporate center with e-business encompasses four distinct stages (Figure 10.6).

**Stage 1: Assess the center** The first stage is to analyze and classify headquarters' current activities and processes. The classification should assign

| Analysis | Implementation | | |
|---|---|---|---|
| 1. Assessment | 2. Design principles confirmation | 3. Design blueprint | 4. Transformation |
| **Purpose:** To establish clear understanding of the business context and parenting opportunities. | **Purpose:** To ensure the leadership team agrees the value proposition and principles for change. | **Purpose:** To translate principles into a practical design, risk assessment and implementation plan. | **Purpose:** To implement and manage the change, and drive out value. |
| The purpose of the assessment stage is to understand the scope, structure and size of the present corporate center, corporate ambition, opportunities for parenting and industry structure characteristics. | During this stage, the top management team confirms the design principles which will set the framework for the corporate center design:<br><br>• Strategy and corporate center value proposition<br>• Leadership style<br>• Size and structure guidelines | The design stage utilizes the analysis from the preceding stages and includes:<br><br>• Processes and activities<br>• System and technology employed<br>• Organization structure and style<br>• People skills and competencies required | The transformation stage enacts the design in a phased approach, identifying key milestones and deliverables.<br><br>Corporate center performance measures and management framework are agreed. |

Figure 10.6 *The transformation process*

activities or processes to one of the three performance arenas: core, value-added, and shared services. This stage also involves reviewing the center's current e-initiatives and comparing them with its other projects. This process evaluates not only opportunities for change, but also how alternative ways of conducting corporate center activities will affect business as a whole.

Bearing in mind the conditions for adding value, as well as how the parent company's value propositions can be adapted to e-business, the assessment will:

- *Identify core initiatives* for using technology to improve the center's functioning and value (changing the balance between activities, setting up a B2B marketplace, outsourcing, etc.).

- *Do an e-parenting analysis* to determine which opportunities the center will be eager to parent, and by which method (e.g., intrapreneuring, venturing, incubating, partnering).

Stage 2: Confirm the design principles    Senior management validates the principles governing the corporate center's design. These principles include characteristics of industry structure and future e-development; corporate center value proposition; and attitudes to risk and leadership style.

The design principles, agreed upon with the CEO, bring into focus the vision for the new headquarters. Here leadership draws out the new paradigm, detailing what it wants and how it will manage, including key messages and policy matters regarding shared services (e.g., outsourcing, centralization).

Stage 3: Redesign the center    The design blueprint translates the new principles and vision into a practical plan. At this stage the new paradigm is compared with the old, and a route map for moving from one to the other is planned, including:

- *Processes and activities* to be undertaken by the center as part of the group's e-infrastructure (what will be outsourced or made into a business unit; parent or portal; etc.).

- *Systems and technologies* to be adopted by the center as part of the group's e-infrastructure (remembering that these are enablers and not ends in themselves).

- *Organizational structure*, including the shape and handling of e-ventures. Emphasis shifts away from hierarchy and management to networks and coordination. Deliberate efforts are necessary to tip the balance of the organization and its initiatives toward the emerging e-agenda.

- *People and competencies*: we evaluate what e-skills we have and where we will get the e-skills we need. What do we offer in return? How can we make ourselves into an attractive e-partner?

A robust design is essential so that the company will not be distracted from fulfilling existing operational objectives. It should take account of practical constraints: potential value destroyers and how they can be eliminated. Cultural issues should never be underestimated; the aim is to bring the center up to e-speed and make it radically more entrepreneurial. As a matter of urgency, the center must find ways to develop its feel for e-business. Finally, it's important to consider how change will affect risk and project management.

Stage 4: Transformation   It is time to implement the design in a phased approach, identifying key milestones and deliverables. By now the new corporate center's management framework and performance measures should be well established. This stage requires that effective change management be put into practice by making hard decisions regarding elimination of activities, outsourcing, reengineering, contractual relationships, and other change management decisions.

Above all, the redesign process must be systematic. External input may be beneficial, bringing with it objectivity and a wider understanding of the e-business arena. In the final analysis, the overarching goal of the transformation process is to *create value*, rather than simply "to do less of what we are doing now." Consider the following case study.

CASE STUDY
The Virtual Corporate Center

*One of the world's leading private investment companies specializing in management buyouts and equity investments has a business philosophy based on deep-seated beliefs. Value is created, the company believes, by focusing on a few fundamentals: solid management, operational excellence, optimal capital structures, and a solid long-term investment program.*

*The company believes that success depends not only on identifying and consummating acquisitions, but also cultivating and nurturing them. After a deal is done, its professionals work closely with management to realize the full potential of its acquisition. The company's focus is corporate restructuring, redesigning the business and its corporate center from top to bottom. In effect, it becomes the newly acquired company's virtual corporate center. Its professionals team with legacy management to:*

- *Determine where value is created*

- *Identify the company's value drivers*

- *Analyze how profits are made and costs can be reduced*

*The team also works together on cash management, clarifying line of sight through transparent financial systems and developing insightful information management.*

*One example of the company's corporate center transformation process is its recent acquisition of a large financial services firm. Despite its size, the firm was vulnerable to its two biggest competitors. Industry consolidation, convergence in financial services, and the potential competition of Internet sales also challenged the acquired firm's future.*

*The parent company's professionals moved swiftly to augment financial and performance management, guiding the acquired firm as it redesigned its corporate center. The goal: to transform it from a directionless, expensive operation to a focused, cost-effective, integrated center with a strong underlying financial system.*

*Developing a thorough knowledge of the firm's businesses was integral to the corporate center's redesign. The combined corporate team determined that customer/business profitability could be enhanced by clear customer segmentation. They saw that they could encourage value-added behavior by changing the firm's compensation structures and offering new incentives to the top 200 executives. The parent is accelerating the center's restructuring—jettisoning budgets, forcing in new systems, accelerating new incentives, and overseeing rigorous cost reduction. The firm faces the challenge of managing these cost-cutting activities without losing revenue share.*

*As the transformation continues, the combined corporate center will divide head office activities among core, value-adding, and shared services. When roles and accountability are determined, it plans to introduce a new performance management regime focused on reducing costs and leveraging new business. Change in the service industry takes time because the focus is on changing behavior rather than closing factories or reducing suppliers. But, as with all its investments, the parent is focusing on the long haul and expects to realize a good return on its investment.*

---

## REMAINING VIGILANT: MEASURING CENTER PERFORMANCE

Corporate centers tend to suffer from a number of debilitating diseases. Left to themselves, they quickly lose effectiveness because of *bureaucracy creep* and *overconfidence.* These diseases are especially dangerous in the fast-forward world of e-business. The only antidotes are vigilance and the willingness to dish out tough medicine when necessary.

- Bureaucracy creep manifests itself as a kind of managerial amnesia, in which center managers forget that their main focus should be on adding value and wealth, rather than administering and developing company procedures. It is difficult to diagnose because the value that centers add can be hard to measure.

- Overconfidence is the opposite of bureaucracy creep. Center managers believe they can add value to anything. They diagnose problems that businesses are facing as having developed because the center was too hands-off. As a result, more and more decisions become centralized.

The CFO needs to be armed with robust performance measures. Core activities are particularly prone to bureaucracy creep and excessive cost. The core should therefore be defined, sized and capped by headcount and inflation-adjusted cost. Increases to the cap should require explicit CFO approval, whether alone or in committee. The core progress objectives should aim at annual cost-efficiency improvements, which should be consolidated into the cap. The best corporate centers expect their cap to be constant or falling in real terms. As a reality check, the core should be subjected periodically to a benchmarking exercise to verify that it is still in line with peer companies.

On the other hand, center value-added activities are apt to suffer both bureaucracy creep and overconfidence. Here the main concern is not cost but the danger of destroying, rather than adding, value. To combat this, companies should subject their center's value propositions and implementation to an annual review. As with most reviews, an objective perspective will likely enhance its rigor. Without a perspective independent of the company power structure, the CFO may never discover his or her own blind spots. Regular feedback from business units is also useful. While allowances need to be made for "them vs. us" differences, feedback is crucial for spotting areas of value destruction.

Shared services are usually easier to monitor. If they have been set up as internal profit centers competing with outside suppliers, then customer input will normally be enough to keep them healthy. Even if the shared services are not full profit centers, customer–supplier relationships will act as an early warning signal if something is wrong. Each service should have the following items as part of its self-management: customer service contracts, clear measures of customer satisfaction, and continuous improvement targets. A diligent CFO can call for these items to decide whether a more detailed review of a particular service is needed.

Ultimately, each facet of the corporate center can be measured and monitored through a performance management framework. Since the corporate center is the responsibility of top management, it should set an example for the entire organization. If a CFO is demanding top-tier performance from his or her business units, it will clearly be unacceptable for headquarters to be second- or third-tier. Only a commitment to continuous vigilance will keep the corporate center on its toes.

The advent of e-business is a breakthrough event in corporate history. From the CFO's viewpoint, it offers the tantalizing possibility of bringing the corporate center up to the speed of *e*. The following step changes are possible:

- Reducing fixed and working capital requirements across the group.

- Reducing transaction and supply cost of sales.

- Dramatically improving timeliness within the company and across the network, as well as the accuracy, availability and usability of management information.

- Increasing the speed and flexibility of response, both financial and competitive, to threats and opportunities.

In short, it's about igniting the corporate center and turning it from a brake on the company's progress to a dynamic asset.

# eCFO CHECKLIST

## REVIEW THE CENTER'S PURPOSE AND CAPACITIES

Does it add value as an e-center? Or is it destroying value through excessive costs, lost opportunities or damaging influences?

## ANALYZE THE FIVE AREAS IN WHICH THE CENTER MAY ADD e-BUSINESS VALUE

Can it build, link, stretch, leverage, or select? Choose areas in which the center has a realistic chance of becoming skilled. Avoid having headquarters do what business units can do better. Cast the net of possibilities as widely as possible.

## ARTICULATE VALUE PROPOSITIONS

These should clarify where and how the center will contribute to meeting business unit needs. Make sure the propositions are well understood by business unit managers.

## REVIEW THE CENTER'S SIZE, STRUCTURE, AND CULTURE

Keep these two objectives in mind: using e-business technologies to speed up, streamline or outsource activities; and making headquarters leaner, more entrepreneurial, and more cost-effective.

## REDESIGN AND TRANSFORM THE CENTER IN SYSTEMATIC STAGES

Lack of time is not an acceptable excuse for putting off this change. At e-speed, the 80:20 rule applies.

## SERIOUSLY CONSIDER CENTER STAFFING

In a transformed entrepreneurial headquarters, there is no place for passengers or time servers.

## ESTABLISH CLEAR PERFORMANCE MEASURES FOR ALL CENTER ACTIVITIES

Include measures for core, value-added and shared services activities; then hold to them. Regularly review and benchmark progress.

# CHAPTER 11

# B2F: The Virtual Finance Function

## HOW FINANCE IS OILING THE WHEELS FOR SHELL

*Stephen Hodge, Director of Finance*
Royal Dutch/Shell Group

*Shell is moving rapidly into all the e-business areas: business-to-business, business-to-consumer and business-to-employee. We have developed and managed new e-business channels inside the existing businesses—with names like Ocean Connect and Level Seas handling bulk transport, commodity exchange and the like. There are also much wider-ranging, transformational initiatives.*

*For example, we set up Shell.com in publishing and TellShell, a conversation site to allow people to say what they think about us relatively uncensored. We also developed Web-based internal communications, covering a whole spectrum of organizational issues such as project management, performance scorecards, office booking, and pension information. In some areas we have set up trans-action systems on the Web, embracing third parties; indeed one of our big successes is Trade Ranger, an exchange owned by 14 companies.*

*Trade Ranger is an example of our most successful adaptation to e-business. It was set up as a separate business with just five of the companies represented on the board yet we still realized this powerful e-alliance in just a few months,* overturning the traditional view of the oil industry's competitive hostility and slow pace of change.

All of this goes beyond simply moving to e-business on the Internet. The expression "digitization" has been used by some to capture the wider implications of embracing the fundamental changes in our whole business.

*The challenge to financial management*

However, with up to 100 initiatives in progress across the United States, Northwest Europe, Australia and probably many more elsewhere not declared, there was renewed concern over resource allocation. This was emphasized by the large outlays associated with setting up certain e-business ventures—exchanges can easily cost in excess of $150 million—which were being written off as operating expenditure around the globe. Were the risks assessed? Were standards consistent? Were the benefits understood? What about duplication and the other consequences of uncoordinated developments?

> **We set up Shell Internet Works as a response to the need to manage our portfolio of e-business investments with a better focus on value creation.**

The main challenge has been to filter the huge number of ideas and manage the promising ones to successful implementation before the expenditure is lost in operating costs. We set up Shell Internet Works as a response to the need to manage our portfolio of e-business investments with a better focus on value creation. Shell Internet Works handles dialog with potential partners and investors, participants, and employees; and it runs a council that brings together the heads of the e-businesses, IT, and services to consider strategic matters only. Our GameChanger approach helps us to coordinate strategic fit and narrow down ideas through a defined qualification process; take the short-listed ideas into a state where venture capital could be justified; then mobilize expertise to support the ideas through to setup or IPO.

This still leaves an important role for the finance function in managing how the chosen ideas fit into the still present legal and fiscal requirements. The different ways of doing business are not always consistent with current business models, resulting in conflicts in commercial practices, reward, performance appraisal and many other matters. For example, we had to develop new ways of remunerating people involved in both the new e-businesses and our specialist financing operation, Shell Capital, and then manage the reaction from some people in the traditional businesses who felt these remuneration packages were unfair. This is just one of the areas where finance must help manage value creation.

We certainly have realized cost savings from both our sizable investment in enterprise resource planning (ERP) and our e-business development. For example, ERP has reduced our costs by some 15% and e-auctions have yielded savings of 5–20%. But if we can go a step further, exploit our ERP investment and, for example, integrate our trade exchanges to create a seamless end-to-end trans- action, the payback should be enormous. Finance needs to be right at the heart of the business, leading such initiatives.

## A vision for the finance function

We anticipated the effects of digitization some while ago when we crafted our vision for finance. We recognized that the concept of a finance function with the right to exist was obsolete—finance would need to earn and maintain its standing as a supplier to the businesses, leading Shell's digitization by enabling e-business process design across the whole value chain.

Our goal was to become the "top performer of first choice," effectively part- nering the business streams in creating and enhancing value. So we came up with a vision to deliver world-class execution of finance. We wanted our finance people at the heart of every business.

This meant refocusing effort away from transaction processing to decision support, while continuing to acknowledge our role in proactively managing systems development and integration to ensure we would get the basics right.

To support this vision, we have now formed Shell Finance Services. Its mission is to provide specialist finance management and decision-support skills to the operating businesses, organized as a virtual business in a few global locations and in competition with external providers. Perhaps seen at first as a *threat to our future, we have found that against this competition, our people have an advantage—they know our businesses and can react to their needs as finance customers.*

## What's new in our finance processes?

*We are fast changing our core processes. For example, we are continuing to build up shared services and outsourcing these services to an even greater extent, using the Net to create virtual shared service centers. Ultimately, we will be able to eliminate the need for transaction processing activity completely, re-placing it with Web-based systems maintenance and audit. We are also developing our corporate finance M&A capabilities to help us structure finance effectively across our geography.*

*e-Business brings us new risks and revisits existing risk priorities. We must deal with risks associated with global customer reach, access to new suppliers, credit risk issues associated with auction versus catalog channels to market, etc. So there will be a new challenge in risk management; we do this already but it will become a higher priority.*

*All this change puts a fresh emphasis on the requirement for rapid and flex-ible access to information on a global basis. Taking advantage of the Web, we are using Web-based information portals to enable our people to make more informed decisions at the times they are needed. These new decision-support tools are underpinned by the investments we have made in ERP. But the business will need to address how our technology architecture is to develop as we overlay existing systems with the requirements of e-business in areas such as customer relationship management or logistics. Finance Services is taking on much of this development.*

## Does the finance function have a future?

*Looking forward, we cannot ignore the promise of vastly simplified electronic transactions reducing and even eliminating related activity, nor the ease of bringing together information from diverse sources into an increasingly virtual finance organization. Therefore I think finance will still exist in the future, but in a very different role. It will continue to become a smaller, smarter outfit. It will be a fascinating place to work because it will function across the business and be instrumental in creating whole new businesses and then managing systems integration.*

*Clearly, we are going to need some high-quality finance people to ensure the systems keep on working; to interpret and comment on the information these systems reveal; and to manage the risks to the business. There will also be financial transactions to originate, treasury transactions, financing transactions, and so on.*

*To make this vision work, we will need to maintain a pool of high-quality people with a new way of working. People who are capable of living in a world where finance is not a room full of green eye-shaded clerks filling in figures in a ledger, but more equivalent to a refinery control room, monitoring immense flows of transactions and controlling them just by exception.*

---

Like Stephen Hodge of Shell, many of the CFOs interviewed for this book see a trend toward "an increasingly virtual finance organization." The evolving finance group that Hodge envisions at Shell will be "a smaller, smarter outfit." It will be extremely proactive and have access to decision-support data gathered seamlessly from diverse sources. Finance will be deeply involved in risk management, creating entirely new businesses, monitoring vast transaction flows, and managing systems integration. These demanding new roles will be supported and enabled by ever more sophisticated e-business capabilities.

What will this virtual finance function look like and how will it operate? How are tomorrow's business demands redefining finance's mission and focus today? To answer these questions, this chapter begins by framing the emerging business-to-finance (B2F) agenda. Then we explore what it will take to translate this agenda into reality. In this context we look at how the drive toward virtuality will transform core finance tasks, from transaction processing to decision support.

## FRAMING THE B2F AGENDA

A survey of 100 CFOs asked them to vote on the future of finance; 25% of the CFOs in the sample said finance would cease to exist as we know it. So how will the finance function evolve? "In six years time finance will be a virtual capability … at the center of a web of relationships … less than half its current size … global, based on products/markets … integral to all key decisions … with the CFO as venture capitalist, analyzing the future not the past … new disciplines and new frameworks … adding value in its own right."

The finance function's move toward virtuality is already well under way. The experience of major corporations indicates that the finance agenda is evolving in four distinct stages or waves:

1. The trigger for the first wave of change tends to be an intervention or disruption, such as a new CFO appointment. If the business is growing rapidly and globally, the operational organization is often complex with differing finance infrastructures and cultures. The CFO tends not to bother with a sophisticated vision, but focuses on getting control, simplifying processes, and fostering collaboration across the finance community.

2. The trigger for the second wave is the creation of a shareholder value agenda, the adoption of best practices, and the search for cost saving through upscaling, possibly through shared services. The goal: finance becomes a value-adding business partner. Its agenda is typically based on initiatives and supported by a value creation message. The finance community is encouraged to move into decision support as rationalization through shared services and outsourcing materializes.

3. The trigger for the third wave is e-business. The organization is pre-occupied with identifying and mobilizing new e-business opportunities. The existing finance change program is put on ice as the CFO comes to grips with new business start-ups, new strategic alliances, and acquisitions, implementing new best-of-breed software. Finance as a function seems to have a lower visibility than customer management, supply chain, and human resources, all of which seem more affected by the Internet. Finance's change agenda focuses on e-business awareness training and the harmonization of existing ERP systems. The finance community is increasingly encouraged to be proactive in leading new e-business ventures.

4. The trigger for the fourth wave is the impact of e-business on finance –the theme of this book. The challenge across the corporation is to

grow share price. The finance vision is more about creating value from finance itself. The finance agenda encompasses decapitalization, seamless transaction processing, increased outsourcing, and integrated decision support. Systems architectures are rationalized, accounting processes take a further dramatic drop in cost, and a new market emerges for finance services over the Web, spawning the development of *application service provision* (ASP) evolving into full *business service provision* (BSP).

Most CFOs find themselves operating somewhere between the second and third waves. They have articulated a shareholder value creation agenda and communicated it enterprise wide. Now they are focused on using e-business as the primary vehicle for achieving their shareholder-value-building objectives. A select group of forward-looking companies have begun to ride the fourth wave by leveraging e-business capabilities to mine more value from finance, transforming finance's primary role from that of gatekeeper to opportunity seeker.

Managing this evolving agenda is a deliberate and creative process, bringing together the financial and business communities, and increasingly, external partners. The finance agenda acts as a bridge, linking initiatives and goals from the old economy and the new. It becomes an integral part of business strategy, changing and growing as fresh value propositions emerge. Over the next five years, we expect the finance agenda of more and more companies to focus on mastering the creation of value from finance itself. Ultimately, this involves four prime areas of "virtual" activity: transaction processing, working capital, treasury, and decision support. Let's look at each more closely.

## TRANSACTION PROCESSING: WEB-ENABLED SHARED SERVICES

Shared services evolved during the 1990s, as large decentralized companies pushed to reduce headcount, cut costs, and improve underlying processes and customer services. Shared service centers (SSCs) are now well established in many companies across geographies and business units. Our five-year benchmarking study looked at more than 80 companies and 1,600 business sites across 50 countries; it revealed that shared service programs have dramatically improved efficiency on many fronts:

- *Procurement*: cost savings of 30% have been realized through new supplier agreements.

- *Customer invoicing*: processing changes have led to cost reductions approaching 40%, primarily in the area of lower personnel costs.

- *Accounts payable*: shared service centers require 60% less personnel.

- *Accounts receivable*: 100% improvement in processing efficiency and 34% reductions in processing costs have been achieved.

- *General accounting*: the required staffing levels have been reduced by 50%.

Most companies with shared service programs find themselves confronting a moving target. There is always more to be done in terms of process, scope, geographic reach, and technology improvements. It is important for the company to be clear about its objectives: do you want a shared service center that is geographically or process/systems based? This clarity of purpose is crucial to success. Figure 11.1 sets out the development routes that companies typically follow:

- *Route A:* shared services focus at first on consolidating local activities into one geographic center to achieve economies of scale and then shift to implementing pan-regional processes. Companies following this route tend to have CFOs who are proactive in persuading the finance community to change. The imperative is cost saving.

- *Route B:* the initial focus is on implementing pan-regional processes and systems with commensurate improvements in consistency and standardization. The geographic consolidation benefits come later. Companies that follow this route place a higher priority on following a clear IT strategy, typically ERP harmonization, than on achieving finance headcount savings.

- *Route C:* this combines geographic consolidation and systems standardization. Doing both concurrently can lead to confusion, increased complexity and failure to keep the program on track. However, some of the most committed companies do succeed via this route and the impact of the Web may make it more viable in the future.

Choosing the best option depends on commonality of processes, systems consistency, and management's appetite for change. For those interested

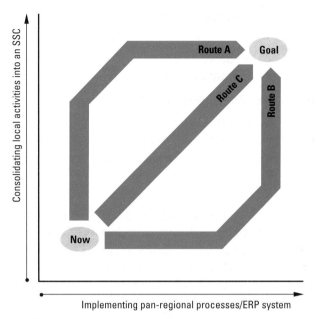

**Figure 11.1** *Shared service center migration routes*

in the move toward virtuality the question is, How are e-business and technology driving the evolution of shared services beyond this point? Web design advances promise to eliminate much of the transaction processing traditionally handled by shared service centers. By shifting finance, human resources and other functions to individual employees and managers on a self-service basis, and even out to suppliers and customers, the Internet should enable shared service centers to off-load time-consuming data entry duties. This will free up personnel to focus on customer service, exception handling, and process improvements.

Will ERP implementations be needed to support full shared services? Yes and no. Web browsers and middleware may be able to integrate disparate systems as effectively as ERP but without massive process re-engineering. However, most companies still view ERP as essential for creating common processes and data standards.

If shared service employees can be freed to concentrate on exceptions rather than routine transactions, they can spend more time helping business units improve their performance. Shared services can assist with problem solving as well as process reengineering. A well-run shared service center can act as an outsourcing business in its own right.

The trend toward convergence of shared services and outsourcing is likely to continue. Transferring an entire accounting function to an independent provider is possible with Web technology, allowing easy access to information both within and across company walls. Clearly, the Internet hasn't evolved to the point where the physical shared service center can be done away with altogether. But that time is fast approaching. In principle, how will a virtual shared service function operate? Here is one prediction of the future.

Virtual shared services are managed seamlessly, enabled by technology, telecommunications and the Internet/intranet. This virtual entity requires no (or very limited) physical relocation and recruitment. In other respects it is still based on proven shared service principles: it's run like a business, with common processes and standards; there are service-level agreements and rewards are team based. Success is predicated on management's commitment to invest in and accept new technology. A culture based on collaboration and networking is a prerequisite. End-to-end processes are the norm; functional barriers don't exist. There is a single common ERP technology backbone; e-business software provides for self-service and tiered delivery. There is a common data model, fully integrated IT architecture, and a data warehouse with the latest analytical tools. Intranet and Internet portals provide access to the shared services.

This may be the future of shared services, but today's realities are far different. The virtual shared service center faces formidable obstacles: local behaviors, culture, consistency and standardization. Nevertheless, the journey to virtuality is inexorable.

Potential shared service operating models are set out in Figure 11.2. Most companies view their development cycles in three-year chunks. Where you arrive in three years depends on where you start. Companies such as Bristol Myers Squibb have the infrastructure, multifunctional process approach, and ERP investment to leverage the full potential available. Other companies which depend more on legacy systems or lack shared service experience, start further back. The jury is still out as to whether they can leapfrog the conventional development path with the new Web technologies available.

The operating models in the figure address the expansion of back-office shared services to incorporate front-office activities:

- *Scenario 1:* the regional back-office model. Typically this is the model currently in operation involving back-office finance activity. Business

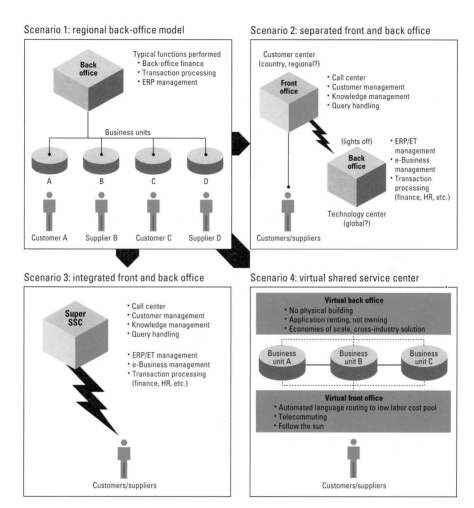

**Figure 11.2** *Shared service operating models*

units (based in countries) are supported by the regional shared service center.

- *Scenario 2:* separated front and back office. Shared services' scope is expanded to include servicing both customers and suppliers from a regional center. In this scenario the front office is separated physically from the back office, which in turn may have been further developed into a global center that is increasingly automated (lights-off processing).

- *Scenario 3:* integrated front and back office. The "super shared service center" (automated and possibly global) includes sales administration and customer management, procurement and other externally focused activities.

- *Scenario 4:* the virtual shared service center. There is no physical office since services are provided over the Internet. Where staff are required, they are provided by a low-cost location with full global language capability. Applications may be rented over the Internet and the service could well be outsourced in its entirety.

In summary, e-business will have a significant impact on shared services. Shared services will become more strategic in providing a business offering to preferred customers and suppliers through an extended enterprise model.

## TRANSACTION PROCESSING: BUSINESS OUTSOURCING

Cost reduction is still cited as a major driver for outsourcing, yet 75% of large-scale outsourcing agreements do not appear to yield savings. Outsourcing can typically cost 10–15% *more* than a large-scale internal service center. What benefit does outsourcing offer? Increased focus on core competencies. CFOs can concentrate on building world-class capabilities and accelerate the benefits of reengineering. An external outsourcing solution makes sense in the following circumstances:

- Your primary intent is strategic, not just cost-focused

- You have already captured internal economies of scale

- You do not have and cannot build competitive internal resources

- Your organization is ready to give up internal control of support functions

Companies that benefit most from outsourcing start with standardized IT programs and process best practices already in place. Successful companies manage the outsourcing process *from beginning to end* by pursuing the following approach:

1. Explicitly define service items or offerings. A detailed analysis of scope with clearly defined responsibilities is critical (including a profile of the baseline business).

2. Establish service-level agreements that support robust processes and attain mutual agreement concerning criteria that are relevant, realistic, controllable, and measurable.

3. Structure an agreement that is flexible enough to reflect:

   –changes in transaction volumes
   –performance measures (including quality)
   –opportunities for partnering

4. Partner with a provider that offers full value on several fronts, including best practices and process improvements.

5. Understand that with outsourcing you are paying for services (transaction processing) instead of internally dedicated employees.

6. Communicate desired objectives and outcomes for your outsourcing initiative.

7. Create a blueprint to support strategic initiatives versus transaction processing.

8. Demonstrate a sense of urgency, moving quickly to drive value across the organization.

9. Build a performance dashboard: revisit performance measures and reporting tools.

10. Proactively seek new ideas and implement them aggressively.

To make outsourcing work, *gain-sharing* has become increasingly popular. This approach ensures that both sides benefit from the results generated. Most contracts are renegotiated within two years. Outsourcers expect these adjustments and build them into their initial project timetables.

Add e-enabled technology into the mix and you can not only reap further improvements in service quality, but also create a seamless end-to-end transaction environment. Taking full advantage of technology, shared services and outsourcing, the process vision in Figure 11.3 shows how the outsourcer performs most of the activity in buying (purchase-to-pay), selling (order-to-cash), and accounting/reporting. The Internet

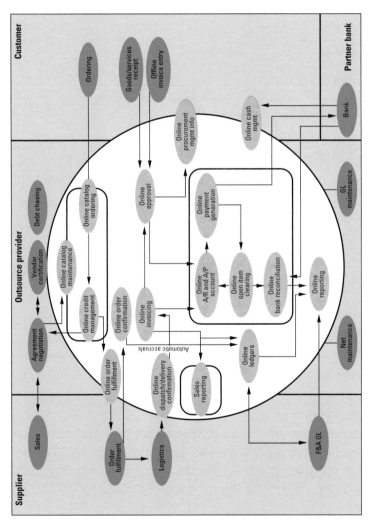

Figure 11.3 *A vision of online, outsourced accounting service provision*

links customers, suppliers and a partner bank; the outsourcer does the rest.

Consider the following futuristic case study based on an actual company's outsourced services operation and its plans for development. Positioned as if it were written by the CFO in the year 2006, the scenario looks back at what has been achieved: lights-out processing, a back office shared with business partners, and a fully integrated front and back office.

CASE STUDY
Leaping Forward to 2006

*Our journey started 10 years ago, when the focus was on performance and value creation. We were committed to moving away from commodity account-ing toward silent running—the smooth, efficient operation of back-office pro-cesses. In 2000 we outsourced most of our accounting activities, but manual intervention was still required both by us and our outsourcer. Nevertheless, we had achieved significant cost savings and a low-risk operation. The challenge was twofold. First, how could we further reduce traditional finance costs: personnel, the time required, and back-office management activity? Second, how could we grow the value-adding role of finance and move into the front office, taking our business into a new growth era?*

*When we launched our next wave of improvements, decision making took place at the business unit level. Business processes varied among the business units, countries, and even across different customer groups. As a result, our back-office functions were unnecessarily complicated. With our outsourced partners, we had already simplified the finance function. The next step was to do this across end-to-end processes, e.g., order-to-cash. Buy-in from the businesses was vital. There were three critical success factors: a group strategy that focused on growth (this encouraged the businesses to "let go" of their back-office operations); the size of the prize was communicated well (and was big enough to grab everyone's attention); and finance led with practical solutions.*

*What did we do? We standardized and simplified back-office processes across the business, although doing so in parallel was difficult. We automated pro-cesses internally using the next-generation ERP solutions, best-of-breed pack-ages and bespoke Web applications. We implemented common solutions and automated the interface between our company and business partners using Web-based information, electronic commerce, e-markets/exchanges and e-enabled customer relationship management. The new solutions were shared across our businesses—one outsourcer supporting two business units with the same processes. And solutions were shared with our business partners—we built shared back-office capabilities with suppliers and strategic alliance partners. Critical ingredients included end-to-end process reengineering across business boundaries, fundamental reappraisal of ownership of processes and data between partners, trust, mutual benefits, codependence, and culture.*

*We used to keep our own books, operate our own processes, maintain our own systems and data and jealously guard our view of the correct picture of the world. Today, with our more enlightened business partners, what was "your order-to-cash" interfacing with "my purchase-to-pay" is in reality "our transaction-to-settle" process. Payables, receivables, operational movements, and inventory are all part of one system.*

*A single outsourcer services both our company and our business partners on one systems platform—known as business infrastructure provision (BIP). We collaborate with our business partners through the outsourcer; the operational transactions are fed into the general ledger. The BIP is also our finance and administration (F&A) process outsourcer and maintains our data warehouse. This F&A arrangement applies to some of our partners, but not all.*

*In 2000 we decided not to follow the e-market hysteria; it was unreasonable to create a single e-market for all our transactions (both buy and sell). Instead, we now participate in a number of collaborative trading markets. We rely on our outsourcer to integrate our data and books of account from these different markets in order to give us a full picture.*

*We have also achieved a full integration of our front- and back-office activities. The front office includes sales, customer management, strategic pro-curement and supply chain management. Today finance participates in strategic decision making, our product portfolio, and customer relations.*

*The front-office change program could not be separated from the back-*

*office footprint. Many of our back-office changes—adjustments in our end-to-end processes and our trading interfaces—gave us both the information and the time we needed to redefine our role in the front office. In stark contrast to the late nineties, we no longer focus primarily on our operational performance.*

*Finance now focuses on options, portfolio management, structure, and partner relationships. Now our decisions are based not on financial criteria alone, but on human capital, brand capital and intellectual capital considerations. Finance manages our risk profile, we do have some high-risk ventures but the rewards can be correspondingly high.*

*In 1995 some 85% of finance activity was focused on historic transactions and data; only 15% was forward looking. After our first round of changes, 75% of finance activity focused on data collection, preparation and presentation while 25% focused on analysis and decision making. Today, the year 2006, we have 70% that's forward looking and overall more than 90% focuses on analysis and decision making. In 2006 we finally achieved our goal of lights-out processing.*

*Finance was once an unwelcome visitor in many parts of our business, particularly the front office. Now the front office is our home. Looking back over the last 10 years, one of the barriers was time; we were slow in supporting decision making, time was against us, and resources were not available. Information was also poor, but data warehousing and automated analytics improved this situation. Our mindset was also against us. We used to be reactive, now we anticipate.*

---

## WORKING CAPITAL-LESS

Beyond achieving virtuality within the finance function, the Internet provides the opportunity to reduce investment in finance itself. The decapitalization concept can be applied to working capital as well as to physical, fixed assets. Working capital exists for two reasons:

- *Inefficiency:* customers and suppliers typically do not work efficiently together, resulting in unnecessary buffer stocks, as well as payment and collections delays. Linking information systems between customers and suppliers via the Internet can decrease these inefficiencies.

- *Time:* executing transactions can be time-consuming. It can take five days to prepare a check (resulting in five days of payables) and five days to make a product (resulting in five days of inventory). The time lag between payables and production creates the need for working capital. If this transaction activity is accelerated via the Internet, less working capital is required.

If transactions are *instantaneous*, there is no need for working capital at all. We call this the working capital-less model. Although working capital-less may be a valuable goal to aspire to, there are several practicalities stopping CFOs from getting there. There will always be exceptions; instant settlement may be the target, but customers and suppliers will make errors and these are likely to get in the way of executing the perfect transaction. In effect, the size of the transaction processing operation and the finance tied up in working capital must be adjusted to address the error or exception rate. So what does the working capital-less model mean in practice? For *traditional* products it means five things:

- *No accounts payable*: a buyer enters an order and payment authorization is automated.

- *No accounts receivable*: funds are transferred via the bank or direct debit.

- *Customized production*: an order triggers sequenced release of material from all vendors.

- *WIP inventory only*: product is made to order and shipped direct.

- *Reserves only*: any exceptions are manually processed.

For *digital* products the working capital-less model can also be extended to a no-inventory position, since digital products can be transmitted and received over the Internet.

As we've noted elsewhere, new Internet-based business models provide better connectivity between customers and suppliers. This means less investment in inventory and debtors, more scope for outsourcing elements of the supply chain, improved velocity through the supply chain, and perhaps even digital distribution. Transaction processing over the Web will mean a substantial reduction in clerical touchpoints (reducing payables and receivables), fewer errors and reconciliations, and quicker, more effective payment and settlement routines. With electronic billing presentment and payment (EBPP) and new electronic forms of cash, less cash is tied up in the corporation and a lower cash float is required in the banking system.

The benefits of the working capital-less model are amplified not only within the balance sheet but also on the income statement. Payables and receivables processes alone can represent 60% of the finance function's cost. Working capital can represent 40% of a typical company's total assets. Taking advantage of the Internet reduces costs and improves capital utilization, accelerating cash flow and enhancing shareholder value. An optimal working capital position is a good indicator of strong management. Improvement initiatives require cross-functional management skills and sharing of information.

Externally published results for investors provide working capital benchmarking opportunities. Using illustrative data from the late nineties, Figure 11.4 takes the working capital position of established companies like Lucent and DuPont, and contrasts it with newer companies like Yahoo! and Gateway. The vertical axis charts the company's terms spread

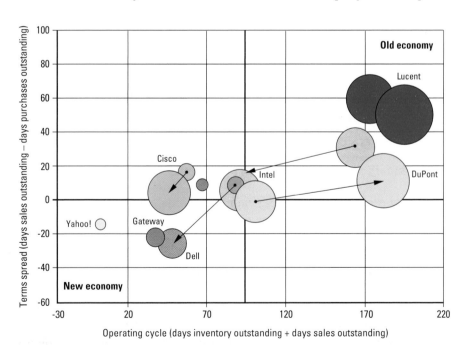

**Figure 11.4**  *Benchmarking working capital (illustrative examples)*

(days sales outstanding less days purchases outstanding), a measure of *external* collaboration; the horizontal axis tracks the company's operating cycle (days inventory outstanding plus days sales outstanding), a measure of *internal* efficiency. The goal for companies is to move to the lower left-hand area of the chart, i.e., reduced terms spread and reduced operating cycle. The bigger the circle on the chart, the bigger the total investment in working capital; arrows indicate the trend over a four-year period. These examples show Intel in the higher working capital area but trending well, as a large capital-intensive company which is decapitalizing. Dell, Cisco and Gateway are in the lower working capital area and getting better, reflecting decapitalization as their strategic goal; because these businesses have grown, the absolute size of their working capital investment is bigger, but their relative working capital efficiency is improving. Yahoo! is in the best position of all; it has no trend because it wasn't around at the start of the period.

> *The finance function is rapidly becoming a customer service organization. Its primary purpose is to convert data into decision-support information and to resolve exceptions.*

The CFO can evaluate working capital performance using currently available diagnostic tools. One such tool supports the following steps:[1]

1. Compile data across regions or businesses.

2. Determine working capital process consistency across business units.

3. Benchmark your company against its peer group.

4. Identify and prioritize initiatives.

5. Set performance improvement goals.

6. Implement best practices.

This tool provides qualitative best practices as well as quantitative data for benchmarking. Results can be compared not only with external companies, but also across business units internally. These diagnostics can be made available online to business units in a global company which is driving toward common processes and integrated performance reporting.

Information-based services such as these can also be profitably deployed in e-markets. Consider this futuristic case.

CASE STUDY
Taking Working Capital out of an e-Market

*A global consumer manufacturing company has networked its systems with its business partners over the Internet, creating an electronic marketplace where all participants share data on a real-time basis. Speed of communication and reduced error rates have eliminated inventory. Errors in forecasting are substantially reduced through the use of common real-time data. Just-in-time supply chain practices result in the right component quantities showing up at the right time. The speed of the network is fast enough to allow all products to be made to order. Point-of-sale data triggers replenishment up the value chain.*

*Instant settlement has eliminated payables and receivables. Funds are electronically transferred at the moment of sale. The business has no bad debt exposure. The finance function is rapidly becoming a customer service organization; its primary purpose is to convert data into decision-support information and to resolve exceptions. Only the exceptions are processed—reconciliation on each normal transaction is carried out computer to computer. A clearinghouse between the e-market participants ensures that 80% of transactions are reconciled automatically. Therefore only 20% are treated as exceptions and processed traditionally.*

*Electronic statements are posted monthly in lieu of purchase orders, invoices, checks, and shipping documents. Finance executives can get real-time management reports from anywhere in the world. The result? They have access not just to operational information about their own business in each region, but also to crucial information about their business partners, including supplier and customer performance data. The latest brand of integrated analytic software interprets and filters the data, highlighting what is important and suppressing unimportant metrics.*

## THE VIRTUAL TREASURY

The journey to virtual finance can be extended from the working capital-less model into the world of virtual treasury. The CFO's corporate treasury function is in a strong position to support the evolution of B2B. Further cost reductions and process efficiencies can be achieved by taking advantage of the latest software developments, settlements over the Internet, and new or alternative banking services. Furthermore, the trend toward outsourcing key services now includes treasury activities.

Where are corporate treasuries today? Many are still sorting out their conventional banking arrangements: dealing with a plethora of different banks across the world with all their associated inefficiencies in pricing and in managing liquidity and balances. Steps to rationalize the number of banks and enhance their efficiency are under way, but they are not complete. The corporate center is still responsible for the more complex aspects of financial risk and funding. But a new trend is developing: corporate treasuries are becoming more actively engaged in operational banking and commercial payments. ERP implementations and the growing number of shared service centers are making this possible.

Today's corporate treasuries are not fully exploiting available information about underlying exposure, cash flow, and working capital (internal and external). Why? Lack of data integration. But new tools are becoming available for performance modeling, treasury information management, and reporting as well as for supporting connectivity to external banking information systems. Yet corporate treasury specialists remain scarce and are not integrated into financial accounting programs. Treasury tends not to be an integral part of the corporation's e-business strategy. It is not usually a top priority when setting up B2B exchanges. Banking and cash are often afterthoughts.

What corporate treasuries need is a vision for taking advantage of the Internet. The recommended route for moving toward a virtual treasury is shown in Figure 11.5. The four phases are defined as follows:

- *Phase 1*: transfer back-office treasury systems to an external information service provider (ISP). The ISP provides treasury information and data management, consolidating underlying exposure and transaction flows with treasury position data. The ISP also provides application hosting using the preferred treasury management package systems. The benefits? Reduced operational loading and risks for the treasury team;

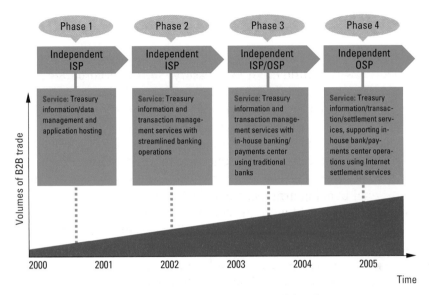

Figure 11.5   *Potential evolution of treasury and banking*

improved information for decision making (a treasury dashboard); reduced technology infrastructure cost; and a flexible platform for future
development.

- *Phase 2*: streamline access channels to banks to give *single-pipe access*
  for corporate treasury flows and flows at the affiliate transaction level;
  this increases liquidity and reduces payment costs. Take advantage of
  external banking service providers such as an independent bank
  service, clubs of banks, or one of the leading international banks that
  offer extended domestic banking services. In this phase the new B2B
  markets are emerging, but from a treasury perspective, they are supported by traditional systems and bank links.

- *Phase 3*: take advantage of shared service accounting center developments by extending the treasury ISPs into *in-house bank and payment
  factories*, possibly also outsourced to service providers (OSPs). Combined ISPs/OSPs provide working capital management information and
  asset securitization information. They can also support B2B exchange
  activities over the Internet. This phase would still rely on traditional
  banks for settlement. The benefits? Cost reductions through streamlining payments, opportunities to leverage shared service centers and
  savings, particularly in working capital, through the B2B exchanges.

- *Phase 4*: this phase incorporates streamlined treasury management, extended use of B2B exchanges, and additionally embraces *Internet settlement*. Banks are retained for collateral purposes only; B2B settlement is undertaken through an independent intermediary known as a trusted third party (TTP). The benefit? Immediate value transfer, eliminating the significant delays associated with a traditional banking settlement.

Consider this case study, then compare it with where you are today and where your treasury function may be headed.

CASE STUDY
Statoil Moves to Internal Banking

*Statoil used several external banks. It relied on these external banks for settlement (including internal settlements) and certain treasury deals were executed with the external market on a suboptimal basis. Payment and receipt activities were owned and managed by subsidiaries; information processing and usage differed from company to company. Statoil had several opportunities:*

- *To achieve economies of scale by rationalizing banking arrangements and renegotiating banking agreements.*

- *To optimize the use of the financial market by netting risk and internalizing intercompany settlements.*

- *To optimize working capital in the company by controlling cash.*

- *To improve the efficiency of consolidating key information.*

*To meet these objectives, Statoil implemented an internal bank supported by a suite of treasury software modules and has achieved the benefits of full integration with its core ERP system. It rationalized external banking arrangements and ensured that the banks worked to international standards. Statoil also instituted an internal cash software program to establish internal current account banking arrangements for subsidiaries and to support centralized payments. Intragroup commercial payment traffic is now internalized.*

*All external treasury transactions are managed by the internal bank. Deals are entered by the front office and processed, on a straight-through basis, through booking and settlement. Internal treasury transactions, foreign exchange settlements, and intercompany loans are managed by the internal bank. Statoil's new system generates the treasury accounting entries at both corporate and affiliate level. Risk is pooled on a corporate basis and only the group's net risk is handled in the external market. External banking transactions for internal settlements are eliminated, and bank balances are zero-balanced on a daily basis to accounts managed by the internal bank, enabling centralized control of cash as a corporate asset. Statoil has successfully integrated treasury into its corporate value chain.*

---

So far, the virtual finance journey has taken us from transaction processing and outsourcing to a working capital-less environment, and a plan for the virtual treasury. The emphasis has been on taking cost out, improving speed, and taking advantage of the Internet in streamlining the accounting process. But what about decision support? Will that go virtual too?

## ONLINE DECISION SUPPORT: i-ANALYTICS

Our CFO research has shown that decision support is the one area in which the finance function as it currently exists is expected to expand and develop within the corporation. As noted time and again in this book, e-business is speeding up the need for information and broadening the scope of the information required, making decision support more complex. While technologies exist today to facilitate more advanced decision support, analytical processes and skills haven't yet caught up. Many companies are in the early stages of implementing strategic enterprise management (SEM) concepts. They are on the journey toward i-analytics—provision of integrated information and intelligence to decision-makers over the Internet.

Decision-support activities are currently based on data from underlying corporate ERP and other types of system. These data repositories tend to stand alone; they are not part of a company's value chain but focus more on functional hierarchies *up and down* the organization. They are positioned as *islands of data*, supposedly providing users with insight. Portals and data access tools improve access but they do not address a fundamental flaw—today's decision-support systems present users with problems not solutions.

For the CFO this means decision making has to be intuitive rather than explicit. It is based on individual mental models (i.e., on an individual's experience and understanding) instead of collective corporate experience and understanding. Here are some key questions that decision-support systems will need to address in the future:

- How can you communicate and implement strategy throughout the organization?
- How can you help managers make informed value-based judgments on predictive information?
- How can you educate managers in decision making based on what works best across the organization?

i-Analytics, or integrated analytics, is the collection, aggregation, management, distribution, and analysis of balanced information that positively addresses stakeholders' decisions. Every organization has data. Companies that transform this data most effectively into useful, timely information and then act upon it to serve their customers better will achieve true competitive advantage. The integration of a company's "actionable" information, combined with best practices and collective experience applied to specific decisions and solutions, is the essence of i-analytics.

Ultimately, using i-analytics will be like turning on the lights, something you do without regard for the complexities of power supply. Analytics will be embedded in what you do and in the way you run your organization. The processes, tools, data and underlying logic and technologies will all be hidden from view. All levels of an organization will be empowered to make economic decisions based not only on real-time data, but also on sophisticated cause-and-effect relationship models. Figure 11.6 shows an outline of such a cause-and-effect model.

Analytics such as these will be based on a deep understanding of the business and will be self-adjusting. They will draw on two major resources, agents and alerts. An *agent* is a piece of automatically activated software that will search and build relationship models. Agents will

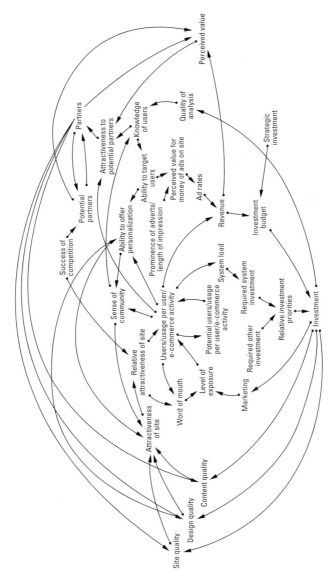

Figure 11.6  *Analytic drivers for an Internet business*

actively analyze performance behaviors and provide early warnings. An *alert* will keep track of changing performance characteristics. These self-adjusting cause-and-effect models will be built up from the lowest statistical level, perhaps an individual customer interface.

At the highest level, these i-analytic models will be strategic, providing active evaluations of strategic options and corporate objectives; at the operational level, they will support day-to-day operations. The tools will all use the same basic technology: self-building cause-and-effect modeling, strategy mapping and communication tools, and integrated i-analytic engines based on the lowest level of granularity (the transaction). Advanced technologies will support collaboration and calendar planning, allowing colleagues to share information instantly (video, content, whiteboarding, etc.) to enrich debate and analysis. i-Analytics will have the following features:

- Economic analysis of customers and customer segments, products and product sets, and process efficiency.

- Shared information across an industry value chain (myAnalytics, yourAnalytics, ourInformationValueChain).

- Instant availability (e-close timescales and Internet delivery).

- Sophisticated natural language queries (you ask, it tells).

For the CFO these exciting advances will provide solutions not problems. Once a problem is identified, systems will search (internally and externally) for relevant strategies and answers. The results can subsequently be shared by all interested parties, not only internally but also with strategic partners and potentially across an entire industry. Discussion, debate, and collaborative decision making over the Internet will ensue.

CASE STUDY
Introducing Integrated Analytics

*The CFO of a fast-growing food retail company is today focused, with board-room colleagues and business partners, on launching e-ventures to extend and develop the range of services they offer customers. He realizes that he could* scarcely have contemplated tackling such initiatives six years ago, when he first became CFO. First, he and his colleagues knew very little about their customers: why they bought or what they valued most. Second, there was no time to focus on customer needs; they faced more pressing issues around running the company.

Looking back, it was surprising that he could even manage the business using monthly information and paper-based processes. He remembered the complaints from the field when he sent out data reports six weeks after the fact. He recalled the huge effort his staff had to make to answer queries from the chairman. Back then, just to answer a simple question, he often had to mobilize a team of 10 people for a week or more to scour their systems and extract information.

The biggest improvement the CFO had made, in terms of overall impact on the business, was to give all employees access to a company information portal (CIP). This gave people the information they needed to do their jobs, as well as tools to analyze data in answer to questions from senior management. Operational information was provided in real time; monthly results appeared less than 24 hours after the period end—the result of moving from the old once-a-month adjustments to a more continuous approach.

What was left of the finance department, after eliminating manual analysis, had a very different focus: looking forward and analyzing trends to help the business refine its strategies. Budgets went some time ago, replaced by performance targets and rolling forecasts. The CIP allowed the entire management team to review individual balanced scorecards, giving complete visibility about the responsibilities and accountabilities of everyone on the team.

Of course, the new business processes and systems helped; these had been implemented not only across the company but also across all its partner companies up and down the supply chain (it referred to these as the extraprise system). With these new processes, suppliers could quickly tap into the company's sales forecasts to make sure it never ran out of stock or was overstocked.

Suppliers and other partners also had access to details of upcoming promotions, as did all the company's managers, via the CIP. They were also linked to the company's point-of-sales systems and new in-store scanning capabilities. Cashless, automated Web payments eliminated transaction processing related to customers and dramatically reduced the finance staff involved.

*Among the biggest beneficiaries of the shift to virtual decision support were regional managers. Not too long ago, they were unable to get information until they got back to the office and tracked down the paper they needed. They found out just how powerful workflow could be, especially when combined with wireless and other communication methods. Now they could send alerts to people in the field, via public networks, mobile phones, and hand-held organizers, to notify them of poor results in one of their operations, of something that needed urgent attention, or a situation they needed to prepare for. Field staff could access the CIP homepage whenever and wherever they needed to.*

*The service center played a big role in making all this possible. The company had resisted shared services for some time. This attitude changed once stand-ardized data and systems were implemented across the organization. The service center was a first stop for transaction processing. Later this function was completely outsourced, along with some other noncore services, such as tax and treasury. As time went on, the service center focused more on managing data standards and portal content, including external information and bench-marks. It also provided help to analytical, decision-support, employee, partner, and customer self-service facilities.*

> **The company had resisted shared services for some time. This attitude changed once standardized data and systems were implemented across the organization.**

*The CFO made significant use of the shared service center during the com-pany's newest acquisition. In order to assimilate new brands quickly, the center assessed the acquired company's support needs, negotiated contracts, put in place service-level agreements, and modified the CIP to bring new manage-ment online from day one.*

*On the service front, new cashless systems allowed the company to collect deeper customer information. Patterns around who bought what, when, and how often became more obvious. This data proved invaluable, coupled with interviews and Internet feedback on what people liked and disliked about their experience. It led the company to modify its ten-year strategy and invest more wisely to cultivate the most profitable customer groups. These moves allowed the company to regain the high ground competitively after many years in the wilderness.*

---

Like the CFO in this case study, you must be willing to rethink every aspect of your business from an e-business perspective. Beyond this, you'll need a road map to navigate the development path required to achieve a virtual decision-support environment. Here are some suggested milestones that may prove helpful.

In two years

- Base internal i-analytics building blocks in place

  −customer profitability
  −product profitability
  −process analytics

- Technological backbone in place

In four years

- Integration of myAnalytics/yourAnalytics (extraprise information value chain)

- Self-building cause-and-effect modeling

- Dynamic rebuilding of i-analytics systems

- Integration of internal and external content providers focused on solutions

## SO HOW DO YOU MAKE THIS JOURNEY TOWARD VIRTUALITY?

What does all this add up to? The drive for lights-out processing, out-sourcing, and i-analytics is moving finance relentlessly toward the *virtual close*: seamless, end-to-end business cycle planning and execution via the Internet.

Up until now, this chapter has approached the finance agenda from a business or content perspective. But achieving the agenda described here will demand new and unfamiliar leadership skills. Past performance will not guarantee future success. The implementation path ahead will not be linear, but iterative and adaptive. It will require building on ideas and experiments that work, and channeling resources into solutions which are treated as investment options.

What's needed is for the CFO to explain the journey's rationale and overall direction; remove major obstacles, and create the initial momentum. Navigation must be continuous, focused on the *direction* rather than the *destination*. Based on frontline research, here are six priorities you must address to meet the virtual finance challenge. By pursuing these priorities with intent and enthusiasm, you can provide leadership to transform them into reality.

Frame the challenge Communicate the end-to-end scope of the *virtual close* and the magnitude of benefits represented by the next 50% cost reduction. Explain the nature of the e-business threat and opportunity, and present a vision of the industry changes it will trigger. Set the bar high and clearly convey the approach the corporate has mapped out to meet the challenges ahead.

Set direction  Describe the *virtual close* as the overall direction being taken rather than a precise destination, so people can make their own navigational decisions. Be sure they understand that both strategy and tactics will remain flexible and evolve.

Unblock change  Remove real and perceived obstacles (such as performance measurement issues and system blockages) quickly and for good. Use partners and centralized projects to speed progress but involve staff to gain buy-in.

Target innovation  Start experiments in selected areas to foster learning, stimulate change, and create initial value through quick wins to fund future projects. Tie these to existing initiatives when appropriate.

Sustain momentum  Seed and nurture experiments to build and sustain momentum. Maintain a productive environment. Contract for change internally and with third-party partners. Focus closely on behavior and culture.

Navigate the journey   Monitor progress and review objectives. Refocus direction as necessary. Manage the change portfolio to maintain alignment, balance risk and keep options open. Seek out and invest in change agents. Use a *strategic staircase* as a practical navigation tool (the further the time horizon, the higher the uncertainty and the more ambitious the change).

## The eCFO: Anticipating the Benefits

The virtual finance function may be little more than a concept today, but the drive toward virtuality is fast approaching reality. Every activity we've discussed here is moving inexorably in this direction. Transaction processing is headed there. Shared services are headed there. And so are working capital management, treasury and decision support. In the not too distant future these activities will play only a minor part in the finance function's realm of responsibility. CFOs who are slow to embrace virtuality will find this trend threatening; those who anticipate and pursue its benefits will find it liberating.

# eCFO CHECKLIST

## BUILD YOUR VISION FOR B2F
Recognize that finance must carve out a new, more proactive role in the rapidly evolving e-business environment. Resolve to make finance a value-creating proposition in its own right. Begin to identify the parameters of a truly Internet-enabled finance operation. What would it look like and how would it work? How would it affect corporate strategy and business planning? What about strategic alliances?

## PLAN YOUR JOURNEY TO VIRTUALITY
Embrace the benefits that building a virtual finance function will offer you and your trusted finance associates. Map out a B2F agenda that is both ambitious and achievable. Determine where you want to be two and four years down the road and then work backward to identify the incremental steps you'll need to get there.

## TAKE THE BIG LEAP INTO TRANSACTION PROCESSING EFFICIENCY
Fully support shared service initiatives and act aggressively to ensure that nonstrategic finance tasks migrate to your service center quickly and efficiently. View outsourcing not as a threat, but as an opportunity to transform your existing finance group's core capabilities. Aim for lights-out processing.

## STEADILY DECREASE YOUR RELIANCE ON WORKING CAPITAL
Commit to eliminating working capital from your asset base and work relentlessly toward achieving this objective. This will push you to increase your efficiency in many areas and to redefine your attitude toward cash flow and value chain management. Decide what the working capital-less model can mean to your business and then identify best practices in other industries that can help you get there.

MIGRATE YOUR TREASURY OPERATION TO A VIRTUAL ENVIRONMENT

Develop a blueprint for moving to a virtual treasury. Have as your goal streamlining treasury management to the point where your relationship with the banking community is almost totally redefined. Take full advantage of the Internet to enhance your information management capabilities and boost operational effectiveness. Approach this process in stages and carefully weigh the benefits of outsourcing your treasury activities.

GO ONLINE WITH i-ANALYTICS

Recognize that more and more emphasis will be placed on finance's contribution to decision support, or what we call i-analytics—integrated information and intelligence. This will be one of the key facets of the CFO's role as a strategic business partner to the CEO, and one of your immediate challenges will be to implement an advanced decision-support program. Meeting this challenge will require extensive systems building, new and fresh intellectual capacity, and advanced analytical resources.

# Notes

## Chapter 1

1. PricewaterhouseCoopers Financial & Cost Management Team (1999) *CFO: Architect of the Corporation's Future*, Wiley.
2. Grady Means and David Schneider (2000) *MetaCapitalism: The E-Business Revolution and the Design of 21st Century Companies and Markets*, Wiley.

## Chapter 2

1. Gary Hamel (2000) *Leading the Revolution*, Harvard Business School Press.

## Chapter 4

1. The section on *Enhancing Customer Value* draws on the work of VisionCube, specialists in customer lifetime value techniques and software.
2. Brand Finance is a London-based consultancy organization specializing in brand valuation.
3. The approach described is based on the work of Sibson & Co., specialists in compensation and performance management.

## Chapter 7

1. Grant Norris, James R. Hurley, Kenneth M. Hartley, John R. Dunleavy, and John D. Balls (2000) *E-Business and ERP: Transforming the Enterprise*, Wiley.
2. Martin V. Deise, Conrad Nowikow, Patrick King, and Amy Wright (2000) *Executive's Guide to E-Business: From Tactics to Strategy*, Wiley.
3. For more on evaluating corporate software packages, including assessment of vendors as potential business partners, see PricewaterhouseCoopers Financial & Cost Management Team (1999) *CFO: Architect of the Corporation's Future*, Wiley.
4. For further discussion of the impact of e-business on sourcing for production and other supply chain strategies, see PricewaterhouseCoopers (2000) *E-supply chain: revolution or e-volution?* Euromoney Institutional Investor (part of the series on information and technology in the supply chain).
5. PricewaterhouseCoopers Technology Center, *Technology Forecast: 2000*, April 2000.
6. H. Dresner (2000) Enterprise business intelligence suites segment heats up. *Intranets and Electronic Workplace (IEW)*, 2 May.

## Chapter 8

1. PricewaterhouseCoopers innovation survey.

## Chapter 9

1. Mark L. Feldman and Michael F. Spratt (1999) *Five Frogs on a Log: A CEO's Field Guide to Accelerating the Transition in Mergers, Acquisitions, and Gut Wrenching Change*, Wiley.
2. Garth Alexander (2000) The man who dreamt up the biggest merger in history. *Sunday Times*, 16 January.
3. Mark L. Sirower (1997) *The Synergy Trap*, Free Press.
4. Adapted from Adrian J. Slywotzky (1996) *Value Migration: How to Think Several Moves Ahead of the Competition*, Harvard Business School Press.

## Chapter 11

1. The PricewaterhouseCoopers working capital benchmarking service.

# Index

TNT Post Group (TNT) 67
total shareholder return (TSR) 65–6
TPG *see* TNT Post Group
trademarks 109–14
transaction processing 12–22, 294,
      330–62
Transora.com 43–4
treasuries 16, 348–51
trust 30, 64, 191, 261, 350–1
trusted third parties (TTPs) 350–1
TSR *see* total shareholder return
TTPs *see* trusted third parties

uncertainty 10, 144–8
      *see also* risks
Unilever 304–5

VACs *see* value-added communities
valuation 8–11, 56–8, 64–90, 131, 273,
      279, 282–6
   brands 101–6
   cultural fit 290–2
   customers 96–101
   evolution 64–6
   intangible assets 93–125
   intellectual capital 94–6, 109–14,
      117–23
   investment appraisals 7–10, 54,
      64–90, 129, 142–8
   limitations 64–90
   portals 48–9
   R&D 106–9
   reputation 114–17
   ROV 10, 64, 69–73, 79, 131, 133,
      144–8
value
   chain integration 5–7, 136–48,
      199–203, 238–9, 354
   diligence 280–2
   drivers 64–6, 70–1, 79, 121–3,
      139–48
   propositions 19–20, 310–15
   scorecards 84–7, 174, 288–90
   staircase 282–4
value creation 5–7, 56–8, 78–86, 92–3,
      127–63, 265–97, 308–9
   business models 27–60, 78–84
   corporate centers 299–326

EVA 9, 61–90, 104–5, 121–3, 127–9,
      133, 163
   finance functions 20–2, 332–3
value-added communities (VACs) 5–6
value-added networks (VANs) 210
value-based management (VBM) 62, 67,
      174
VANs *see* value-added networks
Vantive 206
VBM *see* value-based management
venture capitalists 54–8, 80, 131, 138,
      149–51, 313
Virgin 101, 312
virtual concepts 1–26, 94, 168–9, 224,
      327–62
virtual private networks (VPNs) 204–5
vision 13–17, 54–8, 185–228, 243,
      276–8, 329–31, 339–62
Vitria 218–19
Vodafone AirTouch 313
Volvo 175–6
VPNs *see* virtual private networks

WACC *see* weighted average cost of
      capital
Wal-Mart 2, 49, 154
Wallander, Jan 164, 188–90
Web *see* Internet
Webonomics concepts 7–11, 70–84
weighted average cost of capital (WACC)
      7, 65–6, 142–3, 246, 283–4
Welch, Jack 82, 164, 311
working capital 8, 22, 139–42, 343–7,
      359–61
   concepts 8, 76–7, 343–7, 359
   value drivers 65–6, 71, 76–7,
      139–42

Xerox Technology Ventures (XTV)
      150–1
XML *see* extensible markup language
XQL *see* extensible query language
XTV *see* Xerox Technology Ventures

Yahoo! 70, 94, 101, 220, 345–6

zero-based budgeting 169
Zurich Insurance 152